BUILDING A KNOWLEDGE-DRIVEN ORGANIZATION

BUILDING A KNOWLEDGE-DRIVEN ORGANIZATION

Robert H. Buckman

McGraw-Hill
New York Chicago San Francisco Lisbon
London Madrid Mexico City Milan New Delhi
San Juan Seoul Singapore Sydney Toronto

This publication is designed to provide accurate and authoritative information in regard to the subject matter covered. It is sold with the understanding that neither the author nor the publisher is engaged in rendering legal, accounting, or other professional service. If legal advice or other expert assistance is required, the services of a competent professional person should be sought.
>   —*From a Declaration of Principles jointly adopted by a Committee*
>   *of the American Bar Association and a Committee of Publishers*

McGraw-Hill books are available at special quantity discounts to use as premiums and sales promotions, or for use in corporate training programs. For more information, please write to the Director of Special Sales, McGraw-Hill, 2 Penn Plaza, New York, NY 10121-2298. Or contact your local bookstore.

 This book is printed on recycled, acid-free paper containing a minimum of 50% recycled de-inked fiber.

CONTENTS

Contents

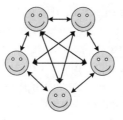

INTRODUCTION

Pooling Your Organization's Knowledge

Everyone who lives ought to be wise; it is as good as receiving an inheritance and will give you as much security as money can. Wisdom keeps you safe—this is the advantage of knowledge.

—Ecclesiastes 7:11

Knowledge has always meant power: power to survive, power to adapt, power to thrive in a hard environment. Ever since the first human clan enjoyed the warmth of the first tame fire, it's been true that knowledge shared is knowledge multiplied. The more a group knows of what its members know, the better it can perform in the world. But it's also true that the more remote people feel from one another, the more risky knowledge sharing looks and the more tempting it is to hold knowledge for private advantage.

Buckman Laboratories has been in the specialty chemical business—that is, the *knowledge about chemicals* business—since 1945. Solving customer problems by applying our knowledge to them is how we generate our income streams.

At first, the knowledge we could offer a particular customer was largely limited to that held by the employee who worked most closely with the customer. Over the years we came to realize that we could multiply the power we could bring to bear if we could focus more than one mind on solving a customer's problem, and still more if we could look collectively at a whole industry's problem. We recognized that encouraging people to share knowledge about problems as they arose would allow us to come up with better solutions to those problems—and that the faster our collective knowledge could spread, the faster we could meet our customers' needs. We had to learn how to move knowledge around the organization to the place it was needed in time for it to be useful. And that required not just the capacity to move information but the ability to find it and the culture to assure people that sharing (rather than hoarding) was right and natural.

Along the way we have accumulated our share of recognition and awards for our efforts. Individually, I was given the Knowledge Management Leadership Award by Business Intelligence in 1996, named a Distinguished Delphi Fellow as the visionary behind one of the most widely cited knowledge management initiatives to date in 1998 by the Delphi Group of Boston, and named as one of the top 10 Most Admired Knowledge Leaders for the year 2000 for world-class knowledge leadership contributions to my company and to the New Economy by Teleos and Work Frontiers International. In addition, I have received awards and honorary degrees from various institutions of higher learning for leadership in this area.

Collectively, Buckman Laboratories has won several awards for its knowledge initiatives. In 1996 we received the Arthur Andersen LLP Enterprise Award for Best Practices in the category of Knowledge Sharing in the Organization. In 1997 we received the Computerworld Smithsonian Award for visionary use of information technology in the Manufacturing category and the APQC Award for Use of Information Technology to Support Knowledge Management.

However, the award we regard as the highest honor is the global Most Admired Knowledge Enterprises (MAKE) program administered by Teleos, an independent knowledge management research company based in the UK. The MAKE research program consists of the annual Global MAKE study—the international benchmark for best practice knowledge organizations. In addition, MAKE studies are conducted to identify leading knowledge organizations at the regional and national level. Currently, Teleos is conducting MAKE studies for Asia, Europe, Japan, and North America.

The Global MAKE winners are chosen by an international panel of *Fortune* Global 500 senior executives and leading knowledge management experts. They are rated against a framework of eight key knowledge performance dimensions, which are the visible drivers of competitive advantage. Global MAKE Winners are recognized as best practice exemplars in the following:

▶ Creating a corporate knowledge-driven culture
▶ Developing knowledge workers through senior management leadership
▶ Delivering knowledge-based products and solutions
▶ Maximizing enterprise intellectual capital
▶ Creating an environment for collaborative knowledge sharing
▶ Creating a learning organization
▶ Delivering value based on customer knowledge
▶ Transforming enterprise knowledge into shareholder value

According to Teleos, "Only 18 organizations ... belong to the select Global MAKE Hall of Fame: Accenture, BP, Buckman Laboratories, Cisco Systems, Ernst & Young, General Electric, Hewlett-Packard, Intel, IBM, Johnson & Johnson, McKinsey & Company, Microsoft, PricewaterhouseCoopers, Royal Dutch/Shell, Siemens, Skandia, 3M, and Xerox. These organizations have been Global MAKE Finalists for the past five years." In those five years we achieved first in the world three times. And in 2003, we captured the top position for the second year in a row. We are very proud of that accomplishment.

"With everything else dropping out of the competitive equation," Lester Thurow says, "knowledge has become the only source of long-run sustainable competitive advantage, but knowledge can only be employed through the skills of individuals." That is true for specialty chemicals and for many other industries and services. Individual knowledge, essential as it is, isn't enough for success; its true value emerges only when it can be taken up and used as needed by a whole organization.

This book tells the Buckman story—how we converted a world-spanning but fragmented collection of information into a seamless array of knowledge that we can apply whenever and wherever we need it. As a sample, consider this ... call it a conversation:

Ricardo: I need all the information about foam gun usage, specially using BSP xxxx foam generator. I would like to have some consumers' references, what dosage is used and how efficient this equipment is.

Jan: This has been a good application for a number of our reps in several countries so you should be getting some direct replies. Have you checked the new case history file? It is much easier to use than the old version. Let us know if you do not find any case histories or get any replies to your question. Our Buckman Europe reps have a very nice portable system which uses a portable handtruck with a drum of Busperse xxxx, a coil of water hose, the foam gun, and the needed connectors to make it work. Water and air pressure can be fine-tuned to make the foam very heavy and thick or quite fluid and viscous depending on your needs.

Terry: Dr. Adams should have a file in his office (my old files) on this either under the Lafferty foamer or foam gun apparatus. There will also be some pictures of carts assembled by Joe Doaks and Rich Roe here in the lovely USA. There should be a variety of information there, suggest you obtain a copy of the file. Please let me know if I can be of further assistance. For Ricardo's sake I would bet that Busperse yy or zzzz would generate more 'clinging' foam than BSP xxxx. The case histories you mentioned should back this up.

Sam: Busperse yy or better yet zzzz would probably be the best bets. Arnie Sparks has a good program going with BSP zzzz. He is using the Buckman-supplied equipment. Good Luck!

Doug: We have used the foam gun with BSP www and zzzz. Both give excellent foam for specific applications. The generator is very small and you need only three things: (1) chemical (2) air line (3) water line. Actual dosage rates should be determined by adjusting these three parameters. You can obtain the desired consistency for your specific application. We have used it for barium scale and machine cleanup and it worked great. BSP xxxx will also work great in the foam gun, but you have to be careful about the surface you're working on; it'll eat the floor if it gets a chance. If you have any more questions please contact me.

Fred: Contact Arnold J. Sparks in Tacoma, Washington. We are using the foam gun at a paper mill there. He can provide the information and references. Hope this helps.

Jim: Bulab Canada has a great deal of experience with foam cleaning in paper mills, both in acid and alkaline papermaking conditions. We have designed and built portable foam cleaning units (heavy duty stainless steel construction) for use with our products. Main products used are BSP zzzz (alkaline foam) and BSP vvvv + BL qqq (phosphoric acid) (that is, acid foam for PC-filled alkaline paper). We can sell you a unit at cost or provide blueprints to allow local fabrication. If interested contact Robert G. McMullan, who designed the unit. For more detailed info on foam cleaning chemical applications contact Tim Morris and Sanjay Kapoor. We'd be glad to help you.

Harry: Here is some additional information on foam guns, and the products available. We have many products that are available for use with a foam gun. Some other replies have given you some information, including products available in Canada. Here's info from Buckman R&D: we have several alkaline products that have worked well: BSP yy and BSP zzzz (very similar to yy, but more caustic) are foaming caustic cleaners; BSP www is another alkaline product, but www has a lot of chelating power and has been effective in removing barium sulfate scale; BL bbbb is a mildly acidic product which is effective in cleaning aluminum surfaces; BL aaa is a very strongly acidic cleaner for cleaning calcium carbonate from a surface. We probably have more, but these are the ones I can remember right now. All of these can be made by Buckman anywhere in the world with no trouble in manufacturing. Let us know if you need more information.

Angus: Another parameter you may want to keep in mind if you experiment with the foam gun is nozzle size. I have found that varying the nozzle diameter will not only adjust the range of the gun but also the characteristics of the foam itself.

This exchange may not sound all that different from the sort of job-related chatter that often makes a coffee break the most productive part of a workday, except perhaps for the amount of specific information the participants have at their fingertips. But these workers aren't sitting at a table or standing around a coffee machine; they're scattered across the world. Most of them have never seen one another. From beginning to end, elapsed time is about 48 hours.

What you've just glimpsed is a mildly edited thread from the Buckman Laboratories intranet, a forum where any associate (the word we now use in place of *employee*) with a need for information can ask for assistance—and any associate with information on the topic can reply. This sharing of knowledge across time and space, when needed and where needed, has become our preferred method of solving problems as they arise.

A Knowledge-Sharing Culture

To achieve this level of knowledge sharing, we had to change our whole style of operation. Like most companies founded right after World War II, we started out with the straightforward command-and-control organization that came naturally to the people involved. For many years, we did very well. When customers presented issues too complex for individual customer representatives to resolve, we passed the problems to a team of experts with the required specialized skills. We would fly these highly educated people (most were Ph.D. chemists, microbiologists, or engineers) around the world to teach others what they knew and pick up new knowledge as they went. It worked, but it was a costly and time-consuming process for acquiring and transferring knowledge.

In the early 1980s our customers began demanding faster and faster solutions. Our expert team couldn't move fast enough or cover enough places to meet the customers' rapidly changing needs. We had to speed up our problem-solving process still further, and it became clear that we could not do it by having our people travel more or by hiring more people. It had become a physical impossibility to meet our needs by relying on face-to-face meetings.

In essence, we could no longer depend on the sequential world of command-and-control to provide the speed our customers demanded. What we needed were horizontal cross-connections that would link our experts, wherever they happened to be, to our people working on customer problems, wherever they happened to be and whenever they happened to need solutions. To move to this networked organization, we found that we had to develop a whole new basis for dealing with one another, taking advantage of the then-new technology of online interaction to set up "open space" meetings on the network across time and space. This allowed people to raise any issue at any time and for others to provide whatever suggestions and solutions occurred to them at that moment. It was a dynamic system. The whole thing was chaotic enough to worry those of us who'd grown up with the orderly predictability of command-and-control, but it got the job done much faster.

It also led us to begin to break down our organizational silos—to question the relevance of our long-established departmental structures in our new marketplace. This process is ongoing, and we've come to realize that an organization positioned for the future will have to be organized around *knowledge*—how to create it, share it, capture it, and apply it—rather than around *structures* and *processes*. Once everyone in the company is in the network for the business at hand, it takes only a slight shift of thought to open the way to an organic organization. To achieve this organic organization requires major culture change, but it comes more and more easily as individuals learn to assume responsibility for making things happen for themselves.

We've continued to grow and thrive for over 20 years with the new system. In the process we've worked out these essential principles for successful knowledge sharing:

- ▶ Focus on the most critical need of the organization. Your systems should support your strategy.
- ▶ Build trust by emphasizing fundamental virtues rather than values.

- ▶ Share knowledge and best practices.
- ▶ Solve customer problems rapidly.
- ▶ Allow associates to solve the problems they encounter without interference by management.
- ▶ Inject customer feedback into the new product development process.

Critical Needs

The critical need of most organizations is to generate cash flow on the front line with the customer. Without that it is not possible to stay in business. What is your strategy for doing this? Do your ICT systems support your strategy? Don't you wish your people would assume responsibility for making your strategy come alive and produce results? Don't you wish your people would come up with their own ways to radically increase their productivity? How can you redefine your business equation to improve your productivity with your customers? These are some of the questions that this book is intended to help you explore so you can get the most out of your organization in delivering on the promise that your strategy holds.

Trust

Knowledge sharing in business calls for a level of trust not far removed from what most of us feel with our immediate family and close friends. This poses an ongoing challenge in the face of the diverse cultures, backgrounds, and experiences found in a global organization. To build the trust needed for sharing knowledge across the organization, people must focus on what they believe, both individually and collectively. The terminology of values turns out to be an awkward tool for this purpose, because the words people use to describe what they value differ radically from time to time and place to place. Nonetheless, almost all cultures prize certain dispositions and kinds of behavior:

- ▶ **Justice:** Acting honestly and fairly, keeping promises
- ▶ **Temperance:** Acting with self-discipline, avoiding overt self-service
- ▶ **Prudence:** Displaying practical wisdom and the ability to choose well in any situation

▶ **Fortitude:** Showing strength of mind and character and the courage to persevere in the face of adversity

These fundamental virtues evoke admiration even among people of cultures wildly divergent from each other. When members of a group can rely on their associates to act accordingly, they begin to look past differences of personal taste, language, and appearance and see one another as worthy of trust.

Is the culture of your organization conducive to the rapid movement of knowledge to meet any need at any time? If not, how should it change?

Spreading Best Practices

When you're trying to solve a problem, you want to be able to tap into the best that your company has to offer. The challenge is to locate the best information that exists. For years, the better companies have written down and documented "best practices" to be used for training and guidance in the future. Companies have taken the time and applied the best expertise they had to make sure that what they were doing was correct and appropriate to the task at hand, but they've done it in a leisurely, centralized fashion that worked well in stable markets.

Is your market static enough that you can give a group of specialists the time to look at all sides of a marketing or manufacturing problem and come up with the best solution? Or will the opportunity where you encountered the problem—and perhaps your whole business—be gone in six months or a year if you wait that long to do something useful about it?

Solving Customer Problems

Customers with millions of dollars at stake for each hour of delay will go to whoever first comes up with a workable solution to their problem. They would like to have the best solution, too, of course, and you might woo them back if you come up with it after they've made another choice. At that point, however, you have to offer enough of an advantage over what they're using to make it worth the effort and expense to change. That's a tough sales job with a customer who is thinking, "Good enough is good enough!" and moving on to a different problem. So it is much better to be first and OK than last and best. That means that your front-line people do not have time to kick something upstairs or to consult everyone in the organization who might have an interest individually before deciding what to recommend.

To keep up in today's markets, your people have to be able to think on the spot and get the information they need to make a decision. And it turns out that allowing them to proceed in this fashion does not sacrifice quality. By connecting all the players to the network, we were able to speed up our responses. And as we drove for more and more speed in our responses, we found that the answers we were offering were generally as good as those that had been developed previously, and often better—on-the-spot understanding gets people straight to the aspects of the problem that make the most difference.

Can your people use their own knowledge to best advantage? Can your people advise your customers quickly enough to hold on to their business?

Distribute Problem-Solving Authority

We have found that the fastest way to get a solution to a customer problem is to empower the associate who sees a need to fill it. The associate on the spot is the one with the greatest interest in closing the gap: meeting the customer's needs will improve the associate's standing with the customer, level of engagement with that customer, job satisfaction, and potentially personal income as well—all powerful incentives. By giving associates the freedom to raise customer issues with anybody in the organization at any time, you let them take control of the outcome. They can drive it toward a conclusion as fast as their priorities dictate.

This is where the networked "open space" meetings really shine. When a company has associates around the world, the sun never sets for it—every moment of the 24 hours, someone somewhere is in a position to answer any question that may come up. (It is the associates who answer the questions, not the office.) All the channels are direct, with no need for gatekeepers and bureaucratic controls.

When your people have a question, how long do they wait for an answer?

Customer Feedback in New Product Development

Customers are the real experts on what customers want and will buy. An important and unforeseen by-product of encouraging dialogue among individuals in marketing and research on a global basis is that the current needs and views of our customers are expressed throughout the organization. Our speed of innovation on products and services has increased dramatically as a result.

Would your market share benefit from a swifter response? As your company progresses in its ability to share knowledge from place to place, try thinking in terms of developing the kind of organic organization that responds automatically to whatever need arises anywhere in the world. Think what would happen to your speed of response if you could develop a culture to do this within your company.

Making the Change

"An individual without information cannot take responsibility; an individual who is given information cannot help but take responsibility." That maxim, from Jan Carlzon (former chairman of SAS Airlines), is what we have used at Buckman to govern the change to our new culture. We knew we needed to move to a networked organization that was built around the flow of information and knowledge rather than geography, so we had to look for a new way to get people to assume responsibility.

Getting people to assume responsibility for making things happen is what knowledge sharing is all about.

The first requisite is to develop the culture of knowledge sharing within your organization to the point where the response to the customer (or any other need of the organization) becomes automatic. You have to create an organic organization that responds to any and all needs as they develop, with no central command structure to compel people to take action. Knowledge about any subject must flow smoothly across organizational boundaries.

The second requisite is to develop online learning so that it can be delivered over your network to anybody in the organization, where and when needed. How fast can your organization learn how to do new things that your customers want? The answer is—

only as fast as your people can develop themselves.

The third requisite is to put all this together so that your associates will have the confidence level to do whatever their customers need, even including assuming responsibility for part of a customer's operation. As you achieve this level of responsibility, your increased value added for the customer is self-evident.

The ultimate payoff of the change to a knowledge-sharing organization is that you learn to react to your customers' needs as they feel them—perhaps even before they feel them—cementing your relationships and enhancing your income at the earliest possible moment. That's a startling development, but we believe it is the wave of the future for the world's successful businesses.

What this book describes is a journey. It is a journey of taking advantage of the changes in communication technology to pursue a strategy with a broader reach as an individual and as an organization. By capitalizing on the knowledge base that is between the ears and behind the eyeballs of everyone in your organization, you can redefine your value added to your customers and achieve a competitive advantage.

To achieve these advantages, organizations have to be willing to change how they function on a day-to-day basis. It is no longer face to face but offset in time and space. Always remember that this is a journey and not a project. It is a journey that will never end if you wish to continue advancing your competitive ability.

With this book, we hope to show you what we were able to accomplish at Buckman Laboratories and how we did it. But that is just the beginning. We also plan to give you all the methods and secrets that we have learned along the way, so that you can figure out your own path to your future. We want you to feel comfortable as you start the journey toward *becoming a knowledge-driven organization.*

ACKNOWLEDGMENTS

The thoughts and ideas expressed in this book are the result of millions of interactions among associates in our company over more than 20 years. This is their story about the learning that we took away from a lot of hard work and a lot of fun as we tried to improve our ability to compete in the crazy world in front of us. This book would not have happened without their efforts over the years. Therefore I dedicate this book to them—all of them.

When I started this project of putting our learning onto paper, it was the encouragement of folks like Alison Tucker (our first sysop), John Burrows (my assistant for many years), and Mark Koskiniemi (that guy at the back of the room) that kept me going. Their assistance and suggestions through all the modifications and reviews were invaluable. We rarely see each other today, as I have moved my office away from Alison, John is retired in the U.K., and Mark is now head of our operation in Australia and New Zealand. So, we have produced this book as we have operated over the years—virtually.

Then there is Hilary Powers, our developmental editor, who helped us convert some vague thoughts into a book that will communicate to all of you. She lives in Oakland, California, and we have never met. Again, everything has been done virtually.

And Barbara McConville, my assistant, who pried the free time out of my schedule so that this book could get produced.

And my wife, Joyce, who taught me how to give power away through trust.

A special thanks to all of you that have made this possible. It has been quite a journey.

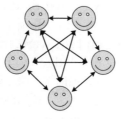

CHAPTER 1

The Buckman Labs Journey:
How We Broke Down Our Hierarchies and Built a Global Strategy Around Knowledge Sharing

> Knowledge is power, which is why people who had it in the past often tried to make a secret of it. In post-capitalism, power comes from transmitting information to make it productive, not from hiding it.
>
> —Peter Drucker

W here did it start? When did the insight strike that has transformed the organization and culture that is Buckman Labs today? People often ask me when we got the process going; 1984 is the date that usually comes to mind.

But looking back, I see I really began to think about what was possible much earlier than that—indeed, long before I inherited the company and was in a position to do anything with the insight. Back in 1967, John Pera (our head of research) and I attended a three-day IBM workshop on information systems, looking for a way to organize research notebooks so R&D could get at the knowledge in them instead of redoing the same experiments over and over. The trip did not solve that problem—the technology just wasn't there yet—but I did learn something that took my thinking to another level.

One of the lecturers made a flat prediction that the day would come when we would all be spending more money on network charges than on hardware and software. In other words, the movement of information and knowledge would outstrip the cost of the systems it ran on. The guy could point to some clear trend lines, but even though I was a statistics-oriented MBA, I still figured he was stretching things a bit; the idea seemed too far-fetched to be plausible. This was the era of mainframes and mainframe thinking. Nobody was doing much with the client/server concept and the Internet wasn't even a dream. (Funding for ARPANET—the military system that became the nucleus of the Internet—didn't begin until 1969.) Talk about a prediction into the future!

Even though I dismissed it at the time, the prediction stayed at the back of my mind. Then, in early 1984, I attended a Tom Peters Skunk Camp on the concepts in Tom's *In Search of Excellence.* One of the key elements I came away with was a point made by Jan Carlzon, former chairman of SAS Airlines: *"An individual without information cannot take responsibility; an individual who is given information cannot help but take responsibility."*

This struck home. I was now head of a global organization facing some major problems and lack of information and knowledge seemed to be at the root of a lot of them. My father, Dr. Stanley J. Buckman, had died in 1978 and my brother John a year later, leaving me to run the family business.

In my father's time, Buckman Labs was a classic top-down organization. All significant issues came to my father for determination of what should be done. His decisions then went out from our home office to the various operating companies for execution. This system worked well in the early days, but it had been under more and more stress as the company expanded and distributed its operations around the world. Now I was the guy in the hot seat—and it was no longer appropriate for one person to decide everything that needed a decision. We needed decisions too fast to permit us to stick with the old pattern, so we had to change it!

I spent the next two years trying to prove Carlzon's assertion right or wrong. I concluded that it was substantially correct. Not 100%, but sure enough to bet the farm on it. Moving in the direction of getting everybody to assume responsibility for making stuff happen became our game plan for the future.

Buckman Labs: A Quick Overview

Today, Buckman Labs has 1400 associates working for 23 companies that operate in more than 15 languages and it has customers in more than 80 countries. Most customers run paper mills, water treatment plants, or leather production facilities. Buckman Labs provides the chemicals they need to operate, and often chemical management and other technological support services as well.

That's vastly different from the company my father founded in 1945. He started with one plant in Memphis, Tennessee, producing one product, a liquid designed to control microorganisms on the wet end of a paper-making machine. He established a marketing company in Canada in 1948 and began setting up distributors in Europe, Latin America, and Asia. The product line expanded into different chemistries and different applications. But, it wasn't until 1964 that he set up his first plant outside the United States, in Ghent, Belgium, followed closely by an operation in Mexico City. He continued to consolidate and grow, establishing operations in South Africa and Brazil in 1971. After I became CEO, we began expanding in Australia and Southeast Asia as well.

When we took our first formal steps along the path to knowledge sharing in the early 1980s, we were providing a fairly limited range of chemicals to a much wider variety of customers than we have now. We had 500 associates and our operations were in seven countries—and that seemed like a lot.

It was rapidly becoming clear that every time we added another operating company in another country it improved customer service in that country, but made it harder to move knowledge and experience across the organization. And that was a problem, because we derived most of our new business and kept our existing customers happy by the creative application of knowledge—often using lessons learned in one part of the world to help customers in another. We kept teams of experts on the road, traveling around the world to solve problems and cross-pollinate local expertise, but the more locations we had the longer it took to get our experts to places that needed help.

A Short History of Our Journey

One evening in 1983, Dick Ross (vice president of marketing) and I were having a beer after a hard day's work in South Africa. He had just spent hours teaching industrial microbiology to groups of associates—and, as usual, had learned several new things in the process.

We began to speculate on how we were going to get that knowledge around the organization to where it was needed. It was at that point that we finally realized that our current methods were not good enough anymore. After our second beer, we decided to begin looking for a better way to move information and knowledge around. We did not know how we would do it, but we were sure we had to learn how if we were going to continue to grow effectively.

At the next annual Planning Meeting, the Buckman Labs leadership—the general managers, international department heads, and I—decided to set up a modem bank in Memphis where we could exchange electronic communications, then only just beginning to be called e-mail. Everyone at the meeting agreed that we would share best practices with each other and move knowledge that way.

What happened? Nothing!

In the first six months, all these good intentions amounted to no more than a few e-mail messages to see if the system worked. Not one "best practice" was shared across the organization using the system. It was then that we realized that top management has no need to know details of the new best practices in the application of our products, so top management would never find time to pass the word around. It was the folks on the front line who needed this information. We had to figure out a way to expand our system to reach them directly.

Bringing in the Front Lines

We decided to have Corporate Marketing set up a program to pay for the production of best practices. But the results had to be really "best." It wasn't enough to pry the knowledge out of somebody's head or file cabinet and put it into a medium where others could get at it. It needed to be reviewed and brought up to a standard that would give us consistency in what was seen as a best practice around the world.

We went down this path with vigor and enthusiasm—only to realize that it was a dead end. It did let us organize a lot of critical information and make it accessible, but we soon found that the marketplace was changing faster than we were producing best practices. We were taking about six months to grind out a best practice document—far too long to meet the needs of the front line. In addition, the process inevitably left a lot of tidbits of information and knowledge on the table, because they were of relatively limited use and the idea was to make the best practice perfect and universal. As a result, people quickly learned that the best practice docs were of limited value, because they could assume that details critical to their particular problem had been left out.

It seemed like the harder we worked at producing best practices, the poorer the job we did of transferring knowledge. All we'd done was whet the front line's appetite for improvement, without actually delivering anything new and useful to satisfy this hunger.

Establishing the Network

After a couple of years of floundering around with best practices, we brought in a consultant from Christian Brothers University in Memphis to help us find a way out. He recommended that we set up a network, which sounded like the perfect answer. But at the time—in 1986—that turned out to be a much bigger challenge than seemed likely at first glance. We wanted to give everybody a PC that could connect to the mainframe in Memphis, so that they would have access to our databases, and we wanted to make e-mail available to everybody. That sounds simple enough—and it would be relatively simple now—but it got more and more complicated the more we looked into it.

We set up a system we called Fastpath on the mainframe, building what would now be called an intranet long before the Web came along. This was an expensive excursion onto the bleeding edge of technology, but it helped us understand where we wanted to go with online interaction.

Access proved a major stumbling block. We had a mainframe shop, of course, and the people who ran it had urgent reasons to maintain control of what they regarded as *their* system. We also had a long-standing pattern of governing access to information according to status in the corporate hierarchy. Now we were talking about allowing people outside the building to dial in to our massive and sensitive computer systems. We had to make sure that the people who took advantage of this facility were authorized to do so—that they were Buckman Labs associates and not outsiders and, further, that they were authorized to see the information they were requesting.

It turned into a major turf war, fought under the banner of security. (I was constantly amazed at how well turf could be protected in the name of security. The creativity expended in this area was awesome.) We finally got to where we had six levels of security, with individual passwords for each level changing every few months.

The IBM Adventure

After a lot of discussion on ways and means, we went with IBM's networking system for access to one another and our databases. For the first time, we had global e-mail in the company and our people could reach databases on our mainframe, both from within the office and from outside. This was a great advance beyond our do-it-yourself modem bank, but we quickly learned that it did not take us where we needed to go.

The IBM network posed some technical problems that made life difficult for us. For one thing, it was set up for IBM-style operations and not for gypsy users who moved from country to country. Users had to keep track of a different ID and password for each country in which they needed to connect to the network. They also had to make separate phone calls to use e-mail and to connect to the mainframe databases.

Although database access lagged behind, as people were rarely willing to go through the hassle of making a second connection to the system, we did get reasonably effective e-mail service from the IBM network. In response, our speed of innovation, as measured by sales of new products as a percentage of total sales (discussed in detail in Chapter 16), took a big enough jump to make us hungry for more. We began to think of other ways to improve our communications across time and space.

We worked with the IBM people for several years, trying to persuade them to change their network to allow for IDs that would work from any country and to permit both e-mail and database access from a single connection. In this we were unsuccessful, as the network served their needs as they saw them. Around 1991 we began looking elsewhere for a new approach.

Knowledge Base via CompuServe

What we were after was a way to allow our associates to connect to one another at their discretion, as easily as possible, wherever they were. That requirement precluded use of much of the otherwise most effective software and hardware of the day, as it was locked into the office and our people—as discussed in more detail in Chapter 8—simply weren't there enough of the time to make such systems worthwhile.

It became clear that we needed to think in terms of ways to link up laptops, because laptops were giving us a much better return on investment than we were getting from desktop systems. Even though they were very crude at that time, the laptops that we had were already producing results for us. My first one weighed 17 pounds, but I lugged it on several trips and was glad to do so. It was heavy enough to be a nuisance to haul around, but so much better than having to work only in the office that it fueled the desire for something lighter, smaller, and faster. The search was on.

Then I was laid up at home for two weeks with a ruptured disk—after a jogging accident. Tiring quickly of daytime television, I propped my laptop on my stomach and began to get some work out while following my doctor's orders to stay flat on my back. As I thought about where we were and where we wanted to go, I came up with some characteristics of an ideal knowledge-sharing system that have stood the test of time:

> ► Reduce the number of transmissions to *one* so as to achieve the least distortion of the knowledge transmitted.

- ▶ Give everyone access to knowledge.
- ▶ Let everyone enter knowledge.
- ▶ Make sure the system works whenever and wherever anyone wants to use it.
- ▶ Make the system easy to use.
- ▶ Allow communication in any language.

I'll go into more detail on each point in later chapters, but this list is enough for now to describe the criteria we used to guide our search for a replacement for IBM's network.

Of the options then available, we decided CompuServe had the most to offer us. It then took us three months to persuade CompuServe's management that we knew what we were doing when we proposed to give every Buckman Labs associate ID access to everything CompuServe offered at that time. We saw this as a way to demonstrate trust in our associates and to train them in the very systems that we were going to use for the sharing of tacit knowledge across the organization. The CompuServe reps believed we would be so overwhelmed with network charges that we would abandon the system as soon as we got started. But we wouldn't take any restrictions and they finally agreed to the contract we requested.

Network charges did soar for the first few months. But they slowly settled into the activity range that we expected when we signed up for the service. I also still had in the back of my head that forward-looking idea that network charges were supposed to exceed the cost of hardware and software at some point in the future—and even with this expansion we were nowhere close to that number. So I was not worried about the volume of traffic.

Some of our operating management continued to worry about the costs, however, so I made sure the CompuServe charges were centrally billed and buried to remove any incentive to try to control costs by reducing communication. Controlling costs by restricting the use of the system would have been the wrong thing to do.

When we went with CompuServe, we established our own private Forums to address Buckman Labs' business needs. Our associates rapidly began sharing both explicit knowledge (the sort of thing we'd been trying to do with the best practice documents) and tacit knowledge (the insights people realized were valuable only when they learned others didn't already have them) across time and space in response to the problems and opportunities that our customers were bringing us. We called them clusters of conversation around our needs. (Today, these would be called Issue-Driven Communities and Communities of Practice; see Chapter 12.)

Our speed of innovation soared again, but we also ran into two major problems that interfered with full use of the system. People *could* share information freely, but the mind-set and culture of the organization made them reluctant to do so: knowledge was a source of personal advantage, and therefore something to be hoarded rather than given away. In addition, controlling the flow of information and knowledge to and from the front-line associates was the power base—indeed, the reason for being—of the middle managers, who were understandably reluctant to let go of the bedrock of their jobs no matter what they were told it would mean to the company.

The next three chapters go into detail on what we did to deal with these cultural problems. For now, it's enough to say that we were able to do so—and that's the basis for our continuing success.

Knowledge Transfer—a New Department

In March 1992, we created a new department, called Knowledge Transfer (KT), consolidating separate Information Services and Telecommunications departments and merging them with the Technical Information Center (the company library). This was an epic shake-up: Information Services had reported to Finance and the Technical Information Center to R&D and Telecommunications was part of Office Management. By bringing these groups together and then having their head report directly to the CEO, we simplified the lines of authority and made it much easier to move in the direction we desired to go.

KT's mission is to respond to global knowledge needs by planning and managing the resources necessary to rapidly disseminate collective industry, technical, and market knowledge. More specifically, KT is charged with accelerating the accumulation and dissemination of knowledge within the company, providing easy and rapid access to the company's global knowledge bases and sharing best practices with all Buckman affiliates.

K'Netix

In 1994, we introduced something we called "K'Netix, The Buckman Knowledge Network" as our service-marked term for the way we used the CompuServe interface. It gave an identity and marketing advantage to a capability unique to Buckman Labs that could be applied to bring value to our customers. The term is still in use even though we've moved on to other systems.

K'Netix became the umbrella under which different programs and systems—some old, some new, some compatible, some not—were housed. It covers electronic forums, online libraries, a knowledge base, e-mail, Internet and World Wide Web access, our intranet, project-tracking systems, customer relationship management systems, groupware, bulletin boards, and virtual conference rooms, as well as the databases that capture institutional memory that is then made accessible to all associates. K'Netix is available 24 hours a day seven days a week, with easy laptop access for associates all around the world.

Because we were able to piggyback on CompuServe's technology and network, launching K'Netix took us only 30 days. We just used what was already there—no need to build the system from the ground up. That let us achieve worldwide connectivity at a fraction of the cost of building it ourselves. We spent our money on network costs and not on infrastructure. This shift in approach allowed us to radically increase the ability of our associates to communicate with each other and with anybody else in the world. And that is what has enabled us to become a knowledge-driven organization.

The increasing interaction among our workforce brought two key concepts to the fore: *span of communication* and *span of influence.*

Span of communication refers to the geographic reach of the communication system, which is governed by the technology used. That is, face-to-face meetings need no technology to increase their reach. The developments of the past century—telephones, in-house computer systems, dedicated networks, the Internet—have made it possible for people to communicate individually or in groups at greater and greater distance. However, although technology determines the maximum possible span of communication in any given situation, the actual span of communication is also shaped by social forces. The online interactions permitted by modern technology eliminate physical distance as a factor and at the same time greatly reduce social distance, making issues such as positional power, age, and ethnic and gender differences easier to set aside.

Span of influence follows from span of communication; if anyone can talk to anyone, what matters is who listens—and why. Influence—power—accumulates around the people who make the most sense, and the whole social structure begins to slide into new patterns. As individual span of influence expands, power and value to the organization expand along with it. People become respected on the basis of what they can contribute to others.

This recognition has a lot to do with why people will go to the trouble of putting their knowledge out there for others to use across time and space. Buckman Labs has thrived as a result of giving all associates the same opportunity to expand their span of influence—and then applying constant encouragement year after year to make sure that people at every level understand that they not only can but should take advantage of the opportunity.

As the title of Chapter 2 proclaims, *the technology is the easy part.* The cultural change we required to make it work was an epic effort, but one we found well worthwhile.

Beyond Forums

As we moved into 1994, it had become obvious that we had created a great learning tool in the Buckman TechForums on CompuServe. Our associates were learning from each other as they solved real business problems and dealt with real business opportunities. (Reality has no equal when it comes to improving the learning of those involved.) And because we could capture the lessons learned almost as fast as they came to us, we could radically increase our knowledge base of best practices that made a difference on the ground. Our knowledge bases were evolving on the fly, based on the current situation with our customers.

In addition, it became obvious that the network was much more powerful than we had imagined. It was allowing us to radically redefine the *time equation of work*—the widely shared but unspoken assumptions found in any group about how long any given task or combination of tasks ought to take. Instead of days and weeks, we now could do things in hours or at the most in a few days. We began to wonder what other areas of the business we could redefine.

Because our TechForums had already improved learning for our associates, we wondered if we could use the network to redefine their formal educational opportunities as well. After much discussion, we realized that we needed to bring in some experts in software development if this question was going to be addressed. We worked for a time with the Lotus Institute, then went ahead on our own to develop our Learning Center, which opened in 1997 and now provides a huge variety of educational opportunities using Web technology across our network.

The Learning Center is a continually evolving basket of opportunities that provides much more today than it could when it started. I believe we have seen only the beginning of a transformation of the whole approach to education—both within the company and in the larger world. Changes are coming faster and faster as new and better techniques are developed. The quality of the education delivered is going up and will continue to go up until it exceeds the face-to-face model of the past. (For more on the Learning Center and its implications, see Chapter 15.)

We continue to take advantage of the spontaneous communities that form online to solve problems and pounce on opportunities that our associates notice in the course of their work. In addition, we've begun to put serious effort into developing ways to form virtual teams—groups of people who can take on an assigned task and bring it to successful conclusion without sitting down together in the same space—altogether virtually. Developing the level of trust required for effective group work is much easier when you bring people together so they can work face to face for a while, but it's feasible at long distance once the people have the skills and cultural base to support it. (Chapter 13 describes these efforts in some depth.)

We couldn't have plunged straight into the networked culture; the technological network has to be the first step, as that's what allows people to develop new and different approaches to the business at hand. By addressing business questions in a new way, people develop the skills to work more and more effectively at long distance. When their span of communication expands beyond their face-to-face circles, their span of influence has the potential to expand to match, but it takes a cultural change before that has a chance to happen. Both the technological and business networks necessarily precede the organizational network, and the organizational network is essential to a truly knowledge-driven operation.

At Buckman Labs, we began with the desire to reshape our ability to provide our customers with faster and better service—that is, more prosaically, to break up the whole corporate bottleneck structure and get me out of the job of bottleneck in chief. The search for a single, final solution to the problem of access to knowledge has evolved into a never-ending journey. One of the key lessons is that this is not a project; it is a complete and open-ended transformation of the organizational model. It redefines and keeps redefining the time equation of work, improving productivity, and creating still more new opportunities with our customers.

So what have we gained? It's important to measure the outcomes of such an effort—something I'll address in detail in Chapter 16—but it's equally important not to try to measure too much too soon. As a society we get in too big a hurry to measure everything, even before we understand where it is we want to be going. You can call it the "Are we there yet?" syndrome.

I still couldn't begin to put a total dollars-and-cents figure on the value of the Buckman Labs knowledge network, but I can see its results in the speed of innovation metric and other bottom-line figures. Other effects are literally invaluable. It has allowed us to transform our operations in ways that we never envisioned in the beginning. The ability to apply our collective knowledge across time and space has allowed us to compete globally with rivals many times our size, and it may well be what has kept us in business as the market changed around us. It has allowed us to redefine the customer interface into one that plays to our knowledge

The Death of Fastpath

This message was sent on November 25, 1998:

> This message is being sent to all Buckman associates. If you do not use Fastpath, you may delete the message.
>
> All Fastpath applications except for PIMS will no longer be available after 5:00 p.m. (Memphis time), 3 December 1998. This action is in preparation for removal of the mainframe, which will significantly reduce costs in the next fiscal year. If this will cause any critical business problems for you, contact KTCenter via email.
>
> JM
>
> KT Support

Even though we'd started to move away from Fastpath almost a decade earlier, as soon as we found commercial applications to take its place, it lingered on. I insert its demise here to illustrate how long some things stay around once you get them started in this area—even after they prove to be ineffective. It also illustrates just how far in front we were trying to be in the early days. We could see the benefit of intranets long before they were commonly available. We had already been there in our thinking.

Do not be afraid to explore directions before the technology is available. That's how you learn what you really want from your software suppliers.

Operations of a New Form

> Knowledge makes resources mobile. Knowledge workers, unlike manufacturing workers, own the means of production: they carry their knowledge in their heads and therefore can take it with them. At the same time, the knowledge needs of organizations are likely to change continually.
>
> —Peter Drucker

What I have described here is the total transformation of an organization over time. It began with a technological network, evolved into business networks, and then transformed again into a fully networked way of life.

advantage. We have changed from a multinational into a truly global organization. We have become knowledge driven—and knowledge is still driving us. The journey continues today.

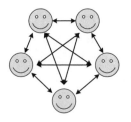

CHAPTER 2

Technology Is the Easy Part:
It's Culture Change That's Hard

The real issue is, how do we use technology for competitive
advantage? That's where people missed out.

—Michael Porter

Moving knowledge around is more efficient than moving
people around. It's as simple as that: knowledge can
travel at the speed of thought and it doesn't need an
expense account or a visa. In practice, however, it often isn't simple at all.

Humans are hardwired to prefer to deal with people they
know and can see; this inbuilt preference for face-to-face interaction cannot be ignored or mandated out of existence. But for
today's world-spanning organizations, it has become very expensive, both in money and in sheer human energy.

For example, as I write, I'm still a little groggy: I left Memphis
the Saturday before last for Australia to make a presentation at a
conference and talk with a few people. Then I flew to New York for
a board meeting. I didn't get home until Monday night, having
spent almost a week and a half on the road—traveling or recuper-

ating—so as to be able to spend four days working with others. Is that efficient use of time? No! But our habits of thought often make it necessary. It is this face-to-face approach that an organization needs to change if it is to redefine its allocation of precious personal time.

Modern communications—online interactions, collaboration, videoconferencing, and the like—make it possible to come close to the feel of a face-to-face meeting, allowing a group to reduce the amount of time it requires to reach a conclusion on an issue facing the company. Unfortunately, the advantage often seems illusory; it takes a great deal of organizational attention and adaptation to begin to reap much actual benefit. Many organizations have taken the first steps in this process by introducing what they refer to as *knowledge management* programs—by which they mean any of a variety of related concepts (see Exhibit 2.1).

Exhibit 2.1: What Is Knowledge Management?

Definitions of *knowledge management* crowd the pages of current business literature. The following selection barely begins to cover the diversity of thought on the subject:

▶ *American Productivity and Quality Center (APQC)*: Systematic approaches to help information and knowledge emerge and flow to the right people at the right time to create value.

▶ *Ikujiro Nonaka (author of The Knowledge-Creating Company: How Japanese Companies Create the Dynamics of Innovation and other books and articles focusing on his model of knowledge creation)*: Knowledge management is the tacit and explicit knowledge framework for a dynamic human process of justifying personal belief toward the truth.

▶ *Karl-Erik Sveiby (author of The Know-How Company, one of the first books on knowledge management, published in 1986, and the more recent New Organizational Wealth: Managing and Measuring Knowledge-Based Assets)*: Knowledge management is the art of creating commercial value from intangible assets.

▶ *IBM Consulting Group:* Knowledge Management is a set of

> practices that allows/enables organizations to better create, understand, and utilize what they know.
> ▶ McKinsey & Co.: Knowledge management is to enhance performance through a purposeful and systematic approach to the creation, development, and application of knowledge to the value-creating processes of an organization.

All the definitions seem to share a sort of innocent faith that knowledge can be treated as a substance, processed and stored and shipped from place to place with little or no attention to the vessels and media—the human minds—in which it exists. Only the first two even mention people as part of the concept.

Nonetheless, knowledge is first and foremost a matter of the human mind, and human minds are inextricably intertwined with human foibles and ancient reflexes. Notwithstanding the fact that human progress always results from pooling and building knowledge, individuals often find it most congenial to hold what they know for their private benefit. ("I taught him everything he knows. I didn't teach him everything *I* know!" isn't a stock line in drama and fiction for nothing. Everyone can relate to it.)

Knowledge Management vs. Knowledge Sharing

Communication is human nature; knowledge sharing is human nurture.

—Alison Tucker

At Buckman Labs we've found that knowledge can't be managed like electricity or raw materials—yet it has to be treated as something real. Of all of the definitions in Exhibit 2.1, we are most comfortable with the first one. It describes what we do, yet we have never used the term *knowledge management* to describe life at Buckman Labs. Instead, we focus on the concept of *knowledge sharing* across the organization to meet our needs anytime and anywhere as the critical path to success.

Alison Tucker's definition describes our behavior toward each other. She came up with it off the cuff one evening in 1996—and saved my bacon. We were at the Arthur Andersen Enterprise Awards ceremony in Chicago. Buckman Labs was scheduled to receive a top award for the sharing of knowledge across the organization and I had to make an acceptance speech.

There were a thousand things I could say and I did not know what to focus on. So I turned to Alison (who had been the driving force behind the success of our program) and asked her, "What does knowledge sharing mean to you?"

Without hesitation, she said, "Communication is human nature; knowledge sharing is human nurture." That quote crystallized my thinking and became the basis of my speech. It captured in a few words what we had been trying to do all those years: help each other succeed in meeting the needs of our customers. How the members of a group collaborate and share with each other to succeed, both individually and as an organization, will determine how fast and how completely they can redefine the equation relative to the competition. Individually, people are all vulnerable to being beaten. Collectively, a group can win in any situation if it can work together more smoothly and effectively than its opposition.

It's essential to harness the minds in your organization so they can pull together to meet your needs anytime and anywhere. This is the most powerful weapon that anyone can have in today's competitive arena. But you can't pour minds down a pipe or run them through a wire; you have to work with people in their cultural matrix to make it happen.

Process Orientation and People Orientation

> The key notion to sharing knowledge is that however strong your commitment to knowledge management, your culture is stronger.
>
> —Richard McDermott and Carla O'Dell

What it comes down to is that the term *knowledge management* is a misnomer. It is a term that fits well with what consultants can provide their clients, but it implies that organizational change can be achieved by simply organizing what is already known. In other words, manage the explicit knowledge of the organization and success will follow. Focus on the processes.

This does help, at least initially, by causing knowledge that has been written down to be organized and made available to the organization. Useful as that step is, however, we've found that it is not sufficient to achieve success. It can deal with no more than a small fraction of the knowledge in the company—perhaps about 10% of the total. The dynamics of a company don't change when it organizes its explicit knowledge. The step lets people speed up some existing processes, but it does not change the way they work. Productivity improvements are minimal. You cannot achieve quantum leaps in human productivity by using technology to do the same things faster. You have to focus on redefining the time equation of work and do the things that were not possible before.

We found that the vast bulk of the knowledge in Buckman Labs was in the heads of our people—and it was changing every minute of every day. It was not written down. Therefore, if we wanted to achieve success in the fast-changing environment confronting us, we had to learn how to engage people and arouse their interest and trust, making them willing to move their knowledge across the organization to where it was needed, when it was needed.

After all, it is this focused movement of knowledge in response to a specific need that stimulates the creation of value. And when knowledge moves, it becomes accessible: it can be captured in transit and made explicit, that is, written down or recorded for future reference. Since we have not figured out how to manage the knowledge that is in somebody's head, we have emphasized the concept of *knowledge sharing*. We have encouraged this movement of knowledge and the synthesis of new knowledge to meet a need of the organization.

Trust Is the Basis for Knowledge Sharing

> You have to be able to trust the information that you receive to be the best that can be sent to you, and those that send it to you have to be able to trust that you will use the information in an appropriate manner.
>
> —Buckman Laboratories Statement on Trust

In a fast-moving networked organization, people need to trust the information they receive implicitly. And that means that the people need a high degree of trust in each other. After all, if you are trying to get something done rapidly, you do not have time to check everything several times over, nor do you have time to wait for some central authority to vet the information for you. You have to have faith that you have been given good information to meet the need that you have brought forward. And those who have the information you need have to be willing to share it with you.

Thus everyone involved must be confident that whatever information they get from the network will be the best that can be sent and must also be confident that the people who get information they send out will use it properly. That is, they all need to participate in a *culture of trust.*

That culture doesn't just happen, and it can't be developed in a purely businesslike manner. Instead, it is built up through many interactions across the organization over time. It starts with an element of play and the sharing of trivia and gradually moves to more substantial matters. In the face-to-face world, people build trust as they socialize with each other—by going to the break room and sharing jokes, telling stories, or doing business over a cup of coffee. They belong to teams that play sports together, learning to rely on each other under stress that is not less real for being part of a game. They recognize each other as fellow members of Rotary, Kiwanis, and various other service groups. They play golf together and much business is done on the golf course.

Buckman Labs has discovered how to do the same thing in the virtual world. We have an electronic break room where trivial stuff can be shared across time and space—not surreptitiously and in fear that the boss will be outraged by the misappropriation of company equipment, but openly and with the boss's favorite jokes making the rounds with the rest. That makes it easy to go beyond trivia when people need to do so.

We even redesigned a major award system for our sales associates, online in front of everybody, across time and space. That shocked a lot of people at the time—it was 1994 and we were just getting used to the power of virtual interaction. The discussion ran for more than two months, and covered all sorts of possibilities, relevant and irrelevant. Here's the concentrated essence of the stream:

Grover: Without doubt, the field believes the RTR award is impossible for 90% of the people to ever have a chance to win. We have asked for either a reformulation of the RTR award or another award that will represent people that contribute in other than just sales numbers. ... This award, as it is applied now, is the biggest demotivator at the annual sales meetings....

Doug: I have heard the word "demotivator" many times when discussing the RTR awards. This feeling is widespread, and something should be done about it. Perhaps spreading the money out, over 20 or 50 people, would be a more effective motivator.

Gordon: As our needs as a company change and as what motivates us becomes more focused, the RTR rewards will also become more refined. Most reps work just as hard whether they have a chance of winning or not. I'd like to think that this is the type of person we hire. These people need to be recognized as well. I have heard of no less than 11 different scenarios for adjustment....

Bob [yes, I'm in this one]: Gordon, I am glad to see you in this discussion. I know there have been many suggestions for changes in the RTR award in the past and currently. You and I have had some of those discussions. I am going to try and give you the background. [Details snipped to save space.]

We can always increase the number of monetary awards so that something is provided for the top 10 rather than just the top three. This will increase the probability of getting a monetary award. Is this a direction that you feel we should go?

I have heard many comments on how demotivating this award is from this thread. If it is in fact demotivating to the individuals on the front line, then we should eliminate it. I have never had the feeling, though, that the award was demotivating from the individuals that have received an award under it. Can we make it a more meaningful award? I suspect we can. How? Gordon, you won this award two years ago and you have listened to all the arguments. What do you think we should do?

I am particularly interested in comments from those for whom the award was intended but others are welcome. Thoughts please.

[Four or five proposals came in from various people in response to the preceding request.]

Gordon: Bob, I wondered how long this string would go, without you jumping in. Thank you for the invitation. I have been with Buckman for six years. During three of those years I was fortunate enough to finish 1st, 9th, and 48th in the RTR running. I didn't work any harder during the years I had the opportunity to be ranked than in any others. [Detailed proposals snipped to save space.]

Bob, maybe these suggestions are not what will please everyone, but I've tried to incorporate what I've heard and experienced. I've also tried to keep in mind where you and Dick were heading when it was implemented in the first place. Thank you for the opportunity to speak frankly. Whatever the outcome of our discussion worldwide on this topic, the exercise alone reassures me that in Buckman *we* are the company and *we* are responsible for its success or failure.

Jeff: It appears to me, as a relatively new Buckman sales rep (two years), there is a misunderstanding as to the rewards available to the rep who maintains his base without the "growth" necessary to win the RTR. As I understand it, the main reward for maintaining your customer base as well as expanding it is the commission and bonus dollars earned from each account....

I have no complaints with the current system and think we should spend more time trying to sell new business and maintaining our existing business than to worry about this award.

Grover: Jeff, your proactive attitude is great. However, there are some of us that have been trying to change the inequities of the awards for several years. I want my reps to have an equal chance and, as their leader, feel responsible to push the wheels that tend to change exceedingly slow. I believe that the thread "Rewarding Yourself" gives everybody that equal chance every day of every year to directly reward the number of long hours put in their district.

Bart: Bob, one of the factors that makes the RTR unachievable for many sales individuals is that they start with a base sales figure that is too high to make a high sales percentage increase and therefore get recognized under the current structure. Often, it is a second-year sales professional that ranks high in the standings. The longer a person is employed, we would hope, the more they should be selling each year. ...

Chris: Gordon, you said it very well. I personally see little to disagree with.

Your plan is the first one I have seen in such a public arena to propose a *detailed* plan for change that seems to cover all the points and concerns. Many of us have whined and moaned for years but haven't really suggested anything more than vague ideas and partial solutions. You have got my vote.

Bob: Gordon, you always stretch the imagination. I find the thought that you express very interesting. I will want to crunch some numbers to see how this will come out based on the last several years' results. ... I have trouble understanding the feeling that the percent increase drives the award. It is not any more important than the dollar increase. The key is that we are putting emphasis with this award on increases. *Growth*!! The award is a mathematical relationship between the two factors that determine *growth* in sales. The percent increase and the dollar increase.

Bob [about a week and a half later]: I have looked at this award from a whole host of angles and the following is where I am coming down at the moment. I need some input before I make the next step.

The only way that I see that we can introduce all the desired attributes into the RTR award is to completely change the approach for the award. Currently the award is based on the multiplication of the percent increase times the dollar increase. Currently monetary awards are only available to the top three with the largest RTR factor.

The biggest problem with the current system seems to be the bias that the percent increase introduces into the decision process. It is difficult to understand and difficult to interpret where one might come out. ... I feel that the only way we can move forward with this award is to base it entirely on the U.S. dollar increase year to year. I also feel that the award pool should be divided among the top 10 individuals based on their percentage of the total of the top 10 increases. ...

Grover: Well said. There are some of us that have been around more than 10 years and, during that time, exceeded the performance of the recent winners but never had a chance at any monetary award. The senior people have held things together with mirrors during the years while covering 12-15 mills and having to get approval for a simple pump. I wonder if anyone appreciates these people?

Brian: I agree with Bob's idea on how the RTR award should be defined. This is much more fair as it is based on real job performance.

The only change I would suggest is to broaden the number of winners even further and consequently reduce the award amounts, perhaps 15 winners. This makes becoming a winner more obtainable without diluting the effect of the desired result. ... Thanks for making the changes this award has needed.

Bob: Hi, Brian, I don't know whether we can expand it to 15 with cash awards or not. We looked at 20 and 10. Twenty became too many for the amount of the award pool. The awards became too small and too close together in amount. This is something worth looking at. Thanks for the thought.

Bob [about 10 hours later]: Brian, here is my second response. We had a meeting this morning and it was the unanimous agreement that the award should be for the top 20 individuals instead of 10. I capitulated and agreed. George will be rewriting the plan and will put it out in the forum very soon. All the best.

Brian: Thanks for your involvement with the RTR award. This new set of rules is by far more fair and productive toward increased sales.

The forum definitely is a help in communicating ideas. Our people can surf the Internet and belong to an unbelievable collection of groups or communities—and we foot the bill, so even the skeptics understand it's OK to take part. By getting involved with each other, people grow comfortable in the building of relationships across time and space. They begin building the trust that will let the dialogue go to another level. Through socialization, they learn how to share substantive matters across time and space.

Eventually, people learn that they can bet their company's reputation and their own on the information they share.

As technology develops, people will be spending more and more time in virtual interactions, because the personal benefits are there and the economic benefits for the organization are there. To get comfortable with this transition, it's essential to think about ways to insert the social benefits of face-to-face interaction into your virtual endeavors.

Effective organizations have places where socializing is welcome in this new virtual space. It does a great deal for a business to create and encourage the use of an electronic break room. When you allow surfing the Internet at company expense and encourage relationship building across time and space, you do as much to build morale and a company culture as any Industrial Age firm did by opening an employee cafeteria or holding a company picnic. Organizations have learned that it pays to spend money on apparently extraneous things that build trust in the face-to-face world, and the same is true in the virtual world.

For example, consider "John Andrews," a Buckman papermaking specialist, who is arguably one of the best in the business. He has worked all over the world, for many international companies, and has a reputation for knowledge and expertise in the industry that precedes him wherever he goes. For more than 30 years, everyone who knows him has thought of him as the man to follow.

When we launched the e-mail system that was the rudimentary beginning of our knowledge-sharing system, John refused to even log on to receive his mail. He certainly would not answer questions or send mail of his own. He was violently opposed to electronic communication and maintained that the best and *only* way to competently communicate was through face-to-face meetings—which kept him on the road for eight months out of 12 each year, every year.

We clearly needed John's buy-in, but he was a hard nut to crack. The system of employee inducements—which were working for most of the Buckman population—did not tempt him. And the rather benign built-in threat—that those who did not participate in the company's growing knowledge network would not be recognized because their work was not visible to everyone—didn't faze him for an instant. He already had an incredible span of influence within the company and among many other companies as well, so he was in a position to ignore us.

Today, some 20 years later, John has his own laptop and is hardly ever seen without it. He participates in the papermaking forums daily, communicates with customers via customer forums, and reads and writes for the company news forums. Why did he become a partner in sharing knowledge when he once was so adamant about staying out of the system?

What got him started was the realization that he could answer a question once and share it with everyone. In addition, he could now concentrate on his love of training face to face—and help solve customers' problems at the same time. He found that even his influence, wide as it already was, didn't begin to have the reach it could gain if he added electronic forums, e-mail, and teams to his arsenal. Had he not found knowledge sharing a personal benefit, he might never have contributed as he does today. He still travels almost constantly, but almost exclusively to customer sites to present new technology to customers. His problem solving is now done on the computer.

People who are at John's level in any organization are rarely in the mood to help all and sundry join them at the top. However, when they get a taste, they often find the idea of developing their reputation for expertise still further, of being seen publicly online, sharing information and solving problems, is a benefit well worth the cost. Meanwhile, the contributions of their expert peers, once hidden as they pursued separate problems in far distant places, add both interest and power to their own work. And some of them rediscover the joys of home and family when they can reach the whole world without having to cross continents and oceans to get there.

Though the vast majority of a company's associates can be either induced or encouraged to join in a new method of work, the vast majority are often not really vital to the success of the system. People like John are the ones who bring one another online, encourage their contributions, and generate a lot of healthy competition among their fellow experts in the lab or in the field.

The level of trust in any organization is a reflection of its culture. Does your culture support the sharing of knowledge?

What Knowledge Sharing Can Do for You

It's worth saying again: knowledge shared is knowledge multiplied. This isn't a matter of how fast people can toss information over one another's transoms by the random bucketful. Effective knowledge-sharing systems don't drown people in information; instead, they speed up the problem-solving process. That allows an organization to reach closure sooner than it could with a traditional hierarchy on the job, thereby improving its chances of turning nibblers into customers and customers into enthusiastic partners—and of leaving its would-be competition in the dust.

Meanwhile, the people in the organization also prosper as their days fill with amusement as well as success. Physical travel won't disappear—some knowledge requires more bandwidth than any virtual system yet envisioned can carry—but much of the drudgery and indigestion of trekking across the world for otherwise routine meetings will become a thing of the past.

As people learn to function as effectively in the virtual world as in the face-to-face world, the organization can begin to think about moving the speed of response toward instantaneity. Ideally, everyone will be tuned in so well that responses are immediate. Instant access to information and knowledge will allow everyone to assume individual responsibility for making things happen.

To do this, we conduct what we call "Open Space Meetings" in an electronic forum. Anybody in the company can raise an issue and anybody in the company can chime in on this issue and offer assistance or an answer. Since this collaboration functions whenever people are available, it is not necessary that participants be online at the same time. They meet asynchronously across time and space. The conversation accumulates as a threaded discussion so that all responses can be seen in context. This collaboration continues until the individual who raised the issue in the beginning is satisfied with the results.

This simple thought is what it is all about—how to put the systems in place and create the culture that supports your people as they assume responsibility for making things happen when they need to happen.

For example, here's how it plays out for us. Say a paper mill in Brazil has a slime outbreak in its systems and can't produce paper anyone will buy. The Buckman associate the paper mill calls on for help has a situation that demands a rapid solution. The faster the solution can be provided, the more money the mill will save and the happier they will be with our service. Everybody involved has to assume responsibility for making this result a reality as rapidly as possible—but there's more to be known about paper and slime than any one person is likely to have encountered.

How do we use technology for a competitive advantage? How do we create a culture where the response is automatic and as rapid as an organism's response to a challenge from its environment? How do we become an organic organization? The next chapter begins to explore these thoughts.

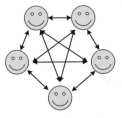

Chapter 3

How to Start Leading a Knowledge-Driven Company

With everything else dropping out of the competitive equation, knowledge has become the only source of long-run sustainable competitive advantage, but knowledge can only be employed through the skills of individuals. The value of an individual's knowledge depends upon the smartness with which it is used in the entire system.

—Lester Thurow

In the glorious rush of consumption and business growth that followed World War II, product was king. Having the latest and newest products and programs was what gave a company an edge. Companies differentiated themselves on products; they were what we now call *product-driven* organizations.

But something new entered the marketplace in the 1980s: the concept of bids and sole sourcing. Having the newest products became less important than having the best cost structure, pricing, and breadth of product line. Companies had to go from producing what they were good at to producing (or at least being able to deliver) everything their customers needed. In many cases that meant picking up the product line from dozens of other suppliers. The *market-driven* scramble was on.

Two decades of this drove margins to all-time lows for manufacturers like Buckman Labs. Eventually, we ran out of ways to bolster margins by cost savings on the actual products. The industry's survivors were all at rock bottom together and all selling each other's output and the world had to find another way to differentiate among them.

When you can't be cheaper or more comprehensive than your competition, you have to be smarter. That is, you have to be able to figure out what your potential customers need right now and get it to them so smoothly and easily that dealing with you makes their own work more effective than it would be with other suppliers. What you know and how well you can use your knowledge become crucial to success and even survival: the marketplace is no longer product-driven or market-driven; it's *knowledge-driven*. And in a knowledge-driven marketplace, knowledge sharing—the pooling of tacit knowledge and understanding from mind to mind across a whole organization—is what separates the leaders from the also-rans.

Moving from Product-Driven to Knowledge-Driven

When they start, most organizations are product-driven. At Buckman Labs, we designed a family of products to accomplish a purpose in the marketplace and focused on being experts in that area of the business. Our knowledge needs were narrowly focused around customers for this limited product line. We built factories and sold their output in the surrounding area, selling the same products in as many industries as the sales force could cover. Economies of scale were achieved as production was pushed out the door at higher and higher rates of productivity. Each organization was known in the industry for the expertise that it promoted. That was how we achieved value added in the marketplace.

As we migrated toward becoming a market-driven organization, we found we had to change our focus. Rather than selling to a broad range of clients, we needed to develop particular markets more fully so that we could become dominant in the industries that we were strong in. That is, instead of covering many industries, we needed to focus more intensively on a smaller number of industries and position ourselves to meet more of their needs. Despite this concentration on fewer industries, our knowledge needs expanded dramatically. Our product-driven strategy couldn't keep up with events in many parts of the marketplace.

This kind of consolidation is characteristic of many businesses in the current economy. It can be driven either externally by the customer or internally by the company. In either case, the change in focus is significant. Companies must look for more opportunity from a smaller number of customers. It is not possible to handle as many different customers as in the past with the resources available. Therefore, it is necessary to look for niches in the marketplace that will allow a company to get more value added into the equation. It's essential to think about crossing national boundaries and learn how this might increase global market share.

This requires a change from working within the stovepipes of the operating companies to functioning on a worldwide basis across the stovepipes of the operating companies. To serve global customers, a company needs global teams that can relate to the customers' global needs. And as a company builds its own global teams, it will soon find that knowledge to meet its needs may be located anywhere in its organization. In research, global teams focus on the creation of new products to meet specific needs of customers; in manufacturing, they work to improve quality on global processes. Meanwhile, global teams in finance work to implement new enterprise software and in marketing they seek to match product to demand for customers that have multiple locations in different parts of the world.

Global customers increasingly want the consistency of global solutions to their problems in different parts of the world. If the customer is thinking global, then the supplier needs to be thinking about customer problems on a global basis to achieve consistency of performance throughout its operation. In many cases, the supplier teams are interfacing with customer teams and they are all functioning on a global basis. Everywhere you turn, in other words, you find a need to pay attention to how customer trends are determining the direction for your own people. And you cannot expect to keep up if your people try to do this face to face.

No one can depend any longer just on the people they know. In most cases the knowledge will not be within that small group, so they must all interface with a larger group, if they are to meet the needs of the customer and the organization. That means the company must start functioning across time and space. As before, it is a drive for increased volume within a segment so as to become a dominant player through increased value added. That involves beginning to assume the responsibility for part of the customers' operation, doing the job more effectively than they can.

This radical change in strategy increases the strain on the organization and requires rethinking the allocation of resources to achieve success. Moving toward more complex forms of customer interaction requires mobilization of an organization's entire knowledge base. At Buckman Labs, we've found that the great bulk of our knowledge base is in the form of *tacit* knowledge (what people hold between their ears and behind their eyeballs). The true picture in most companies probably works out along the lines shown in Figure 3.1—but it can't be captured with any precision because every company's knowledge base is changing every minute of every day.

Figure 3.1. Where knowledge resides

Whether a company is product-driven, market-driven, knowledge-driven, or some combination of all three, you have to clearly identify what that driver means in terms of the needs of the organization. That becomes the strategy of the organization, and the entire company needs to work together to achieve it. In particular, supporting services such as information technology (IT) must have their strategy in sync with the strategy of the organization. IT departments frequently develop minds of their own, which is only natural, dealing as they do with technology that other parts of the company have not mastered and have often actively avoided. But for knowledge sharing to work, IT cannot have an agenda of its own that runs contrary to the strategy of the organization. The best way to keep everybody focused on the strategy is to stay focused on meeting the needs of the organization while executing that strategy.

At Buckman Labs, we realized that what we needed most was the generation of cash flow on the front line. Everything else flowed from that. We needed to beef up the front line with the customer so that we were the place customers would go for what they needed, rather than to our competitors—many of which were larger than we were. We began to build our whole strategy around that insight. And we weren't alone in the effort. In a great article titled "Strategy as if Knowledge Mattered" (1996), Brook Manville and Nathaniel Foote outline a set of operating principles for the knowledge economy that any company would do well to take to heart today:

1. Knowledge-based strategies begin with strategy, not knowledge.
2. Knowledge-based strategies aren't strategies unless you can link them to traditional measures of performance.
3. Executing a knowledge-based strategy is not about managing knowledge; it's about nurturing people with knowledge.
4. Organizations leverage knowledge through networks of people who collaborate—not through networks of technology that interconnect.
5. People networks leverage knowledge through organizational "pull" rather than centralized information "push."

Manville and Foote point out a grim corollary to the importance of tacit knowledge: people will not willingly share it with coworkers if their workplace culture does not support learning, cooperation, and openness. And it is unfortunately true that in most workplaces today, the culture actively discourages such sharing. Exhibit 3.1 provides the details on these principles as Manville and Foote see them; the discussion is still worth attention now, as it's borne out every day in our experience at Buckman Labs.

Exhibit 3.1. Guiding Principles for the Knowledge Economy

1. *Knowledge-based strategies begin with strategy, not knowledge.* The new form of intellectual capital is meaningless without the old-fashioned objectives of serving customers and beating competitors. If a company does not have its fundamentals in place, all the corporate learning, information technology, or knowledge databases are mere costly diversions.

   The old truth is still the best truth: a company has to know the kind of value it intends to provide and to whom. Only then can it link its knowledge resources in ways that make a difference—serving customers around the world in a coordinated, consistent manner; responding quickly and effectively to changing competitive conditions; and offering its products or services to customers more quickly, cheaply, efficiently, and innovatively.

2. *Knowledge-based strategies aren't strategies unless you can link them to traditional measures of performance.* Supporters of intellectual capital are quick to argue that old financial measurements not only can't account for intangible assets, such as knowledge, but also discriminate against them by using obsolete accounting principles. But, the hard truth is that if knowledge can't be connected to measurable improvements in performance—including improvements on the bottom line—then the knowledge revolution will be short-lived, and deservedly so.

   It's not as if we don't already have solid examples showing that knowledge can have a clear impact on measures such as sales, costs, cycle time, productivity, and profitability. One pharmaceutical company, for example, increases sales significantly by sharing physician prescription patterns throughout its national sales force; a computer manufacturer speeds up its rate of new product development by systematically sharing information among its marketing, sales, and engineering departments; a farm equipment manufacturer adds a major new stream of revenue by reselling information about crop yields gathered and repackaged from its agricultural customers.

These successes can be tracked to the superior use of knowledge. And they are much more compelling than the warm and fuzzy argument that companies should adopt knowledge as a philosophical goal since learning and education are "good for the company"—or even "good for society." The point of a knowledge-based strategy is not to save the world; it's to make money. It's for hard heads.

3. *Executing a knowledge-based strategy is not about managing knowledge; it's about nurturing people with knowledge.* Knowledge is also about soft hearts. And here's a key paradox. "Knowledge for knowledge's sake" lacks performance discipline; but efforts to engineer knowledge in some coldly bloodless way subvert the human dimensions of learning. The trick is to balance the "hard" with the "soft"—tapping the knowledge locked in people's experience. This "tacit knowledge" is frequently overlooked or diminished by companies. In contrast, most companies have elaborate systems to capture and share their "explicit knowledge"—the stuff that shows up in manuals, databases, and employee handbooks. This kind of knowledge never translates into a winning strategy. What good is a database if it doesn't include what the employees really know?

There is a corollary to the importance of tacit knowledge: people will not willingly share it with coworkers if their workplace culture does not support learning, cooperation, and openness. One office-equipment manufacturer sought to increase the rate of "knowledge-transfer" among its departments while simultaneously downsizing the workforce. The combination proved impossible. Who wants to share what they know when the boss is looking to cut headcount and consolidate expertise in a smaller and cheaper organization?

4. *Organizations leverage knowledge through networks of people who collaborate—not through networks of technology that interconnect.* Despite endless media hype about groupware and the "interconnectivity of the '90s," computer technology is not the real story. The IT graveyard is littered with companies that followed high-budget, "visionary" CIOs down the path of this or that client-server investment, or rolled out new e-mail systems—only to find that people still didn't want to collaborate to share and develop new knowledge. Interconnectivity begins with people who want to connect. After that, tools and technology can make the connection.

When it works, the combination of people and technology produces networks of people who transform themselves into "worknets"—suborganizations or informal groups whose collective knowledge accomplishes a specific task. The key to this worknet transition is that its members have compelling reasons for finding others with knowledge to share who in turn have compelling reasons to share their knowledge when asked. Which leads to our next operating principle.

5. *People networks leverage knowledge through organizational "pull" rather than centralized information "push."* The engine that drives knowledge development and sharing is the worker's need for help in solving business problems; the power comes from the demand side rather than the supply side. In fact, companies that push information at their people may actually cause information overload, blocking them from developing their own networks.

> The "pull-not-push" principle suggests that problems need to be framed and articulated specifically. For this reason, knowledge-based strategies should emphasize on-the-job learning rather than traditional training. "Just in time" learning, which takes place in the moment or actual need, not only creates the most value; it also makes the biggest impression on the learner and the organization.
>
> Ultimately, learning is up to each individual—it's not something that management can require.
>
> *Source:* Manville and Foote, 1996, p. 66; used with permission.

Culture and Work Flow

"Command-and-control" still describes the operations of most companies around the world. Indeed, companies often feel they have to stick with that tried-and-true (or apparently true) model because the legal systems they work under reinforce it so firmly. When the law of the land calls for an accountability structure that is most easily provided by a table of organization resembling a military hierarchy, it's no simple matter to look for alternatives.

The resemblance to the military is not coincidental—the command-and-control model of organization was copied from the military, which developed it to manage the activities of large numbers of relatively uneducated people. It served the industrial age well for many years, but it was based on a view of the workforce that discarded most of the range of human capacity. Frederick W. Taylor, one of the first great proponents of management theory, made the point explicitly: "Now, one of the first requirements for a man who is fit to handle pig iron as a regular occupation is that he shall be so stupid and so phlegmatic that he more nearly resembles in his mental make-up the ox than any other type." Such human oxen obviously needed to be trained and driven to follow specific procedures with unvarying precision to get their jobs done satisfactorily.

But jobs that keep changing cannot be done with unvarying precision. In addition, communication in a command-and-control structure is simply too rigid and too slow to keep up with the need for new directives to replace the old ones that don't work anymore. The strict patterns of flow that channel information from one level of authority to the next were designed to protect information and maintain its accuracy, but they wind up distorting it instead.

Command-and-control communication structures apply an assembly-line mentality to solution building. A problem comes in and is passed from hand to hand up the line. Information about a problem or opportunity is gathered on the front line with the customer and then passed along sequentially, with each recipient adding his or her own "perceptive wisdom" to make it "better." Finally it reaches some guru who gives the information the benefit of exalted and refined wisdom. The information either starts back down the line or is deposited into the knowledge base of the company. The net result of this cumbersome chain of communication is that the original source of the information would barely recognize it when it comes out the other end.

The whole process resembles a gigantic game of post office or telephone—the one where people sit in a circle, someone starts a message by whispering it into his or her neighbor's ear, and the message is then whispered from person to person around the circle until it returns to the beginning. Even when everyone in the circle makes an honest effort to repeat the message exactly, the message at the end of the circle tends to be hilariously distorted. All rigidly defined channels of communication are subject to the same problem and outside pressures often mean that the transmission of important messages is skewed, as in Figure 3.2. It is not surprising, therefore, that the wisdom provided by the guru is often neither correct nor even appropriate.

And the message isn't just distorted; it's slow. Like any assembly line, the process tends to move at the pace of the slowest point in the line. It fails to take into account the time requirements of the customer or even the options or components the customer may require. In addition, managers and experts are deciding who needs to know what—and it is impossible for managers and experts to meet all the knowledge needs of their people with this approach. You end up—to paraphrase Henry Ford—with a "You can have any solution you want as long as it's black!" mentality.

To compete in a knowledge-driven marketplace, a company's process of communication and thus problem solving needs to be

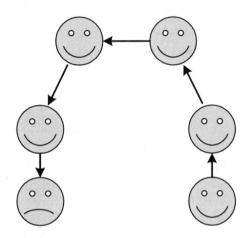

Figure 3.2. Organizational post office

more dynamic and allow for important problems to jump the line and get attention from those parts of the solution-building process that are most suited to the customer's needs of the moment. Command-and-control structures can no longer cope. Fortunately, as the average knowledge level in the organization goes up, such structures are no longer needed.

Today's companies are no longer looking for brawn but brains, because most of today's workers—even those who also need physical strength and endurance to handle their jobs—are really knowledge workers. They can and must think for themselves, so they no longer need managers to control the flow of information and knowledge in an effort to make sure that it is correct. That means their employers can now think in terms of a different model of communication, one where anyone with the need for knowledge can communicate directly with the person or persons with the latest and best knowledge on the topic. A networked model of an organization like the one illustrated in Figure 3.3 can begin to supersede the rigid command-and-control processes of the past.

The challenge is to do this while keeping the legal structures and records in place to satisfy the authorities. Many command-and-control systems and structures can and should be maintained. But in the realm of communications, companies need to move to a networked model that will permit the speed and clarity that are

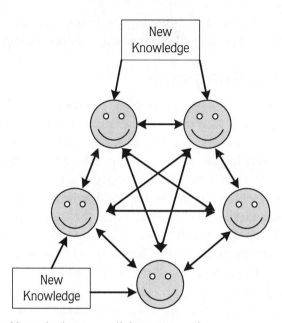

Figure 3.3. Knowledge as a living network

essential in today's fast-changing world. There will still be a need for officers of a corporation and the legal structure that provides that interface with the authorities and the legal system in each country. Legal systems change very slowly and organizational governance issues move at the same pace, so it's necessary to be patient with them as they struggle to keep up with the organizations that they purport to govern.

Meanwhile, it turns out to be possible to keep your communication model separate from the legal requirements and uncontaminated by them. As an initial step, think in terms of poking holes in the rigid silos of command-and-control communication that currently exist in your organization. When you become comfortable with the culture change involved in doing this, then expand the holes and gradually turn your communication model into a network. This will not happen overnight; culture change is a slow process. Keep focused on where you are trying to go and be persistent in going there. Use examples of success achieved by this movement to instill further desire on the part of the organization to continue moving in this direction of a networked model. You will find that people will naturally move in this direction, provided that the culture of the company will support them in this change.

The End of Geography

Legal requirements shape companies in other ways, beyond promoting a command-and-control operating structure. The countries of the world regard their borders as sacrosanct, so they set up their laws with a view to governing and regulating the commercial entities that exist within them. That strongly encourages companies to organize themselves into units that mesh with national legal structures. Unfortunately, such units key into the ingrained human tendency to divide the world into "us" and "them"—with other-country elements of the same international organization falling naturally into the category of "them" unless the parent takes dramatic steps to avoid the split.

And those steps are well worthwhile. Despite the pressure to divide themselves up on a national basis, many customer organizations have discovered global needs; they want suppliers that can provide a consistent level of service across national boundaries. Buckman Labs has found that increasingly it has to function on a global basis if it wants to meet the needs of its customers—and it's far from alone in today's marketplace. That means that the old organizational model based on geography is no longer valid. Instead, a company must think in terms of organizing around the flow of information and knowledge rather than around geography.

The flow of knowledge is what creates value. As you begin to consider moving to a knowledge-sharing organization, you'll find it useful to diagram the way knowledge flows in your organization today and then consider how it should flow to support the changing needs of the customer. You may come up with something along the lines of Figure 3.4b. Think in terms of organizing your systems and efforts around the flow of information and knowledge rather than where people happen to be. Geography is not as important to doing business in the world today as bringing together the right individuals at the right time to meet the global needs of the customer. It is how you bring those individuals to the scene of the action that will determine your success.

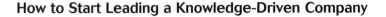

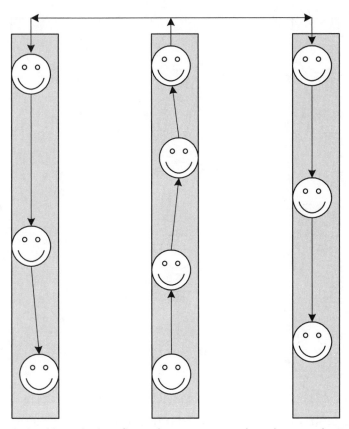

Figure 3.4a. Knowledge flows in a command and control structure

As you review your information flows, these are the key questions to ask:

▶ How do we increase the power of individuals to communicate their thoughts to others in the organization?
▶ How do we do this for every individual in the company?

The factor that does most to restrain the free transmission of knowledge is a concept I call the *span of communication*—that is, the number of places an individual can go for help without specific authorization. In a hard-core command-and-control environment, the span of communication is one: the immediate boss. Even people who work side by side are discouraged from talking with one another, though human nature means they always do. Most organizations these days have loosened up to the point where the whole

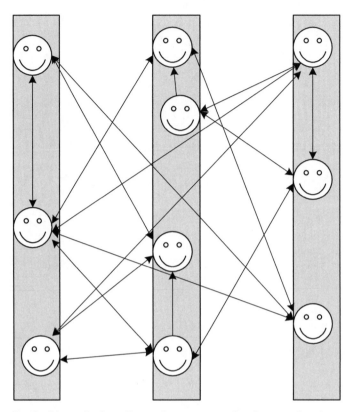

Figure 3.4b. Knowledge flows in a networked organization

team or work group is within the span of communication, and
some have begun to recognize the value of interpersonal networking beyond the face-to-face group as an asset that can be provided
by existing employees and new hires, a point Wayne Baker
describes in *Achieving Success Through Social Capital* (2000).

We need to move forward toward a condition where people
who need information can gather it without confusion or worry
about the appropriateness of the request. To accomplish this, individuals need a radically wider span of communication than most
organizations provide today. What they need is to be able to go
from the immediate work group to the entire company and
beyond to anybody on any network that they need to go to for
information and knowledge. If the greatest database in the company is housed "between the ears and behind the eyeballs," then

this is where the power of the organization resides. These individual knowledge bases are continually changing and adapting to the real world in front of them. It's essential to connect these individual knowledge bases together so that they can do whatever they do best in the shortest possible time.

But you may well be shaking your head as you read this. Yes, it's a grand goal to speak of letting every individual talk directly with whoever has the latest and best knowledge in the organization without having to go through someone else of greater authority. Instantaneous response and problem solving—what could be better? But what does that mean in practice? In most organizational cultures, the results would be gridlock and guarded paranoia, and requests for information would be about as welcome as telemarketing calls at dinnertime.

You can't just throw a switch and go live with a new culture. You can't decree an end to national boundaries and language differences. You can't get there by fiat—but you can lead the way.

Leadership in a Knowledge-Sharing Culture

To get the benefits of knowledge sharing, it's necessary to invest in it. And as with any other investment designed to change an organization, money isn't enough. You have to give it active entrepreneurial support from the top. The people in charge have to settle down and live the change, not just provide the resources and recommend it to others. Asking the IT department to go forth and introduce knowledge sharing is a recipe for disaster, because the effort becomes their proprietary project rather than part of a journey of culture change by the organization, and other groups then have a tendency to dig in their heels and hope the idea goes away.

Knowledge sharing is a strategic change of direction that alters the way the organization will function from now on. It involves all the departments of the organization, not just the IT department. It is not an IT project but a journey involving the entire company. And even for a company that is already relatively open, it is a genuine culture change.

If you want culture change in a department, the head of that department has to lead it. If you want culture change in an organization, then the head of that organization has to lead it. Everybody watches the boss. If the boss doesn't seem to care about communications and refuses to touch a keyboard, mouse, or microphone, then the others will not think communications are important and will not use the array of tools and toys you provide. I do not care how wonderful the statements of direction are, if the CEO does not back these statements up with personal action, then it will not happen in the organization. The one at the top must lead the organization into new ways of working by example.

When we began this journey at Buckman Labs, we were indeed leading culture change in the organization. As CEO, I figured that if people did not see me on this journey, they wouldn't want to go. So, in an effort to get people to use the new knowledge system we were putting into place, I made a point of finding occasions to use it daily.

I also tried something different. I got the system manager to send me a report on Friday mornings, showing users and nonusers and when they had last accessed the system. Anyone who had not accessed the system in the last four weeks got a personal e-mail note from me, asking if they needed help, training, or anything else in order for them to use the system. I added that if they were not getting value from it, then we wanted to know what we could do to turn that around and if they had any suggestions for changes or improvements.

It made a splash; every Monday, I would hear people gossiping about who got notes and who didn't. And every Thursday afternoon, it was fun to watch the user group increase—people knew the report was about to be run and they didn't want to get caught.

I gradually moved the time line forward—when almost nobody sat out for four weeks, I started on the three-week nonusers, and eventually began addressing those who had not been in the system for the last week. In the long run, this really worked. Even those skeptics who only went into the system because they did not want that personal note from me began to find value while they were there. Sometimes you do whatever it takes to change the culture when you know it needs changing.

Where Do You Stand?

Think of a business continuum from product-driven through market-driven to knowledge-driven. That's the direction successful companies need to be heading. Where is your company on that continuum now? Would it be better off at a different place on the continuum? Can you identify the barriers to your moving along it?

Think of your decision-making processes. Are you still operating by command-and-control? How can you speed up your decision making with people who have never met and might never meet face to face? What knowledge resources are required to be an effective player in your marketplace?

Think of your customers. Who are they? What are their real needs and desires? What products do they really want from their supplier? What combination of capital assets and knowledge assets will allow you to develop and be dominant in some new core competency that has a higher value added for the customer?

Think of your knowledge assets. Do you have what you need? Would it be desirable to invest in the development of different knowledge assets that will lead in new directions? Which ones are important for this new strategy?

Finding a Place to Start

What is your most critical need across your organization? I am not talking about just within a department or operating company. I am talking about across the entire organization operating in a global world. This is because all companies operate in a global world today whether they realize it or not. The size of your business is not crucial—size is largely irrelevant. Even if you are not global, some of your competitors are.

Think clear across the entire organization to its furthest reaches. What is your most critical need?

Is your critical need in your manufacturing operations? Is it relative to your customers? In most organizations, the most critical need is the generation of cash flow on the front line with the customer. If you are a private company, then this need becomes even more urgent because you cannot go to the stock markets for operating capital. You have to earn it!

In fulfilling the strategy of your organization, you need to focus on satisfying the most critical need with your systems for the movement of knowledge. It is essential that you begin organizing your systems and efforts around the flow of information and knowledge to satisfy your most critical need, rather than where people happen to be.

As you build your system around the flow of knowledge, look for ways to both encourage and magnify that flow. What you need is a people-centric system that builds trust among the participants so that they will share their innermost thoughts across time and space. Take the time to develop the set of values that you believe in as an organization so that proactive knowledge sharing will flourish, but remember that it will take time to build trust across the organization with people that have never met face to face.

Culture Change

The culture that we create as leaders in our respective organizations has a major impact on our ability to share knowledge across time and space. People need to move from the hoarding of knowledge to gain power to the sharing of knowledge to gain power. We need to create a climate of continuity and trust so that we may have proactive knowledge sharing across time and space. Everyone must be able to trust that the information they receive is the best that can be sent and that the information they send out will be used in an appropriate manner. This climate of continuity and trust, which is necessary to accomplish proactive knowledge sharing within a company, is the same climate of continuity and trust that the company needs to create with its suppliers and customers.

To make all this work, you must deeply feel, understand, and be at ease with the philosophies and concepts that underlie knowledge sharing. The implementation of change can be a pleasure rather than an ordeal—and it must be so, if it is to work at all.

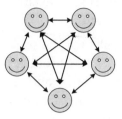

CHAPTER 4

Knowledge-Sharing Bedrock: Building a Foundation of Trust

Communications is human nature; knowledge sharing is human nurture.

—Alison Tucker

Alison's deft statement is probably the best definition of knowledge sharing that I have ever heard, so I quote it often. But it hides a basic and difficult question: Who will provide that nurturing? Or, more to the point, whose nurturing will you accept?

Will it be your boss? How about other associates in the company? The training department? A company needs a nurturing process to keep its people growing as individuals and collectively as an organization. And yet the process cannot be based on force-feeding the individuals—people will resist all attempts to make them learn. They must be willing to accept what they receive as useful or they will not take it in. That willingness implies mutual trust between the giver and the receiver of the knowledge.

Thus—assuming our experience at Buckman Labs is any guide—the entire basis of a knowledge-sharing culture is trust.

And for such a culture of trust to exist in an organization, several key elements must be present:

- ▸ The employees must trust the organization.
- ▸ The corporate culture must reflect the four basic virtues: justice, temperance, prudence, and fortitude.
- ▸ The company's statement of values must govern decisions at all levels, all the time.

Employees Must Trust You

For any organization to function today, employees need at least minimal trust in the organization and what it tells them. Even in the current economy, most people have a substantial amount of choice among jobs. They will stay with an organization only if they feel some degree of trust in their employer. The required degree of trust will differ for each individual. Some will need to be comfortable and confident and some will find they can live with barely enough trust to keep them coming to work. But the higher the degree of trust, the greater the acceptance of the knowledge transmitted between the organization and the individual—and vice versa. Although organizations do survive on minimal trust, they don't begin to reach their potential peak effectiveness when their people are watching their backs instead of their work.

Step back and think a minute. Do you share your innermost thoughts with anyone? If so, who is it? In general, people share most freely with those they trust the most. But how does that trust develop? It is usually based on common virtues and a belief in common values, patterns that develop most readily among family members and close friends.

The challenge for organizations today is to build that same high level of trust with employees. The higher the level of trust between an organization and its employees, the more knowledge sharing will take place.

Achieving this level of trust is the most difficult aspect of knowledge sharing. Over the years people have both taught themselves and been taught by others to hoard knowledge to achieve power and recognition. Schooling teaches everyone how to acquire and use knowledge for a better grade and personal gain, not how to share knowledge. But knowledge has no commercial value unless it moves across an organization and results in new actions. It doesn't matter how many Ph.D. degrees and other forms of expertise are tucked away in various offices and cubicles. All that acquired knowledge is of no value to the organization unless its holders share their knowledge with others.

Today it's essential to reverse the desire to hoard knowledge so as to achieve power. Instead, the most powerful individuals should be those who become recognized as sources of knowledge. They achieve this by volunteering before being specifically asked and sharing with others either what they have or what they can get their hands on. These are the individuals with the most value to any organization in the future.

But how does an organization build trust with its people? You do it one step at a time.

One of the first things you need to do is build values into the organization that are consistent with the values of the people. One key element is the amount of security that you can provide your people against the vagaries of the world they live in. For example, Buckman Labs has run counter to the received wisdom of modern economics by announcing a no-layoff policy—and maintaining it for more than 50 years in good times and bad. Actions speak louder than words.

Another element is the quality of the day-to-day relationship between the company and its people. We demonstrated our confidence in our associates by handing out laptop computers and by encouraging people to use them on their own time for their own purposes. When we went with CompuServe in 1992 and 1993, we gave everyone access to everything available over the CompuServe network at our expense—and suggested they ask their kids for help if they ran into any problems. (We knew that children could be good teachers and getting online would be a family project.) We had a difficult time getting CompuServe to accept that it was OK for our people to have this degree of access. They thought we were crazy and would be flooded with network expense. Their upper management would not agree with our approach and even refused to send us a contract. It took us more than three months of active negotiation to get them to agree to let us give this universal access to our associates. As it turned out, the charges took a significant rise at first but soon settled down into routine use after the novelty wore off. What the extra freedom did was extend our trust of our associates to a new area and radically accelerate their getting up to speed in the use of the new system.

Since the Internet became available, we have allowed access to everything on the Internet (except pornography, gambling, and hate sites) at our expense. While this may seem to conflict with our principles of openness and the trust that we have for our associates, we have always felt that such sites were inconsistent with the values that we espouse as individuals and as an organization in our Code of Ethics. That is why we restrict access to these sites from within our organization. We've purchased a product from WebSense that allows us to restrict access to these selected sites without disrupting other activities.

We pay the network charges. We urge our associates to go play and learn how to explore for knowledge in their favorite areas and build relationships of continuity and trust over the Internet. It is amazing how many company problems have been solved because somebody had run into the answer by surfing on the Internet.

We also have an electronic break room that is open to all. Anything can be shared as long as it does not violate our Code of Ethics. A key lesson that we have learned is that sharing trivia across time and space helps people who have never met and may never meet to build trust with one another, allowing them to share more substantive matters when the need arises. It is part of building communities across time and space.

Another thing you can do is open up windows of opportunity for your people to grow to be the best that they can be over their lifetime. Establishing a culture of continual learning and encouraging people to develop their own skills and knowledge at company expense is a win-win strategy for the individual and the organization. I will go into this more in Chapter 15.

A key issue that all companies have to address is whether you design your communication systems to control those few individuals who have a tendency to abuse the system or open things up to the maximum for the people who want to do things right. It turns out that trust is a self-fulfilling prophecy, and so is distrust. If you expect people to do the right thing, the vast majority—more than 99%—will do so; if you wall the system round with protections, many people will quickly run beyond the limits of whatever protections you have built. At Buckman Labs, we found it much more cost-efficient to build an organization around the majority who do their best for the company every day. We also found that the more open the system, the easier it is for the legitimate users to spot anyone abusing the system. As the abusers become known, they can be dealt with individually.

Trust between an individual and an organization is built one step at a time. It starts with the selection process—hiring someone already disposed to follow the Code of Ethics—and continues for the life of the relationship. It is based on the actions of both parties—not their words. It can be lost in a heartbeat. But, delicate as it is, it provides organizational strength that cannot be built in any other way. Build trust.

Creating Culture Change Around Your Values

A culture of sharing requires work processes built around foundation values grounded in the four basic virtues I described in the Introduction:

- ▶ **Justice:** Acting honestly and fairly, keeping promises
- ▶ **Temperance:** Acting with self-discipline, avoiding overt self-service
- ▶ **Prudence:** Displaying practical wisdom and the ability to choose well in any situation
- ▶ **Fortitude:** Showing strength of mind and character and the courage to persevere in the face of adversity

In my experience, all human cultures recognize and admire these virtues. But I didn't make up the list from my own knowledge and impose it on my organization. Instead, when it became clear that what Buckman Labs needed was a value statement that would speak to all the cultures represented in its worldwide operation, the management team realized that everyone had to establish what they believed in as a group of individuals and collectively as an organization. To determine what we believed in, we went through an iterative process with all of our operating companies in the early 1980s. Eventually, everybody in the global organization took part.

Each operating company met in small groups to determine the top 10 virtues and values that they believed in. These were combined and one list was developed for each company. These company lists were sent in to Memphis and a rank-order master list was prepared, arranging the virtues based on the number of times that each one made a list. This master list was sent back to the operating companies for their concurrence or for new input. Eventually we came up with the Code of Ethics described in the next section.

I believe that if you go through a similar exercise with your own organization, you will come up with a very similar list of virtues and statement of ethics. But that doesn't mean you'd be better off by simply posting the Buckman list on the wall and getting back to work! The effort itself is worthwhile. As people consider what they believe and develop their list from first principles, they realize its importance in their own lives—and as they observe the time and resources you allocate to it, they realize that it means far more than any of the high-sounding programs they've seen in the past.

I think of corporate ethics as a pair of shoes designed to help the organization keep its footing on rough ground: no matter how comfortable somebody else's shoes are for them, they won't suit your feet nearly as well even if they're the right general size. You need to walk your own way into your own shoes. The process is critical.

Code of Ethics

Our Code of Ethics, given in full in Exhibit 4.1, is the glue that holds our company together and provides the basis for the respect and trust that are necessary in a knowledge-sharing environment. We hold these fundamental beliefs as essential to our ability to communicate across the many barriers to communication that exist in our company. This common set of shared values has been critical to guiding the relationships within our organization toward free and open knowledge sharing.

Exhibit 4.1. Buckman Laboratories Code of Ethics

Because we are separated—by many miles, by diversity of cultures and languages—we at Buckman need a clear understanding of the basic principles by which we will operate our company. These are:

▶ That the company is made up of individuals—each of whom has different capabilities and potentials—all of which are necessary to the success of the company.

▶ That we acknowledge that individuality by treating each other with dignity and respect—striving to maintain continuous and positive communications among all of us.

▶ That we will recognize and reward the contributions and accomplishments of each individual.

▶ That we will continually plan for the future so that we can control our destiny instead of letting events overtake us.

▶ That we maintain our policy of providing work for all individuals, no matter what the prevailing business conditions may be.

▶ That we make all decisions in the light of what is right for the good of the whole company rather than what is expedient in a given situation.

▶ That our customers are the only reason for the existence of our company. To serve them properly, we must supply products and services which provide economic benefit over and above their cost.

▶ That to provide high quality products and services, we must make "Creativity for our Customers" a reality in everything we do.

▶ That we must use the highest ethics to guide our business dealings to ensure that we are always proud to be a part of Buckman Laboratories.

▶ That we will discharge the responsibilities of corporate and individual citizenship to earn and maintain the respect of the community.

As individuals and as a corporate body we must endeavor to uphold these standards so that we may be respected as persons and as an organization.

Each of the 10 points in the code represents a careful thought process that is worth exploring further here.

The company is made up of individuals. Each and every person is a "community of one." They are all different in skills and talents and experience, but they can all strive to use what they bring to the best of their ability. It is this collection of individuals that makes up the organization. All are necessary to the success of the organization.

We acknowledge that individuality by treating each other with dignity and respect. As individuals, we are all important to the total that we want to achieve together. To be effective, we need to learn to work with one another in a manner that brings out the best in all of us.

We recognize and reward the accomplishments of each individual. People all grow at different speeds and this is recognized by the company's salary adjustments and the positions that people occupy through time.

We continually plan for the future. Our destiny is in our own hands. It is how we play the game of life that will determine how we come out in the end. We are determined to keep control over our destiny by the efforts we make to shape our future every day.

We provide work for all individuals, despite prevailing business conditions. It is the responsibility of the organization to be creative in its actions so that its collection of individuals will continue to flourish and grow. The steps that the organization will take in protecting the livelihood of the individual members are limited only by how willing the members are to be creative in what they do each day. The last order of business is to let people go because we do not have enough business to keep them employed. After that we close.

We make all decisions for the good of the whole company. Everyone must continually think and act on the basis of long-range objectives and goals. If we chase after the flavor of the month, we will not build the pieces that are necessary to be a successful global company.

Our customers are the only reason for our company's existence. The value added that we deliver to our customers is determined by our products, our services, and our knowledge. How we put these pieces together will determine the total value that we will be known for. This will determine our reward and the cash flow that we are able to generate from these efforts. It is this cash flow that will determine how well we will succeed as individuals and as an organization. Without our customers, we would cease to exist as an organization.

We make "Creativity for our Customers" a reality in everything we do. As noted, it is how a company puts the pieces together that determines the total value it will be known for. In solving customer problems or enhancing the speed of global results or developing new products that open up new markets, it is the creativity that we are able to apply collectively and as individuals that will define our difference as an organization. The speed at which we can innovate as an organization will determine how much distance we can put between us and the competition.

We use the highest ethics to guide our business dealings. The way we work together determines whether we will be proud of what we accomplish together. The values that we aspire to and operate by will determine how we feel about each other. If we want to grow in our relationships with each other, we must continually raise our sights to be the best we can be.

We discharge the responsibilities of corporate and individual citizenship. The way others view us determines our value in the world at large. If we want to be respected as individuals and corporately, we need to do those things and stand for those things that will raise the sights of those around us. We cannot be satisfied with what we did yesterday.

Skunk Camps

Whether you articulate the virtues that you believe in as a formal statement like the Buckman Code of Ethics or you develop another set of values for effective communication, they have to become part of the operating reality of the organization. Otherwise, they are just empty words on the wall.

To establish our statement as an operating reality, each of our operating companies had what we called "Skunk Camps" to articulate the values and to empower our people to function on the basis of them. These Skunk Camps were three-day meetings devoted to going over the changes taking place in the company. (That may seem like a long time to take away from ongoing operations, but it's necessary. Such meetings really need three days and two nights. The first day, no one believes the boss is serious. By the second day, people begin to accept that the program is real. By the third day, they buy into the change. We tried to do it a couple of times in two days, but we never achieved the same level of change that we did with the three-day meetings.) These meetings covered the basic issues of transferring courage to every individual—helping people accept and believe that they were important and that they could make a difference by getting involved. We let them know that it was OK to run and fall. It was OK to fail. The important thing was to keep trying. Keep moving forward.

One image we've found useful is to tell our associates to think of our company as a ship like the one sketched in Figure 4.1, with the Code of Ethics as the waterline of the ship. You do not blow holes below the waterline because you can sink the ship. However, you are free to be as innovative as you wish in changing the superstructure of the ship to meet the needs of the customer. We trust our associates to do this intelligently. Two-way trust is essential, if you are going to have real knowledge sharing.

By following these principles and empowering our associates to take the initiative to meet our customers' needs in every situation, we have become a very adaptable and sure-footed organization. We can define our business as meeting the needs of the customer today because we no longer have to carry the weight of command-and-control procedures that defined the company in terms that suited its environment in decades past.

Create a Living Document

Once you have your statement of values—your code of ethics, if you call it that—you're not done with it. No matter how much work went into it, if you post it on the wall and forget it, it's dead.

To keep it a living document, you have to base decisions on it every day, real live business decisions, including hiring and firing.

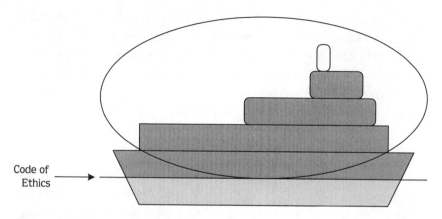

Figure 4.1. The company ship

That is, one of the criteria that new associates must meet is the willingness and ability to uphold the values of the organization. And one of the surest ways to get fired—from any level of the organization—must be violating those values. That's the way we work at Buckman Labs.

But the Code of Ethics should never be accepted as just a standard by which to judge people. It should also be a liberating force in the company, one that encourages individual and collective initiative.

For example, our associates can say anything in our electronic forums provided they do not violate our Code of Ethics. We have had several instances where an officer of the company wanted some message pulled from a forum to make the atmosphere more comfortable, yet the message stayed online, remaining in a position to advance the debate at hand because the Code of Ethics was not violated. By basing all decisions of right and wrong on our Code of Ethics, we have been able to develop a very open society within Buckman Labs.

Where Do You Stand?

Think of your own organization. Who hoards information and who shares it? Which is prevalent, hoarding or sharing? Do people trust each other well enough to share information across time and space with people they have never met?

Think of your company's culture. Do you have a statement of common beliefs that everybody can subscribe to? If not, how would you develop that statement in your organization? How would you make it a living and breathing part of your organization? How would you build trust in your organization so that you could have knowledge sharing across time and space?

The World Won't Wait

The only way a company can really prosper in today's racing markets is to take advantage of all its assets of knowledge and intelligence. That means developing a level of trust that has always required frequent face-to-face interactions to establish. But we don't have the time or the resources for face-to-face interactions on the scale needed now. People must learn to operate with trust and mutual responsibility even though they never see one another, in an environment made up of virtual and asynchronous contacts.

Management can build the framework for that environment and establish it within the company, but then, paradoxically enough, the only way to keep it going is to let go. That's the part of the story I take up in Chapter 5.

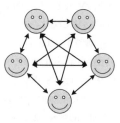

Strip Management of Control over Information

The value of a network increases as the square of the number of users on the network.

—Metcalfe's Law

Knowledge is power—but that adage can lead in a lot of different directions. It doesn't necessarily promote the sort of shared knowledge that makes a company strong in today's environment. Quite the contrary, in fact. In a hierarchical organization, it means that knowledge—control over information—provides a civilized alternative to physical force. Managers at each level can choose what is to be done because they control access to information about what *needs* to be done and about what is really happening. When people don't know what's going on and assume that their managers do know, they're likely to do what they're told.

That outlook suited the pace of the Industrial Age. It wasn't the only possibility even then, however, and it has become less and less appropriate with each passing decade of the Information Age. Nonetheless, many corporations are still organized as hierarchies designed to fulfill management's need for command and control over the organization.

This model causes communication to move in a sequential manner from one level to another in a process replete with checks and balances. Information gathered on the front line is passed to the first level of managers, who add their own interpretation and send it on. If it is important information, then it keeps getting passed up the line, and the process repeats at each level until this modified information (now knowledge) reaches some guru somewhere who pronounces it knowledge of the organization, after which it makes its way back down the line. Unfortunately, by the time it completes this circuit, it's apt to bear little resemblance to the original material.

The more layers this process includes, the more distorted the information becomes. So the more important the original information, the more likely it is to be distorted, because it has to travel through all the layers of management en route to the top. As discussed in Chapter 3, even with the best of intentions at each level, this process ends up modifying the original information before it reaches the person who needs to use it to take action on behalf of the organization—and every step of the way, the people who receive it face a thousand pressures to adjust the message to improve their own relative position or add their own concerns to the stream in the hope of getting action on them as a by-product of the main issue.

A Whole World of Communication

From the point of view of the organization as a whole, it would be preferable for information and knowledge to reach every individual in the communication pathway in a pure and undistorted form. But human nature is human nature. The only way to reduce the amount of distortion is to reduce the number of transmissions, ideally down to one. That goal was impossible when the only instant transmission vector was face-to-face communication, but it's feasible today because global communication systems bring one-link communication within easy reach. And all the older forms of communication are still with us. We now have a choice of modes, each with its own advantages and disadvantages:

▶ Sequential
▶ Parallel
▶ Network

Sequential Communications

Before the advent of electronic collaboration, work moved from one physical space to another in sequence. People "pushed" work, information, questions, or requests to one another and they acted on incoming work, information, questions, or requests as they arrived. Electronic communications don't necessarily change this pattern, as they flow naturally through the old channels. People can move work from one e-mail in-box to the next and on to the next in much the same way they would move paper around the organization, just much faster.

Such enhanced sequential communications can be very beneficial in certain processes, of course. Writing this book, for example, I take advantage of speedy sequential communications to develop and refine each chapter, consulting several reviewers for their input—which must be based on what has been written previously.

But for many forms of business interaction, this process is inherently flawed, and speeding it up just amplifies the flaws. Unintended distortion pours rather than creeps in as information and knowledge move up and back down the line. And things can still grind to a halt—any individual can become the bottleneck in the process of getting something done—without even a paper trail to follow to the root of the problem.

Parallel Communications

Any complex job—from building a factory to preparing a banquet—involves many separate tasks that all have to be completed for the final result. Some must be done before others, of course, but work on many can (and should) proceed at the same time. Managers have techniques such as Gantt and PERT charting to tease out the strings of work so they can get people moving in parallel toward the final goal. Communications likewise run in parallel on such jobs, and even people who are participating in more than one string of work at a time tend to discuss each one only with those who are also working on it.

This parallel processing provides a huge boost in speed compared with the single-thread alternative, where a person or a group does everything needed for one part of the work and then moves on to the next, leaving the output from the first effort to sit and wait until needed. On the other hand, it can get out of sync relatively easily, so that the output from one process won't merge properly with that from another—as in the famous cartoon that shows two transcontinental railway-building crews at the moment they discover the north rail of one track segment lining up on the south rail of the other.

Over the years, middle management has generated much of its value to a company and found much of its reason for being in coordinating the various parallel processes so that they all came out together. Middle managers were the gatekeepers between the processes—and, like any gatekeepers, they sometimes turned into bottlenecks.

Networked Communications

Instead of moving work from one place to another, networked operations put the work in a central space where everybody has access to it as needed. The concept can function with a physical product, as with some complex assembly tasks such as building a modern jet liner, but it really comes into its own with information-based networks that can exist in an electronic environment.

Networked communications rely on the "pull" concept—the direct opposite of the sequential push. People acquire what they perceive they need to do their jobs and feed the results back into the issue at hand, involving anyone who may have relevant input and notifying everyone who needs access to the output. The method can be used by a team, a department, an operating company, or an entire global organization, as long as the technology and the culture can support it. That is, instead of relying on face-to-face communications as in the past, individuals can extend their reach to the global world of the Internet. They can call in help from anywhere in the world, instead of just relying on those who can gather face to face. Whether you are solving a problem or seizing an opportunity, networked communications provide a way to bring the knowledge needed to where it is needed whenever it is needed.

When they work smoothly, networks are dazzlingly swift and effective. They can leave sequential and parallel operations in the dust. But they rely heavily on the knowledge, trust, and diligence of their participants and they can become lost in a morass of irrelevance if not focused on what the organization needs. They also require a dramatic change in the role of middle management, from gate keeping to facilitating exchange; this can be a difficult shift to make. In addition, they require a careful interface with the physical world—people a thousand miles apart can share information and knowledge about a task easily, but they can't all get their hands on the tools and ingredients involved.

Choosing a Mode

Networking is the most powerful model of communication in the world of today. The Internet and the many corporate intranets and extranets provide living examples of the advantages of instant, many-to-many communications.

Metcalfe's Law—"The value of a network increases as the square of the number of users on the network"—boils down this concept into an easily remembered epigram, saying that the bigger the network the greater the value. I can illustrate this with a couple of diagrams.

Figure 5.1 shows the communication characteristics of a network of just five people, illustrating the primary (one-to-one) communication connectors possible in a group of this size. These 10 communication connectors begin to illustrate the power of network communications.

However, the real power shows through when I include the secondary communication connectors, as in Figure 5.2. This diagram shows both the 10 primary communication connectors (one to one) and the 15 secondary communications connectors (one to two).

Suffice it to say, it is this expansion of the number of communication channels possible in a networked model that provides the quality of response in the time frame that all managers need. This is why networks deliver enhanced value so rapidly. This is the power of Metcalfe's Law.

How do we take advantage of this power in our organizations

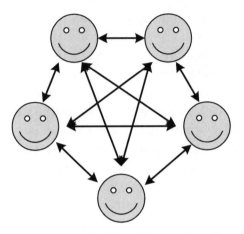

Figure 5.1. Primary communications in a network

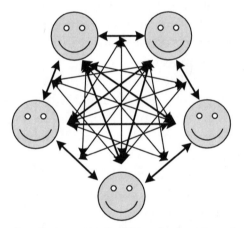

Figure 5.2. Two-level communications in a network

today? As a first step, we need to think in terms of updating the communication model for all parts of the organization. Old habits die hard, so that will almost certainly require significant culture changes within the organization. It will take persistent effort and will have to be led from the top. The CEO, the division vice president, the department head, the supervisor—all leaders in the organization have to be involved.

At the same time, it is not necessary to forsake sequential and parallel communications to make use of networks. Instead, a virtual environment allows collaboration to proceed in sequential, parallel, or networked modes as needed, *enabling everyone to see what everyone else is contributing at any time.* The important point is that all communication within the group should be open to all the participants.

Open systems of communication have many advantages over the secret pathways that exist in many organizations today:

- ▶ *They make it impossible for people to manipulate the discussion to their own ends.* Individuals who blow smoke are found out for what they are and who they are very quickly. You can guide an open discussion and lead it, but you cannot manipulate it.

- ▶ *They dramatically improve the speed at which you can reach a conclusion, satisfy a need, or generate new knowledge for the organization.* At Buckman Labs we went from taking weeks to satisfy a global customer need to a couple of days at the most—and a matter of hours in several instances. We did not have to do a lot of cost analysis to see that we had achieved a significant benefit—the benefits were obvious.

- ▶ *They highlight the high performers.* The individuals who contribute most become known throughout the entire organization very rapidly. They are not hidden in some department in some remote operating company. In addition, their managers cannot divert the credit to themselves—even the temptation isn't there, as everyone knows who is providing the value, and managers draw credit from showcasing the talents within their departments.

- ▶ *They greatly improve the quality of the response to any need of the organization.* Virtual operations involve more people with broader experiences and knowledge in the process, providing a living example of the adage, "Two heads are better than one."

Of course, there's a rival adage: "Too many cooks spoil the broth." The goal must be to create communities and teams that function virtually across time and space more effectively than people do when they stick to face-to-face communications. We cannot do it with the old models for communication. How do we further this process of moving to a knowledge-driven world? We have the technology, but the technology won't do the job for us. It's essential to remember that IT is a tool, not an end in itself.

The Networked World of a Knowledge-Sharing Culture

Nam et ipsa scientia potestas est. (Knowledge is power.)
—Francis Bacon, 1597

The culture in most organizations today promotes hoarding knowledge to gain power. Francis Bacon framed the adage that runs through this book over 400 years ago, and he surely wasn't the first to think along those lines. It seems that people are always trying to figure out how to get knowledge and control it. In hierarchal organizations, it's the foundation of power: the higher up you are, the more knowledge resources you have available to use in maintaining and enhancing your position.

The challenge is to move from this well-worn ground to a culture of sharing knowledge to gain power. If we want everyone in the organization to have access to all the information that they need so they can assume responsibility for getting things done, then we have to recognize that we cannot depend on the knowledge that is in our knowledge bases or electronic files. Too little of what an organization collectively knows is captured in that form, and in a fast-changing environment too much of that limited collection is out of date by the time someone looks at it. In addition, we cannot depend on management or experts to push the knowledge out to the people—it takes too long and it doesn't reach them at the moment they realize they need to know it, which is the only time they'll pay attention in the face of all the competing demands they have to deal with.

What's left? It turns out that everyone in the organization must be able to call on any resource of the organization at any time to meet the need at hand. That may seem like a vision of Utopia—a world where trusted and trusting people freely share their innermost thoughts with each other across time and space. But to the traditional middle manager, thoroughly primed by education and experience to expect to control the flow of information in the name of making sure things happen when and only when they should happen, it's not a happy prospect. It's a nightmare vision of anarchy, impossible to achieve and wrong-headed to attempt.

The Middle Management Challenge

The biggest challenge middle managers face in the implementation of open systems of communication is the attack they perceive on their power base. As I've said, people in management and particularly in middle management develop a lot of their power and prestige by controlling the flow of information and knowledge to and from their people. In this way they can control their people.

They derive their power as managers from this gatekeeping role. They direct what projects and requests should be acted on, where to go, where *not* to go. They set the priorities and generally don't take kindly to the idea that someone else will be able to disrupt their plans and interfere with the activities of their subordinates. After all, *they* are in charge—and should be in charge—here. So when outsiders can put something in an open discussion forum that will reorder the priorities of a unit, it naturally drives a traditional manager a little crazy. And a whole system that allows for discretion for associates to work on something not on the manager's work list looks even worse.

If you want to put in systems for open communication built on the networked model, then you must deal with this power base of the organization and redefine the way it should function. Middle managers don't have to be gatekeepers to survive. They have other avenues for serving the organization and keeping their jobs, but many of them will need help in seeing the opportunities and learning to take advantage of them.

Confused About New Roles and Resistant to Change

The history of electronic communications and networking at Buckman Labs provides a useful case in point. Things went quite smoothly at first, and it took us a while to realize that the whole conversion wouldn't be a matter of natural human instinct.

When we put in global e-mail, we had no problems with the management group. In fact, they loved it—it let them do their existing job better and faster. We improved their span of communication, enhancing their efficiency, and this allowed them to begin to think in terms of increasing their span of influence.

When we gave our associates access to our then-current data-bases and knowledge bases, everyone was still happy. We started by scouring the files for knowledge that we could make available to our people online. We also paid for best practices to be written up so that we could put them in knowledge bases where our people could find them. This electronic access sped up the learning process for motivated associates. As one put it: "In the pre-computer days I would have to wait until I was in Memphis to go through the files in the archive to find out what was going on at other accounts or what had been tried at my accounts years ago. I would get to Memphis about every six months. With electronic access I was able to go through files online when I needed the information, which meant that in the best-case scenario I was six months ahead of the curve!" Again, this gave our associates quicker access to the information and knowledge that they already had access to and they perceived this as a benefit.

However, when we put in global systems for the sharing of tacit knowledge based on the networked model in 1992 and 1993, we ran into a wall. All the middle managers, to some degree or another, perceived the new system as an attack on their personal power bases. They wanted to control all activity by their people in the new system, just as they had done in the old sequential one. We were no longer speeding up a process or making it easier to get access to existing knowledge; we were changing processes to rede-fine the speed and quality of the response that we could give the customer. We were not using technology just to do things differ-ently, but to do different things. We were redefining the time equa-tion of work.

That's when we found out that changing the way people do work requires significant cultural changes in the organization and the individuals involved. It all has to do with power.

Right or wrong, many of our managers had become paper shufflers, and they viewed the introduction of the new networked model of communication as a threat to their jobs. They thought they were being made redundant. And they weren't alone. When I took the problem to Tom Peters and Reuben Harris of the Tom Peters Group in 1993, they said I should just get rid of the middle managers: they'd been replaced by the new communication system and I should recognize that and move on. I told them Buckman Labs couldn't use that answer, for two reasons:

- ▶ These were our best and brightest people and we had promoted them to positions of responsibility based on their previous performance. It made no sense to us to start a wholesale reduction in our best people.
- ▶ In addition, we have a no-layoff policy embedded in our Code of Ethics ("we maintain our policy of providing work for all individuals, no matter what the prevailing business conditions may be") and we take it seriously. It's not window dressing to be discarded the moment it appears inconvenient.

I asked Tom and Reuben to rethink their answer in the presence of these two constraints. Two days later they came back and recommended that we explicitly redefine the managerial role in our organization, from one of controlling the flow of information and knowledge to and from a group of people to one of helping those people succeed in the fast-changing world in front of them.

The middle managers needed to learn to let the new system handle the communication needs of their groups because it produced faster results for the customer than the old system and improved quality at the same time. To get them to accept that sweeping change in operations, we had to show them how they could get value from the new system for their own needs.

Our entry point was the observation that, as a group, middle managers were always pressed for time. The better they were as managers and the more they cared for their people, the more trouble they had finding time to do everything they needed to do. We had many one-on-one meetings showing how they could get value from the system for their people and how they as managers could redefine their own time equation of work. They had to give up power over one aspect of their work to be able to gain more power elsewhere. What it boiled down to was persuading them that they could move faster in the directions they wanted to go and become more important as leaders of the organization if they embraced the new system.

We tried to do all this quietly and not shame anyone in front of the associates who reported to them. At the same time, we championed any success story we could get our hands on. Between these two efforts, we gradually changed the culture of the company in the direction of faster and further communications by every individual. We redefined how fast a unit could achieve closure with the concerns of its customers. These are some of the specifics that were most useful in the reeducation effort:

▶ Each week, I received a list of everyone who had not used the system in recent weeks. I would then write to the whole list to ask what we could do to help them get value from the system. This was followed up with communications by others, systematically working with each individual until we reached critical mass in system usage.

▶ We defined knowledge-sharing effectiveness as a point to cover in each individual performance review and made sure that the people who were the best knowledge sharers in the company benefited accordingly—and that everyone knew what we were doing on this.

▶ We adopted the slogan "Effective Engagement on the Front Line" and emphasized the role that everyone could play by living by that principle.

▶ We went beyond slogans, publishing success stories and downplaying instances of backsliding. That is, we distributed success stories that highlighted movement in the direction that we wanted to go as an organization—anything from a clerical spreadsheet-optimization trick to a new approach to a chemical problem could provide an occasion for general praise and admiration. We knew that we were dealing with culture change and we had to show what the new definition of success looked like for everyone.

▶ Along with others in the management team, I went from office to office and sat with the managers and associates, showing them ways to get value from the new system.

▶ Information Services specialists helped the managers upload their files into the new system so that they could continue to project themselves as leaders of the organization. As soon as they realized how much easier it was to tell people where to get something than it was to make copies and send them out in answer to requests, most managers began to see the new system as a way to expand their influence rather than as an effort to curtail it.

As a result of all this effort, the networked operation became a win/win situation for the managers, the customers, and the organization. When we went into it, we thought we were introducing a straightforward change in communication methods within our organization and that it would be a simple exercise for everyone involved. But it turned out that the cultural aspects of the issue slowed down our progress and almost stopped it.

Changing the way people work is difficult. It does not come with just the installation of some new software. You have to teach your people how to achieve success in the new community of virtual activities—to take the time to teach them and help them realize that this is a permanent change in the way work will be done. It can't be viewed as just something to do for this project coming up; instead, it must be part of the shift in culture so that the organization can continue the journey to better times.

Where Do You Stand?

Think of your organization's middle managers. Where do they derive their sense of purpose? How many are likely to see networked communications as an opportunity rather than a nightmare? What can you do to bring the reluctant managers into a networked world?

Think of your budgets for IT and training. What do they tell you about what's important in your current operation? Will they support you in your new course? Are you willing to invest resources in training your knowledge workers?

Think about the cultural outlook people need if they are to operate effectively in an open, networked communication model. Are you willing to help your middle managers achieve success in a new way? Are you willing to help them increase their span of influence across the organization? Would other managers view such an effort as interference? If so, what would you do about it?

What's Next?

Productivity improvements will not come from just speeding up existing processes. It's essential to redefine processes while taking full advantage of the benefits that technology can bring to the equation—and to remember that, as appealing as it is to play with the technology and look for the perfect application, the great bulk of the effort will be needed in cultural change. The technology component will be the easy part. Behavior change is hard change. Yet this is where the benefit is and this is where the effort will really pay off in terms of bringing the benefits of communication advances to the bottom line.

Your relative expenditures for technological change (equipment, software, connection) and cultural change (training, performance evaluation, and internal publicity efforts) will give you some idea of the magnitude of the problem your organization will be dealing with. How much are you committing to teaching your people how to function in a new and better way? How much of your training is designed to help your people function in a new and virtual world? Remember that this is a journey and not a project. And it is a painful journey. It is a journey of change.

As you move down this path to the future, you will find that your organization will need to encourage and emphasize new patterns of behavior. You will not get there by doing it the same old way. For example, knowledge sharing among individuals has proved to be a critical element in achieving success in Buckman Labs—so critical that we have stopped considering individuals for advancement unless they actively reach out to share knowledge in the organization. It's part of our annual review process now, and I believe that you will find it equally necessary in your organization. You have to reinforce the behavior you want people to engage in if you hope to be successful on your journey.

At the same time, the most effective cultural changes won't bring networked communications to a global company unless you also have the technology to make them work. The technological component may be the easy part when compared with the cultural redevelopment, but it's not necessarily either easy or cheap in absolute terms. The next chapter turns to the technological side, discussing ways to speed up and simplify the process of introducing the tools that make it possible for the new culture to develop in your organization.

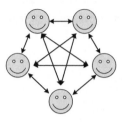

CHAPTER 6

Build or Buy a Knowledge System:
Custom-Made and Off-the-Shelf Solutions

Knowledge is the beginning of practice; doing is the completion of knowing.

—Wang Yang-Ming, 1498

I s your IT director telling you that the department can produce better software than anything on the market today? Self-confident love of the craft like this is what drives a lot of the creativity behind the constant stream of software and systems that compete for our attention every day. It's an attribute shared by the best in the IT field. But it doesn't always serve a company's best interests.

When it tempts people to build something that won't bring in any direct income and therefore won't have a built-in incentive for support, it becomes dangerous. A company that goes down that road is playing an expensive game, one that will at best take resources away from applications that do serve the organization in the pursuit of its strategy.

The Basic Choice

Of course, we all like to think that our business is unique and that we know best what kind of software will serve its needs. It follows that no outsider can do as good a job as our own people when it comes to defining and building software and systems for us. This outlook was reinforced during the early decades of the Information Age, when build-it-yourself was first the only option for creating mainframe systems and then, for many years, still the best option when compared with the commercial products offered.

To this day, many companies keep a corps of programmers on staff. It seems only natural to continue with the traditional thought process and create, in house, whatever is necessary to expand the company's computer systems to support communication and collaboration. Unfortunately, these days custom software and systems rarely provide the payback necessary to justify the expenditures of time and money they require. You not only have to make them, but you also have to maintain them so that they stay state-of-the-art. This takes a commitment of people and resources beyond the economic reach of most companies.

House-written code has another built-in problem: it takes a lot of time to create software and keep it up to date. Business is speeding up more and more, and the time to produce, maintain, and modify software has become an unaffordable luxury for most companies. Remember: the people cost of writing code is not going down. If it is not possible to spread this cost over a greater and greater user base, then it is not possible to get economies of scale when writing your own code. And the only way to get a sufficiently large user base is to have the program compete in the mass market and not just within one company. What would it cost your company to develop and maintain the vast collection of programs distributed under the name of Microsoft Office? Yet you can license the software today at a nominal fee per user.

The size of the user base also determines how rapidly a given software package can be updated to the current state of the art. The current consolidation in the software industry is not over; in my opinion, it will continue until a very small number of software houses dominate the mass market for business application software. Those companies that develop the largest user base will have the economies of scale to provide the latest bells and whistles at the lowest cost. The bottom line: unless you are in the software business, stay clear! It is not your core competency and it is not your marketplace.

Yet putting together software and hardware packages into unique and powerful systems still takes thought and expertise. You don't want to dismiss your IT department and trot off to the nearest computer superstore in search of a universal answer! Instead, enlist your IT department in helping you move as fast as possible in the direction of selecting packages of software that will do your job—and the ideal equipment to run that software—and keeping your people up to date on the use of the software and equipment you provide.

The marketplace of ideas is currently offering an interesting alternative to buying software licenses. Some organizations are moving to *open-source* software—free systems developed communally over the Internet—to serve their needs. Open-source software works under Linux, a free Unix-type operating system originally created by Linus Torvalds with the assistance of developers around the world. It will be interesting to see how far this expansion of the code-writing knowledge base and community to anybody wishing to get involved will go. If business is willing to adopt this approach, then we will have another revolution in the software that we use to run our systems. The cost equation will be radically redefined again.

Whether they license software or go the open-source route, the companies that move most smoothly toward off-the-shelf software and away from do-it-yourself code will gain a competitive advantage in the marketplace. They will be far more agile and adaptable than those with thousands of pages of their own programs weighing them down and providing a constant incentive to make do with what they have.

This Race Really Is to the Swift

It does no good to have a wonderful statement of direction if you do not back it up by keeping your people up to date. Personally, I would not have software anywhere in my company's system that is more than three years behind the state of the art—and preferably not more than two years behind. If you try and stretch your use of software for longer periods than that, you will slow down the productivity growth of your people. The cost savings will be overshadowed by productivity losses.

But because it is easier to measure potential cost savings than productivity improvements, it's always tempting to stretch the software budget by keeping old software in operation, even if it makes people less productive than they might be. In addition, the budget process rarely gives sufficient weight to the potential developments that will occur when people are operating in the forefront rather than several years behind the curve.

If you want to play in the knowledge arena, then you must be willing to put your people on the cutting edge of development. It turns out to be essential to think in terms of replacement cycles far shorter than most companies are inclined to support if you want your people to be effective knowledge workers in the world today.

Now, some of your people will pounce on all the new software and equipment you can give them and go to town with it at once. It's never necessary to twist arms to get the technically sophisticated power users—the real techies—to play with some new software package. They will push each other out of the way for the opportunity to try out the latest and best.

Unfortunately, unless you're in the software business, techies make up a minority of your organization. The challenge is to get the other 80% of the organization up to speed. Most people are not techies; they couldn't care less about all the bells and whistles that some hot new software package might offer. They just want something that works without too much effort. If you give these non-techies software they don't use, it's a waste of time and money—not only will you not get the benefits you expected from the software, you will irritate your workforce and reduce its effectiveness.

So the first step is to find user-friendly software—software that most users can understand and at least begin to apply without reading reams of instructions. You want the cutting edge, but not necessarily the bleeding edge! When it comes to engaging that other 80% of the organization, ease of use and broad acceptance make all the difference. And the more popular the better. The bigger the user base, the easier it is to share in networks that go beyond your company. It helps a lot when your associates can exchange tips with customers, friends, and family. Giving and receiving coaching in a wide field can really speed up the process of getting proficient with a piece of software. It also promotes a natural integration between the business and personal worlds.

Picking a Product

At Buckman Labs, we look for software that is useful at a simple level, on the assumption that most software has many more features than will be used by most of the people in the organization. We also look at a maximum life span for software and hardware of two years. I frankly do not think it logical to let something stay on people's desks much longer than that. Three years is the most that seems reasonable to me these days, though I know that many companies would still regard even that as too fast.

At Buckman Labs, we apply the two-year cycle by replacing half of our hardware each year. We found that waiting longer than two years meant depriving many of our people of the capacity in the box necessary to do what the new software was bringing to them. You need to keep the software and hardware in sync so that they work together.

What I recommend is an active effort to push the best technology into the hands of your people, instead of an effort to get the maximum economic return on current hardware as calculated by the bean counters. Expenditures in this area need to be viewed from an entrepreneurial perspective—that is, as investments—rather than from a cost perspective. You are positioning your people to be knowledge workers, not paper shufflers. The right tools are essential to function in this new world across time and space.

Microsoft Office and Its Predecessors

Today we are using Outlook Express for e-mail and Newsgroups under Outlook Express for the sharing of tacit knowledge. We also use Microsoft Office, which is available in multiple languages and has the support we need, for the balance of our software needs. We went with Microsoft because of its huge user base, which both provides an indication of the user-friendliness of the software and gives its designers the means to afford the continual development of the software necessary to keep up with the state of the art.

Before we went with Microsoft Office, we had multiple programs from a variety of vendors to try to do the same thing that Microsoft Office does today. We had Harvard Graphics for presentations, Lotus Organizer to keep track of stuff, CompuServe for e-mail and Forums, and Lotus 1-2-3 for spreadsheets. None of these applications worked very well with any of the others.

The brilliance of Microsoft Office was that we finally had a combination of applications that everybody could use and each application complemented the next. It is this seamless functionality in working together that is critical in the building of total systems that are world-class. This is one of the most cost-effective packages ever put together for the business user. While we tried to accomplish the same thing through a combination of applications software prior to bringing in Office, we were never able to achieve that functionality.

One area that is missing in Microsoft Office is an area for collaboration and working as a team. Microsoft is trying to fill this void today with Sharepoint and Team Services. Yet it is our feeling that these new offerings have not yet achieved the functionality of Microsoft Office. Hopefully, someday that collaboration feature will be on offer as part of Microsoft Office. It is my understanding that Microsoft will be doing this with the introduction of Microsoft Office Suite 2003, and I'm eagerly looking forward to that development. That would go a long way to improving this important business package.

Another area that needs attention is document management. Many organizations today are required to provide secure storage for documents to meet government regulations, support critical applications, or support legal proceedings. Yet these documents still need to be used on a frequent basis in the activities of the business. This is another feature that should be included in Microsoft Office to provide a seamless interface between these critical pieces of business software.

Outlook Express and Newsgroups

Because it did not and still does not currently support collaboration as part of the package, Buckman Labs decided not to use the Outlook segment of Microsoft Office. Instead, we used Outlook Express, a simplified version of Outlook that had the e-mail functionality we needed at the time and also included a Newsgroups feature that worked like the CompuServe Forums our associates were used to. Outlook can be tailored with the addition of Sharepoint, a more robust but much more expensive and complex system for managing threaded discussions, but we decided not to experiment with it. Maintaining the familiar procedures seemed so desirable that it might well have made Outlook Express preferable even if the Newsgroups feature had involved extra cost rather than being part of the package. As a freebie, it was irresistible.

Newsgroups under Outlook Express opened up the opportunity for us to move from CompuServe to Microsoft software for Forums and e-mail, using a network that was assembled by combining parts from several sources. This simplified our system architecture and let us go on sharing tacit knowledge in a Microsoft environment. As long as we could have a threaded discussion, the tools for knowledge sharing were in place. The "Open Space Meetings" that we have today in Newsgroups organized around the needs of the business are just as powerful as the Forums that we used to have in CompuServe. We can still capture the important threads and save them for reuse by the organization. And there is no additional cost—it all comes with the e-mail system. If you want an inexpensive solution to the collaboration needs of your organization, Newsgroups under Outlook Express will almost certainly fill the bill.

Lotus Notes

Despite what I've said about the need to supply the most advanced tools, the software with the best features sometimes isn't the best software to use. Lotus Notes, for example, looked very promising. It provided a good platform for organizing knowledge and information. It provided a good e-mail platform and it provided good space for collaboration. It provided a platform for distance learning through Learning Space. In fact, it was better than anything else on the market for many years. We were tempted to use it many times, but it had one fatal flaw. If you had to use the server through a dial-up connection—say, through a hotel switchboard—the process of synchronizing with the server was too slow to move very much information and knowledge across time and space and the costs were prohibitive.

The problem was that Lotus Notes was designed for a hardwired environment and not for a global networked environment. Lotus and IBM tried for many years to improve the system's ability to work with dial-up connections, but they still have not achieved the ease of use or speed of synchronization that exists with other systems. With as many as 86% of our associates out of the office at any given time, we absolutely must have systems that work over poor-quality dial-up connections. As a result, most of our operating companies were never able to make effective use of Lotus Notes. Our Canadian company did decide to adopt it—and uses it to this day, though its management is now facing up to the need to change very soon or be left behind by the rest of the corporation. But in general it was one of the biggest disappointments that we experienced in the software that we looked at over the years. It was great software, but it did not do the job we needed. So be careful—don't be lured by superior software if it will not work well in your business environment.

Building a Network

These days, people are not necessarily in the office when they want to engage in work-related communications. In fact, someone who is in the office 40 hours per week is there for less than 25% of the time available in that week. Today's effective knowledge workers don't turn their brains on and off on that sort of schedule; they have to be able to connect to the office anytime. The "office" is no longer the physical space the company provides. Today, people "go to the office" wherever they are, whenever they wish to connect to the network.

Nonetheless, many organizations still want to keep their networks under tight control. They insist that the network be in-house, with access limited to the precious few. Security is the cry. I think this is an extension of the philosophy of hardwiring everything. It seems natural to say, "We have to control who has access and what they can do." Yet if a company builds its own network, then how do its customers connect to it? How do its people get access to information that is outside the organization?

Networks seem to have a built-in bias toward growth. The wider the network, the more people you can reach and the more you can do, regardless of the size of your organization. In many companies—even those much concerned with security—what started out as relatively simple Local Area Networks (LANs) within departments and organizations has expanded into Wide Area Networks (WANs), intranets, extranets, and the Internet. And people routinely use dial-up connections through some external provider of network connections to reach the home office, a friend in another country, or an e-commerce site halfway around the world.

Today's public networks can provide the same level of security once available only in private networks. So why not outsource this need of the organization? In fact, you can outsource the entire network and software requirements of the organization. You do not have to be a big company to get the benefits of secure software and networks that are global in scope—and you don't have to be a little one to benefit by the services of commercial networks.

For example, we used CompuServe for about five years in Buckman Labs with great success. When we switched from IBM's network to CompuServe in 1992, we had everybody in the office dialing into the CompuServe network to get mail in Columbus, Ohio. You can imagine the conversations about sending mail to the office next door by way of Columbus. Yet this is basically the same model that FedEx was using for the distribution of packages. We found it was much more efficient than our previous approach, which had involved using IBM's different network technology in different countries.

Even though we use these public pathways as an integral part of our network, we do not control them. We have never felt that this created a security issue. At the time we went with

CompuServe, Goldman Sachs was using the same network for its communications—and storing highly confidential financial documents on CompuServe's computers.

I do not understand why any company would try to create its own network in today's electronic world, any more than it would try to build a private highway to truck parts from one plant to another. The economics certainly are not there if you have a global workforce with people working in many locations on a regular basis. Taking advantage of public pathways allows us to keep costs down and focus our investments of time and funds in areas that will really take us someplace.

Where Do You Stand?

Good judgment comes from experience, and a lot of that comes from bad judgment.

—Will Rogers

Think about complexity versus usefulness of software. Where is your organization's software now? Do you tend to write code or do you buy packages?

Think about your equipment. Do you provide hardware that is capable of functioning when and where your people happen to be? How will you move your organization in the future to make your systems more people-centric? What changes would you like to make now in your system, if you could?

Think about collaboration. How will you collaborate across time and space? Will you use sophisticated systems like eRoom or Sharepoint Team Services or will you use something simple like Newsgroups under Outlook Express? With the development of Microsoft Office Suite 2003, which combines many of these features into one package, standard software may support collaboration. Will you use sophisticated and costly systems at the cutting edge of technology or will you go for the simplest and cheapest solution that will get the job done? Are you sure you know what's available at both ends of the spectrum?

Think about document management. Will you use a sophisticated system like Documentum or will you use the features of

Microsoft Office Suite 2003 for your needs? What kind of system will serve your needs? How easy is it to move documents from the repository to where you need them? Is it seamless or is it a challenge?

What combination of software and hardware will give your people the greatest facility for productive work no matter where they may be? Do you build the front end for your system or can you use the packaged front end that is provided?

Think about your networks. Can your people use them whenever they need to do so? Or are you clinging like grim death to the banner of perfect security? What would you need to do to be comfortable with the ways that your people work to your company's best advantage?

Becoming a Knowledge-Driven Organization

It's essential to be careful when picking the software and hardware that will provide communication infrastructure. The systems must function 24/7 on both the server side and the individual side. Knowledge work can occur anytime and anywhere. You need a people-centric system that is so easy to use that more than 90% of your people will take advantage of the system.

This ease-of-use criterion more or less mandates buying packages of software designed for the public that are fully supported and maintained at a state-of-the-art level. Equally, everyone in the organization needs hardware that is capable of operating the software with ease, around the clock, day in and day out.

As you begin to look at ways to change your systems to better serve your company, think about how you might change the organization and focus of your effort. I will take up this issue in Chapter 7. Then in Chapter 8, I'll turn to the ways you can achieve security in open systems for communication.

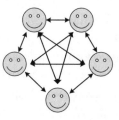

CHAPTER 7

Turning the IT Department into Something New

We are shifting to a knowledge-based economy. ... Expect turbulence, surprises, chance. That's what revolution brings.

—Alvin Toffler

Most organizations have a department they call Information Technology (IT) or something along those lines. But that raises an interesting question. What does the name imply about what the people there do? It's easy to see what Research does: research. Marketing performs the marketing function and Manufacturing produces the product. But what *does* IT do? Do you know what it means in your organization?

I never really figured out what IT was supposed to do at Buckman Labs—and that's not good. I submit that either you have to carefully define what IT does and have it completely understood by all parties involved or you have to change the name of the department to something that describes what its people should be doing. It turned out that we could not get the job done without changing the name of the department so that it was clear to everybody what the focus should be.

We started with a typical IT department, responsible for building and supporting our technological infrastructure: accounting systems, communication systems, knowledge systems, project services, and team services—all of which were theoretically designed to help us fulfill our strategy. But, like most of their peers in the business, our high-powered and knowledgeable IT staff found it easy to believe they already knew what they should focus on to achieve success in the technology arena. With that outlook, it seemed natural to proceed without consulting anyone else in the organization.

Traditional IT Choices

When an IT department goes down the familiar road of relying on its own expertise, the organization winds up with well-designed systems—but many of those systems will be more or less out of sync with its overall strategy. IT specialists tend to select state-of-the-art systems based on what their current supplier is providing—systems with "all the latest features" that promise to solve "all the problems" in a company. The rationale is persuasive: the system is the best that can be purchased from the best supplier (the one we so carefully chose), so it is the system we should have. IT finds it relatively easy to sell the system to the rest of the organization on this basis.

In the early days of computing, of course, the technology was so arcane and so specialized for a given company that IT really was the best at knowing what software should be used. But as more and more software was outsourced, the relationships between IT and the software suppliers grew stronger and stronger. The purchase of software from one supplier would tend to set the stage for more software from that same supplier, thus setting the technological direction of the organization for many years to come.

Whether this meant that the organization stayed with mainframe systems long after they ceased to be the most valuable option or whether it meant that some software was purchased for the organization at a very high price and never used in the manner hoped for, the result is the same. The organization was not supported with the technology that it really needed.

Sound familiar? This same sequence of events has played out thousands of times in companies large and small. I still hear the horror stories today of misplaced assets and directions that did not make sense with 20-20 hindsight, even though the projects were launched with the best of intentions.

At Buckman Labs it played out like this. Back in the 1980s, it seemed that every request anyone made of our IT department was met with looks of pitying disbelief. "You just don't understand," the IT folks would say. And they were right—but they had gaps in their own understanding. The petitioners were looking at organizational needs they had to meet, although articulating those needs was at times difficult. Meanwhile, the IT staff had a system they had spent months and years building and tuning, and they wanted to use it. The last thing they wanted was to rip the thing apart to meet the ever-changing demands that were beginning to rain in on them, and they didn't see why they should have to do so.

This led to endless hassles and miscommunications. The people using the systems did not begin to grasp how long it took to make even apparently minor changes in mainframe software. The people running the systems did not see that the needs of the business were changing faster and faster—indeed, faster than the IT department could respond. This was before the days of servers that were easy to configure and set up for a new direction. Yet we had to move forward with rapid change if we were going to meet the needs of our customers and remain a viable player in the marketplace.

Changing the IT Culture

One key lesson that we learned from those days was that the culture that springs up naturally in an IT group makes it difficult for people to appreciate their role in the larger organization. Our IT staff thought that if they maintained the systems and explained the input and output procedures to the people in the organization who fed the systems and worked with the results, then their job was done. They were happy enough to do more of the same—to process new input streams, control new processes, and generate new reports—but they resisted the idea of coming at their field from a whole new direction. They simply didn't want to hear about organizational and environmental pressures that were pushing us toward moving from a mainframe shop to a client-server shop, feeling (rightly enough) that they would lose control of their systems as soon as we allowed data to be located somewhere other than the mainframe.

This idea of everybody having a computer that could be located anywhere was a novel concept at that time—and an unwelcome one. It was one thing to have computers scattered around the office hardwired to the system, but it was something else if these little beasts could call into the system from anywhere via a phone line whenever some user wanted access. Where was the security in a system like that? IT was interested in controlling the integrity of their systems and the integrity of the data; we were interested in putting more power into the hands of our people: a basic disagreement about where we were going.

And it wasn't just that the IT staff didn't like the idea and saw it as full of security risks; they also didn't have the skills to implement it. Mainframes require a huge and complex body of knowledge to manage and maintain, and relatively little of that knowledge applies in a client-server environment. So we were asking people to move in a direction that they knew about but did not understand. We wanted them to focus on moving knowledge around the organization and not just keeping it safe in a database somewhere. We wanted it to fly to wherever it was needed, when it was needed.

We also wanted the systems to be easy to use, because we had to bring a lot more people into the process. We were not thinking in terms of "management information systems" but of systems that would turn people throughout the organization loose to do their best. We had to improve our ability to generate cash flow. This required us to be able to solve customers' problems faster and better than before. We had to move knowledge to our front line on demand from wherever it existed in the organization—or beyond. We were going to turn the organization upside down and put maximum power in the hands of those on the front line with the customers. Figure 7.1 shows the dramatic change in direction we were contemplating.

Unfortunately, we did not do a good job of articulating this need to our IT department in the beginning and they did not do a good job of helping us think in a new way. In the end we had to let the head

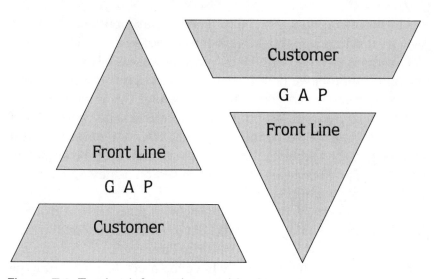

Figure 7.1. Turning information upside down

of the department go, because he simply couldn't shift the department from its mainframe orientation to one of helping each individual in our organization succeed in the new, fast-changing world.

We then pulled in a Ph.D. research chemist, someone who had been heavily involved in moving our R&D department into knowledge systems, to take on the IT leadership role. Needless to say, the shock at the change of management and direction was significant; over the next two years, we lost about half of the old IT department. Most of them wanted to stay in a mainframe shop.

This turnover gave us the opportunity to bring in new people who understood where we wanted to go and how to help us get there. We began taking the first significant steps toward the structural changes that would set the new direction for our old IT department.

Knowledge as a Resource

It was at this point, in 1992, that we changed the name of the department from IT to Knowledge Transfer (KT). We wanted everybody in the department to understand that their role had to be aligned with the strategy of the organization, which was to leverage—not just store and secure—the collective knowledge of the organization to better serve our customers.

I cannot emphasize this difference in direction too much. We had tried without much success for several years to change the department from within. The disconnect that we found in IT was so significant that we had to change direction if we were going to move the company forward through a knowledge initiative.

If you stop and think about it a minute, this shift makes a lot of sense. It's essential to define the role of IT in the organization if you are going to get effective use of its resources for the organization. And those resources must be focused on achieving the strategy of the organization.

Do not be afraid to look for talent with unusual backgrounds to help you move a department off dead center and in the direction that you are trying to go. Leaders who have come up through the ranks in one department usually have too much baggage from the past to move that same department in a new direction. If the new direction requires a complete rethink of what needs to be done, new talent may be the easiest way to move forward.

Knowledge Resource Center

In addition to changing the name of the department to Knowledge Transfer, Buckman Labs moved the corporate library into it, creating a knowledge resource center rather than a depository for books and journals. The library had been part of R&D, but we wanted all the enablers of the movement of knowledge to be in one department with one global focus. Our librarians had to change their focus from their accustomed face-to-face environment, where they handled requests for information that could be found on paper and physically handed to the person who needed it, to one that put them in virtual touch with everyone in the company. They now had to help our people succeed across time and space, processing requests for resources that might involve finding an e-mail message, locating an archive of a discussion, or digging up another electronic file somewhere inside or outside of the organization. At that time, over 50% of our associates were outside the United States (a condition that still exists today) and the only way that the librarians could effectively support our entire company was for them to become *cybrarians* as well.

New Mission of the Knowledge Transfer Department

We developed the following mission statement to emphasize the need to focus on moving knowledge across the organization:

> Plan, organize and manage information system applications, infrastructure and associated resources necessary to rapidly disseminate collective industry, technical and market knowledge in order to gain a sustainable, global, competitive advantage by proactively responding to the information and knowledge needs of Buckman Laboratories worldwide.

Looking at it now, it's hard to believe how pleased we were with this statement—it seems wordy and difficult to follow. But it does cover the ground, and the people who wrote it were engineers and chemists who figured that as long as it was in one sentence, everything fit and it satisfied the mission of a mission statement.

What this statement did was align the KT department's view of its proper activities with the organization's global needs. It was obvious that it was no longer focused on providing information to management; it was focused on the movement of knowledge of all types to gain a competitive advantage that was sustainable and global in scope. We were competing globally and we had to have systems that functioned and provided value globally. And we had to do this without breaking the bank.

Beyond the Mainframe Mindset

> To attain 100, 300, 500 percent improvements, you can't do the same thing better. You have to do something fundamentally different and, in the process, your business will be fundamentally transformed.
>
> —Stan Davis and William Davidson, *2020 Vision*

Much of the transition from IT to KT at Buckman Labs took place at the same time that we were making the transition from mainframes to distributed systems, but the two don't necessarily go together. It's entirely possible to employ today's agile little computers in a cultural matrix that bears a lot of resemblance to the formal, protection-oriented IT of yesteryear. So even if you're thinking, "Oh, we junked our climate-controlled computer room years ago," your IT department may still be working in independent-expert mode.

And that mode is more or less bound to put the brakes on progress now. It was well suited to its own day, but it won't let you take advantage of the capabilities of modern computers, which are really first and foremost *communication* devices.

This communications aspect is what can allow an organization to redefine what I like to call *the time equation of work*—that is, the normal and expected time for getting things done. What factories were able to do in the Industrial Age, replacing handwork with machinery that assisted in the production of goods, we can now do again—completely changing the way modern work is performed and reaping similar (or greater) advances in productivity. We now have the tools to move from face-to-face interactions to a virtual realm that can be extended to include any point on the planet.

But this requires new processes based on networked organizations rather than command-and-control. The focus needs to be on speed, on taking chunks of time out of current ways of doing things. It's no use to defend sacred places here; everything is fair game.

Productivity improvements require everyone to focus on how long it takes them to do what they do and how to redefine their processes so that time to solution or other completion is reduced. Keep in mind that this redefinition may take the form of combining several activities into one because of the reach of our communication systems, returning to something that looks at first glance a lot like the pre-Industrial Age way of creating a product. Or it may be as simple as expanding the reach of an expert to address a global audience instead of just those that can be reached face to face.

Redefining the time equation of work is what will lead to the next round of productivity increases. But it is also what will lead to the next round of fundamental changes in the culture of that work. The revolution is no longer confined to the manufacturing department; it is company-wide.

If you want to give your organization the tools that will let you redefine the time equation of work, then you have to make the people responsible for knowledge transfer—whatever you call them—part of your strategy development process. At Buckman Labs, we have what we call our Planning Team, made up of all the top management of the company: the operating company general managers, all the vice presidents who head up functional areas, and the president, chief executive officer, and chairman of the board. While this makes for a rather large group, it allows our Planning Team deliberations to include both cultural and process changes, with the goal of gaining general agreement on the directions that we have to take.

The KT department is an integral part of this team, and the head of the department reports directly to the CEO. I regard that as an absolute requirement. To lead the culture change in the organization, the CEO needs to have whoever is charged with building the system for that change as a direct report. If the head of KT reports to anyone else, the CEO has de facto abdicated that part of the leadership role in favor of someone else in the organization. The real question is whether the CEO and the Planning Team of the organization have the courage and desire to tackle the culture change necessary to get the advantages these new tools can bring to the scene.

Where Do You Stand?

Think of your knowledge resources as resembling water resources. Do they flow where needed? Or do they sit in protected reservoirs to be doled out upon carefully justified request? Whatever your answer, are you happy with it? Do you want to maximize the movement of knowledge in your organization or not?

Think about the culture surrounding the storage and processing of knowledge. Are you willing to look at the way the organization is currently put together and see if it suits its real needs?

Think about your organization's current productivity—compared with its competition, compared with your own dreams of the way things could be, even if it doesn't seem possible now. Is enough ever enough? Or are you willing to change processes to redefine the time equation of work to aim for those 100%, 300%, 500% improvements? Are you willing to deal with the cultural change necessary to achieve improvements of this magnitude? Are you willing and comfortable in investing *your* time and the organization's money into a knowledge-driven department or system? Are you brave enough to lead a culture change?

Supporting Business Strategy

The best way to predict the future is to create it.

—Peter Drucker

Product-driven companies can focus on their technology and market-driven companies on their customers in a fairly limited and linear fashion. Becoming a knowledge-driven organization, by contrast, requires a vast increase in the role that knowledge plays in the strategy of the business. Increasingly, companies will be using knowledge to differentiate themselves from their competition. Whether that knowledge is used to create products or services, whether it is used to improve a manufacturing process, whether it is used to understand competitors and find a chink in their armor, whether it is used to solve a customer's problem or to satisfy a need, knowledge will be the differentiating factor for the successful organization. And static knowledge won't count. It is through the movement of that knowledge that a company will create value.

The whole focus has to be on the front line with the customers' needs, because this is where the money flows in. All the other departments must learn to track and support that relationship if the organization is to be successful. And knowledge needs will shift over time as customers' needs change; everyone must stay alert to that and watch for ways to respond, pursuing customer satisfaction like independent entrepreneurs.

Drucker, in his autobiography, *Adventures of a Bystander*, talks about "the importance of being single-minded." He states, "The single-minded ones, the monomaniacs, are the only true achievers." Monomaniacs, he says, carry out *missions*, while other people have *interests*. He concludes, "Whenever anything is being accomplished, it is being done, I have learned, by a monomaniac with a mission." Those words come to mind here, when I encourage pursuing customer satisfaction like independent entrepreneurs. We should be like "monomaniacs with a mission."

In addition, knowledge needs grow and change with changing capabilities throughout the organization, providing opportunities and requirements in areas that the customers couldn't imagine but that are essential to long-term customer satisfaction. For example, the Buckman Labs R&D staff used to record their work and insights in paper laboratory notebooks. Around 1994, they were asked to switch to electronic laboratory notebooks—just the sort of device John Pera and I were hunting for in 1967 and unable to find—which proved to be a vast improvement. After running in parallel for a couple of years as we sorted out some cultural issues, we cut over and never looked back. People could search the records easily, so they stopped reinventing the wheel every time they needed to roll into an unfamiliar area.

This may sound like a simple accomplishment, but it was far from straightforward. We had to be sure that we met the legal requirements for research records to protect our dates of discovery. In addition, it took a lot of soul-searching on the part of our research associates to become comfortable with the cultural shift that this change would mean for them. Sharing results is all very well—researchers are used to that—but having the entire background work open to view was something else again.

But this step eliminated the ongoing frustration of having to rerun experiments because the work couldn't be found in the paper notebooks—something that was eating as much as 20% of every researcher's time. Saving this effort gave an immediate increase in productivity of our R&D efforts and a corresponding increase in researcher morale. In addition, our records are now more complete and better organized to support the conclusions reached.

In modern organizations, the basic ability to handle information and knowledge is changing for the better every day. To take advantage of these improvements, it is essential to push the development of knowledge systems that will help redefine the time equation of work. Those are the systems that will build the future you choose.

As you build these systems that will take you in new directions, it's useful to pay attention to some principles that turn out to be critical to achieving proactive knowledge sharing across time and space. I will explore these principles and the handling of security in open systems in the next chapter.

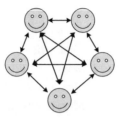

CHAPTER 8

Encourage the Flow
of Knowledge

Human beings have an infinite ability to create knowledge.
Add the convenient fact that unlike conventional assets,
knowledge grows when it is shared and you have the most
powerful features, which will change how we manage in the
Knowledge Era.

—Karl-Erik Sveiby

Muscle workers put down their tools at the end of the workday and go home. They may well mull over job problems on their own time, but they're not expected to do so—and there's little they can do about their conclusions until their next shift starts. The organization they serve is set up from top to bottom on the premise that *work* is something that happens at a certain place during set hours.

Knowledge workers and knowledge-based organizations often proceed on much the same basis, but that's a matter of personal and organizational habit, not necessity. Knowledge workers can function anytime they wish to engage their brains. A fully knowledge-driven organization can follow the same path: work is something people need to be able to do anywhere and anytime it needs doing, and work and play are both acceptable at any point in the day or night. Results are what determine a worker's value, not visible concentration on a task.

But distributing work across time and space poses several kinds of problems. You have to make it possible. You have to make it attractive to people you can trust to do it. And you have to make it safe, both for the organization and for the people in it.

A New Model for a Networked Organization

The value of a network increases as the square of the number of users on the network.

—Metcalfe's Law

The office is not the place where the bulk of the knowledge work of a company is done. It is not the place where knowledge workers spend most of their time. Even those who still put in a traditional eight-hour workday are in the office only a third of the workweek and less than a quarter of their time overall, and they often find that their best ideas occur when they are most relaxed, at home or outdoors, rather than at the desk or lab bench. Those who travel a lot—as I do—spend even less time in an office setting. And a field sales rep who works from home spends essentially 100% of the time outside the office. All need to be able to take advantage of their work-related insights whenever they occur.

If its people are generating constructive work outside the office much of the time, then a company needs to set itself up to capture and channel that work. In particular, since most knowledge work has a large computer component, the company needs to base its computer systems on the realities of distributed use. And that, paradoxically, means resisting the temptation to adopt the latest hardwired application with all its bells and whistles. It doesn't matter that a system is the best if the majority of the people you are trying to support won't be able to use it when they need it. You cannot depend on software that requires the user to be hardwired to function because most of the time people cannot be hardwired.

At Buckman Labs, we knew we couldn't use software that

required a real-time connection to the network to function. Our people must be able to operate as what we call a "Community of One"—independent of the network—because they are not in the office and are not connected most of the time. They need computer support that is equally flexible. So we set things up so their only reason to connect to the network is to send and receive activity and to do searches for information and knowledge, mostly in the form of plain text.

Of course, in some parts of the world we do have high-speed cable modems and DSL connections, but we decided not to depend on that high speed in building our system—videoconferencing and the like is a pleasant add-on, not a way of life. Until wireless Internet access becomes ubiquitous, it must remain feasible to work effectively over a dial-up connection in a hotel room or from home. And although I do think wireless is the wave of the future—many countries are bypassing wired solutions as they modernize—it's not a fast-moving wave. I don't think it will be deployed world-wide to the point where a global company can depend on it in my lifetime. In some countries, it simply will never happen. Companies that develop software that works only in the realm of high-speed connections are playing a game of wishful thinking and companies that stake their future on that software are casually discarding potential customers in whole regions of the world.

Even in 2004, it's safest to design for a practical connect speed of 28,800 baud. While this may sound very slow, I can remember when Buckman started using online interactions; the best we could hope for then was about 900 baud, and we thought it was wonderful. It's best to design systems that recognize the speed constraint and focus on software that functions well in a disconnected environment. That also means maintaining the courage to resist the temptations software suppliers offer every day and stay focused on the practicalities of the real work space.

Organize the Business Around Knowledge Flow, Not Geography

It's obsolete for a company to organize its business functions based on where it happens to be. Instead, the governing principle must be what it wants to do. In a knowledge-driven world, what matters is the flow of knowledge in the organization, not where people happen to be or what operating division or country-based operating company they work in. Organizational units invite improved communications within their defined turf, but it takes planning and care to keep them from raising corresponding barriers where they interface with one another.

The same goes for the different operating companies in different countries. Every country has its own laws and rules for governing organizations that operate within its borders, and a global organization has no option but to abide by those laws. But local requirements—for example, to follow International Accounting Standards Board (IASB) rules rather than the U.S. Generally Accepted Accounting Practices (GAAP)—generate different results and prime the people involved to think differently about how to achieve those results. This creates a unique culture of operation within each country and, again, it takes careful planning to keep that culture open to sharing knowledge with the whole organization.

Whatever it takes, the effort is worthwhile. As the percentage of business activities conducted using networked solutions grows and knowledge moves at a blink of an eye to wherever it is needed whenever it is needed, the speed at which you can operate goes up in quantum leaps. If you are not prepared to take advantage of this in your organization, then you will not get much benefit out of your system no matter how good it is—nor will you be able to redefine the time equation of work.

And redefining the time equation of work is what this entire effort is all about. The focus must be on what the organization needs and how to meet those needs as rapidly as possible. The normal human tendency to procrastinate about change is growing more and more dangerous as the competition is moving faster and faster. For simple survival, let alone prosperity, it's essential to get your decision cycle inside your competitors' decision cycles and to figure out how to meet your customers' needs faster than your competitors can. Think speed!

People often assume that there's a necessary trade-off between speed and quality, but that is a perception thing. The trade-off is between *rushing* and working with quality. When you build the capacity to move faster and faster as an organization, the quality will rise along with the speed. As you build your system around the flow of knowledge, use one that will both encourage and magnify that flow and you'll find that your associates will take advantage of it to maintain and develop the quality of their work.

The Features of an Ideal System

Knowledge networks need as much diversity of thought as they can get, as it is from the interaction of diverse thoughts that they generate the most valuable knowledge exchanges. It is not a question of just being open to all to be nice. Instead, it is recognition everyone was hired for a purpose. If they are going to fulfill that purpose, or some other purpose that they have grown into, then they need to be connected to the communication network. And this connection has to be ubiquitous—and everyone in the network has to be treated the same. Every potential contributor is important if you are trying to mobilize the entire organization to be able to move faster than before. You cannot leave anyone out. If they are important enough to have access to a phone, then they need access to your knowledge network. This is how you will capture the power of Metcalfe's Law.

As you build your system, look for ways to reduce the number of transmissions required to get a communication from one individual to another anywhere in the organization. Make sure everyone has access to the knowledge of the whole organization and that everyone can make their own knowledge available to others. The idea is to bring the flexible, personal communication patterns of a small office building to the networked workforce of a global corporation.

One-Step Transmission. As I noted in Chapter 5, the way to achieve the least distortion of the knowledge transmitted is to reduce the number of transmissions to one. Developing a knowledge-driven organization means moving away from the sequential communication model typical of command-and-control structures and into a networked communication model where all players are equal and Metcalfe's Law rules. What's needed is clarity of communication to all involved in meeting the needs of the organization, not just to the next person in the chain of command. The last thing you want is to recreate the game of post office or telephone (as described in Chapter 3) on the job; once a message makes that sort of round, it's worse than useless. The easiest way to get the required clarity is for everyone to communicate directly with everyone else. That way, everybody gets the same message at the same time.

Universal Access. Any organization's greatest knowledge base is in its people's heads. To capitalize on it, you need to extend one-step transmission across all the organizational barriers to communication. Messages must be able to go through all the structural silos of the organization. Whether these barriers and silos are real or perceived, people have to realize that crossing them is not just permitted but expected. You need to help them make that mental leap if you want to have an organization that functions in a global world.

One guideline is to give everybody the same access in computer networks as they could achieve with a telephone. And these days, telephones are ubiquitous—few organizations still make any effort to control their people's access to the phone system. The next step is to create computer networks that are just as ubiquitous. Everybody should have access to all of the knowledge in the organization, provided it does not violate the privacy needs of the individuals involved or the intellectual capital needs of the organization. Someone who doesn't know what is going on cannot assume responsibility for making things happen. Freedom of access is key!

Universal Entry. Since each associate is part of the knowledge base of the organization, all associates should have equal rights to enter knowledge into the system without filtration. In a fast-moving world, it isn't possible to meet the needs of the organization without allowing everyone to contribute as valued members of the team. People need to be able to expect and assume that their contributions will be welcome or they won't try to make them.

The right to speak is one of the important freedoms in many parts of the world, but it often seems to stop at the workplace door. It turns out that this mental outlook—expecting to contribute as a matter of right—is particularly useful in a global company. When you have a communication system capable of dispersing knowledge from anywhere to anywhere, what you need are people who assume they ought to be using it. Why shouldn't people have that same right when sharing knowledge in a communication system?

Open Around the World and Around the Clock. Another corollary of the human storage of the vast bulk of the knowledge base is the need to provide hardware and software that will allow everyone to connect anytime and anywhere. Permission to reach anyone and offer anything is all very well, but it has to be possible to do so or the freedom is meaningless.

These days, people simply don't know when they will want or need to function as knowledge workers. It can be at any point in the day or night, not just during a scheduled stint in the office. Organizations need to recognize this if they want the best both for and from their people. That means the system ought to be able to function anyplace and at any time. Practically speaking, these days that means wherever there's a phone and a modem, or a hardwired connection to a private network, or a wireless connection to the Internet. Wireless networks are beginning to free us up from the wired world, so a company should provide for their use when they're available—but don't set things up so wireless is the only way to go.

A Network People Will Use

You have to build the network before people can use it, but just building it isn't enough to ensure that they will use it. Open invitations will bring many people in, but many others will assume that such an open system will be too complex to find anything in, or that they won't be able to trust (or perhaps even to understand) whatever they see there, or that if they get mired in it will suck their brains out and they won't have time to do their real work.

As you redefine how work is done, make sure the system is easy and comfortable to use—in fact, easier and more comfortable than ignoring the system—before the level of participation will reach critical mass. People must be able to find using the network more valuable to them than any of the rival uses of their time. That means solving their own problems as well as helping others solve theirs through the use of the network and getting a return from this activity while doing real work. And, of course, you have to recruit and train workers willing and able to use the network responsibly, without getting lost in it.

Ease of Use

Bear in mind that only about 20% of the people in any organization can be considered techies. The challenge is to get the other 80% functional on the system too. Much of the software on the market today is far too complex; that's one of the biggest reasons that companies don't reach critical mass in the use of the systems that they deploy. People rarely use more than a small fraction of the features provided. For example, I regard myself as a fairly sophisticated user, yet I am continually technically challenged either to get results from some feature that I do not use very much or to find where something I need is buried in the software. I am still trying to understand the logic behind some software.

Think in terms of software that is designed for the public and easy to use, rather than software written by techies for techies; that's the only way to get usage up to the critical mass essential to a viable ongoing system. Keep it simple.

Generally speaking, the larger the customer base a piece of software has, the more likely it is to be useful in your organization, if it can be adapted to your needs. We observed this when we used the systems at CompuServe for our business operations, compared with what we had when we were with IBM, and again when we adopted Microsoft Office as a replacement for CompuServe. Initially, we used Outlook Express rather than Outlook to keep the transition simple and give ready access to the Newsgroups. Now we're beginning to migrate to Outlook to take advantage of its new features. The move to Microsoft Office Suite 2003 will be a natural extension of where we are today.

Trust

I keep coming back to trust, because trust is a bedrock requirement at every turn. Besides finding the system easy and congenial, people need to trust the information and knowledge that is sent to them to be the best it can be. They also need to trust that the information they send out will be used in a responsible manner. The quality of the information is best protected by unfiltered transmission, coupled with unfiltered commentary added by anyone who sees it. When you trust everybody to do their best all the time and give everyone equal right to enter knowledge into the system, the resulting interchange will separate the wheat from the chaff far better than any filtration system could. I repeat: trust is essential. Without this degree of trust, you will fail.

And that means that the "system" is far more than the computer system. To make this all work, you need to build a culture of trust backed up by a shared code of ethics.

If you already have a code of ethics in your company, then focus on developing another document, say, a Statement of Values for Effective Communication. This will accomplish the same thing without the necessity of reopening the discussion of ethics, which many people would find unsettling. Whatever type of statement you use, it needs to have teeth—it must be used in hiring and firing decisions and in every aspect of working life. Such a statement will help you get the right people—people predisposed to work well, who will be encouraged by their own expectations and those of the people around them to do so. The higher the percentage of individuals predisposed to high quality in your organization, the easier it is to develop the speed and flexibility you need.

In addition, you cannot expect people to be purely businesslike and business-minded in all their use of the system. Humans need to understand one another on a variety of levels before they will trust one another deeply enough for genuine knowledge sharing to take place; they can't build that understanding if they're limited to discussions of product and customer. For a knowledge-sharing organization, providing facilities for playful interaction is as much a business necessity as providing lights and bathroom facilities in the office.

One of the great advantages of lighthearted and multilevel interaction is that it helps people recognize their own cultural assumptions and those of their fellows. We are all products of the environment that we grew up in, and it takes a while to learn that behavior that is acceptable in one culture frequently is not in another. As they rub shoulders in a worldwide community, people learn how to recognize each other's needs. For example, those who come from cultures where asking a question involves loss of face learn both to respect those who do ask questions and to make their needs known; those who ask freely and figure that anyone who wants something will ask for it begin to recognize the sources of tension and the kinds of cautious generalities others use when they wish to leave an opening for assistance without coming out and requesting it. Until such patterns develop, systems for the sharing of tacit knowledge are unlikely to provide the benefits you may expect from them.

Judgment

When we went to CompuServe, we gave all of our associates access to everything it offered, including unlimited access to the Internet. We did this intentionally to gain training by doing and because we trusted our people to use this access intelligently. When you hire people on the basis of a code of ethics that covers the values that you all live by from day to day, you can be comfortable that they will not violate that code when they surf the Internet. While there is always the potential for someone to abuse the system, we have always felt that it was better to design our systems at Buckman Labs on the basis of the 99.9% of our associates who are trying to do the right thing. In that way, a bond of trust is established with the vast majority and those who do abuse the system become obvious and can be dealt with individually.

Now you may well be wondering, *But won't the lure of gaining worldwide acclaim as an internal guru tempt people to spend their time monitoring messages and solving problems at long distance while their own responsibilities go to hell? How do I make sure everybody's primary job gets done?*

All I can say is that this has never posed a problem at Buckman Labs. On the rare occasion that someone migrated into solving problems online so effectively that the work became more important than what he or she was hired to do, someone else moved in to fill the vacuum. But normally, the old jobs were transformed on the fly as we learned how to get value from our new systems.

We told everyone to use their own best judgment and look for the value delivered by the different ways of working and move toward those systems that provided the most value to them and to the people with whom they interfaced across time and space. We asked them to think about how they would increase their influence across the organization and make stuff happen. But "stuff"—real results that the customers really pay for—was and remains the measure of progress and a major factor in everyone's compensation. Results rolled in and kept on rolling, because trusted and trustworthy people don't deadhead or freeload; when they interact about business problems online, the business benefits.

Multilingual Support

Language creates its own challenges for communication and doing business on a global basis. The literal translation of words will not convey the same meaning in another language. Those of us with English as our native language are lucky that the principal language for communication in the world today is English, and not just because our lifelong familiarity with it makes it easy for us. English has the helpful quality of being an imprecise language: it can be both spoken and written poorly and still be understood. It is a very forgiving language in that respect. If those who grew up with more exacting languages can get past their cultural desires for precision, then they can reach us (and each other) around this barrier more readily than those who use broken versions of precise languages can reach those born to them.

Communication still takes effort, though. Vijay Govindarajan and Anil Gupta capture the point as well as I've ever seen it, pointing out that as CEO of the Sweden-based conglomerate ABB, Goran Lindahl, always referred to his company's official language as "poor English." His intent was "to drive home the point that no one should be embarrassed to express an idea simply because their English is not perfect."

Computer systems can be built to help with the language problem. We're not there yet, but it's possible to envision a computer network that would undo the curse of Babel so that all the participants could communicate with one another without regard to the language each prefers to use. Ideally, the system should allow all associates to function in their native language, with the system providing the translation into the language of each recipient.

At Buckman Labs we work in more than 15 languages as we stretch around the globe. About half of our associates use English as a second language and understand communication in that language at a level lower than in their native language. For some, English may even be a third or fourth language! Since people always learn best in their native language, for in-depth communications we will translate the needed documents. For training purposes, we use up to eight principal languages to improve the learning across the organization.

A Network That Protects Your Interests

All this talk of "open this" and "free access to that" may well be making your skin crawl. With the virus mongers, the system crackers, and the outright industrial espionage agents that infest the online world, maintaining an always-on knowledge-sharing network is apt to seem impossibly risky. But even though security is an ever-present issue, you have to deal with it if you want to figure out how to innovate faster than the competition—and that had better be a goal, if you mean to be a viable player for the long term.

Too many organizations view security as being achieved when someone is denied access to some knowledge of the organization—anyone, any knowledge. Yet when you analyze your true security needs, you will probably find only a few places where access really needs to be denied absolutely. In the specialty chemical business, for example, we have two such areas: legal issues and R&D.

We have to keep access to legal records limited to those who need to know for the defense of the business in a court. Likewise, we have to keep access to personnel records limited to protect the rights of the individual associates in the organization.

Meanwhile, the intellectual capital tied up in the invention of new molecules and new combinations of molecules to provide new attributes is a critical bit of knowledge that has to be protected. To be able to get a patent, we have to be able to prove that the invention is unique to us and has not become common knowledge. Date of invention is also critical to obtaining a patent. And then there are the trade secrets, bits of knowledge that are critical to the product, the process, or the application of the product but that are either not patentable for some reason or so dramatic that they're better protected by not being put in the open disclosure environment of a patent. So, by necessity, these records have to be kept confidential and access has to be limited to those who need to know.

For all the rest of the knowledge of the organization, you need openness if you are going to be able to move fast in the competitive world in front of you. Yet you still need enough security to make sure that this movement of knowledge is secure from prying eyes—you don't want your competitors to be an audience for your network. Your systems must have a reasonable level of security so that everyone is confident that they can share their innermost knowledge across the system. Some of the elements of that system have to do with things the users themselves do to protect their identity, others are built into the equipment and software and work without direct user intervention, and still others take the form of audit and review.

User-Level Security

The human systems surrounding the security issue have been worked out well in recent decades. There's nothing new in what we do at Buckman Labs; it just takes constant application.

Unique IDs and Passwords. Everyone gets a unique, personal ID and password. By assigning unique IDs and passwords to associates, we make reasonably sure that only authorized individuals will have access to company and personal information. This requires someone to serve as an ID administrator and assign the IDs and passwords. The recipients are responsible for choosing a new password within two weeks to replace the one assigned by the administrator. If they do not, then the password is invalid and the process will have to start again. After someone chooses a password, it works for a given period of time; then it is necessary to choose a new one to maintain access to the network.

Password Kept Private. The associates are accountable for any activity attributed to their individual IDs. That reinforces the point that IDs and passwords are for the individual owner's use only and should be kept private. Sharing of passwords is a recipe for a breach of the security of the system. People are repeatedly warned that they should never share their ID with anyone (other associates, family members, or friends) and should never write a password down. Anyone who suspects that a password has been compromised should change it immediately.

Use of Strong Passwords. Passwords should be difficult for someone else to guess or crack. People often have a tendency to forget passwords, so they choose something that has particular personal relevance: the name of a loved one or a favorite car, sport, ice cream—whatever seems likely to stick. Unfortunately, the patterns are so predictable that an acquaintance can make a list of such words and crack a password based on them. All-numeric passwords usually fall into this category as well: birth dates, phone numbers. A password should be something memorable, easy to type quickly and accurately, and made up of a mixture of seven or more letters *and* numbers.

To ensure that passwords are both unique and difficult for anyone but the owner to guess, Buckman uses the following rules for creating them:

Your password must meet the following criteria:

▶ Have at least seven characters
▶ Not be longer than 14 characters
▶ Have at least three letters
▶ Have at least one digit
▶ Differ from your old password by four or more characters
▶ Have no more than two pairs of repeating characters
▶ Not be a dictionary word after all numbers are removed
▶ Not be your username
▶ Not be your username backwards
▶ Not be your username with the letters rearranged
▶ Not be an old password you've used in the last two years

The software monitors these rules and makes sure they're followed. If an associate attempts to enter an invalid password, the system will reject it and provide the rules for review, highlighting the particular problem.

Regular Password Change. By changing passwords on a regular basis, you will reduce the risk of an associate's ID being compromised. At Buckman, associates must change their passwords at least every 180 days. They can't switch to any of their last three passwords or any password used in the past 180 days. When associates log onto our system, a program will run to determine the expiration date of the password. If it is scheduled to expire within the next 30 days, the system will ask for a change. Associates can hold out to the last minute, but they risk getting shut out if they wait too long—once the password expires, they will not be able to log on to the system.

Replacement of Expired or Forgotten Passwords. Of course, people have to go on working and, in the natural course of events, some people will let their passwords expire and others will forget them. The ID administrator verifies that anyone requesting a replacement password is still entitled to have one and then issues a new password and communicates it to him or her in a secure manner. As with all newly issued passwords, the replacement password must be changed by the associate within two weeks.

System-Based Security

Of course, system security gets more and more complicated when you have many PCs scattered around that have relatively open access to your system and other systems. And you also have to maintain the security of your servers to protect them from attacks originating outside the company, with firewalls, spam filters, and so on. However, the benefits achieved by these open systems far exceed those possible on the closed, hardwired systems of the past. Here are the measures Buckman Labs takes to preserve the integrity of its systems.

PC Power-on and Hard-Drive Passwords. Every PC has power-on and hard-drive passwords set before it's handed to an associate to use. Associates are encouraged to keep these passwords active and secure. This minimizes unauthorized access to information on the PC in the event of theft or loss. And the instant we learn that a PC is missing, we shut down the associate's password to prevent any chance that the machine can be used to get through to our network and we do everything we can to recover the lost or stolen PC as soon as possible. However, this is rarely possible. To protect our ability to keep functioning, all our associates back up their hard drives on a regular basis so that recovery is not too difficult.

PC Lockout Screen Saver. Every PC also has a screen saver with lockout password installed when it goes into use. Setting a lockout screen saver to a maximum of 10 minutes will minimize the security risk when the PC is left unattended. But associates are also warned not to rely on this for protection; they shouldn't leave PCs logged on and unattended at all, as giving anyone a chance to use a machine in that state is tantamount to handing out a live logon ID and password.

30-Day Inactive ID Review. Active IDs for terminated individuals are a dangerous source of unauthorized access to the system—a door that should be kept solidly closed. The HR department has procedures that call for notifying the ID administrator when anyone who has had access to the system—whether as an associate, a temporary employee, or a consultant, leaves the company—but, like any human procedure, this one doesn't always work perfectly. The ID administrator therefore gets a regular report listing IDs that have not been used for a 30-day period, reviews them to determine if they are still required, and cancels any that turn out to be inactive.

One Logon per ID. As noted, everybody with access to the system is issued a unique ID. This allows access to those areas that have been approved for the individual and protects the system from unauthorized use. As part of the security procedures, multiple concurrent dial-up sessions with the same ID are not allowed. The system monitors and reports concurrent logon attempts; then the ID administrator investigates to see how the apparent ID sharing occurred.

Virus Protection Current and Active. All PCs have up-to-date virus protection software installed when we issue them to associates; we download and distribute the latest virus signature files at least once a week, and more frequently if events warrant it. In addition, we distribute new engines—new versions of the protection software—whenever the manufacturer releases them. We advise all associates that it is their responsibility to make sure that their virus protection software is active and current and to refrain from knowingly injecting viruses into our systems.

Inactive Dial-Up Sessions Disconnect Automatically. To keep people from clogging the system and running up network charges, we automatically disconnect connections after they are inactive for 10 minutes. This also helps minimize the security risk associated with open connections.

Blocking Inappropriate Material. Because of our desire to make our systems as open as possible on the Internet, we have to restrict access to certain sites. We have found that pornographic and race and hate sites carry their own brand of problems for corporate systems. Their active downloading of software onto corporate systems can bring their own collection of attacks on the system. We use Internet filter software to disallow access to sites included in categories selected for access blocking.

Servers and Firewalls. We use UNIX-based servers, which are somewhat easier than Microsoft servers to secure against unwanted public access, and we restrict Internet activity to different servers from those that operate our internal networks. We also use a hardware firewall to close down access to most system ports and keep unauthorized programs or users from entering our network. To catch viruses early, before there is any damage to our environment, we use anti-virus software from two leading vendors. One provides virus protection for our e-mail servers and the other provides virus protection on our other servers.

Encryption. Thus far, Buckman Labs has not found it necessary to take the step of encrypting messages sent over our systems. However, we're continuing to keep an eye on the subject and may go to a secure transmission setup (like those used by e-commerce sites) at some point in the future. The move to wireless systems may change our view of the need for encryption, as eavesdropping is easier in a wireless environment than in the current wired and dial-up operation.

Audit and Review

Once you've established an open system and encouraged the development of a culture of trust, it may seem out of place to check up on people. Nonetheless, you need to keep track of what's happening and make sure that the system is working to the benefit of your organization and not someone else's. At Buckman Labs, we review both the inner workings of the software and the external operations of the system.

System Security Internal Automated Reports. We also use security audit software to analyze the system and point up changes that will improve overall internal security. Security personnel in the KT department look at summary and detailed reports that show users with administrative privileges, inadequate passwords, locking screen savers, and virus protection software installed. By performing regular audits of the system, we can identify new security requirements as computer systems change. That lets us keep the security policy up to date to reflect the changing needs of the business.

System Security External Audit. Our external auditors provide a summary of our vulnerability to intrusion from outside the company (hackers, denial of service). Here, we look at the adequacy of security measures, identify security deficiencies, and evaluate the effectiveness of existing safeguards. Also provided with this audit should be a summary of recommended changes to improve overall external security.

Where Do You Stand?

Think about your current network. Can your people use it wherever they are? How are your associates able to contribute their knowledge and breakthrough thinking when they are not in the office? What is the disparity between your high-speed connectivity and your "on the road" connectivity?

What proportion of your associates can speak their minds on the network without clearance from anyone else?

What proportion of your associates use the network as casually as they use the phone system? What proportion of your associates use it with suspicion or refuse to use it at all?

Think about your security policy. Does it promote an open dialog in your company or does it contribute to silo building and barriers? Do you care about being able to innovate faster than the competition? Do you know for sure that everyone who has access to your system deserves it?

Breaking Down the Barriers to Communication

A fully functional network takes on a life of its own. In terms of the old command-and-control philosophy, it's downright subversive.

However, if you want to radically redefine the time equation of work and are prepared to accept all its consequences to acquire the benefits of vastly increased organizational speed and agility, then a living network will provide a great tool to unleash the power of the organization. It will help you speed up the way you innovate around the needs of the customer. It will help you come up with new products faster and get them introduced faster. It will help you solve problems faster with your customers and it will help you get closer to the instant solutions your customers desire. It will also help you reorganize your company around the flow of knowledge rather than geography.

But when you turn that switch on, you are starting a revolution in your business. You cannot avoid it. Enjoy the ride! It will take you places that you cannot imagine.

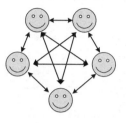

CHAPTER 9

Let Customers Be Your Guide

The race is not always to the swift, nor the battle to the strong—but that's the way to bet.

—Damon Runyon

Who really matters in business? The customers. If they don't buy what you have to sell, you're dead in the water. So who's next most important? The people you have on the front lines, working with your customers and potential customers to make sure they're getting the products and services they want and need.

In a fast-moving market, it is a company's responsiveness to customer needs and its ability to innovate to meet them quickly that determine its ability to improve the value added it delivers. This requirement for continual innovation will determine many of the systems required for effective action. But innovation produced in a vacuum isn't going to do the job. The only innovations that matter are the ones the customer is willing to pay for. Innovation must be based on what the customer wants, so all the company's systems for the sharing of knowledge must be focused on that end.

Inverting the Pyramid

At Buckman Labs, we highlight the importance of the customers in this process by putting them at the top of our organizational chart, followed by the people who deal directly with them. That turns the usual organizational pyramid upside down, as shown in Figure 9.1.

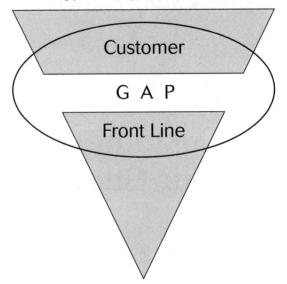

Figure 9.1. Upside-down pyramid

As you can see from this diagram, a broad reach of the organization is available to serve the needs of the customers in a direct way. But in most organizations, it is still less than 50% of the workforce. The rest are supporting those on the front line without much if any direct involvement with the customers. But if you want to put all of the power of the organization to this task, then everyone in it must actively support the needs of the customers by as much direct contact as possible. No one can just sit back and leave that to the people who deal with customers every day. Instead, the organizational climate everywhere from the executive offices to the loading dock must promote an awareness of the customer interface. The front line has to be everywhere and everyone has to be—in the words of the Buckman Labs slogan—"*Effectively Engaged on the Front Line*," because everyone in the company is important to the process of getting and keeping customers.

Not I, you think? But if you are not necessary to help in closing the gap between your company and its customers (its sources of income and its reason for being), then you should probably be asking why you are there.

Being involved in closing the gap with the customer is easier than it sounds. More and more, customers are making decisions about the products and services they use by involving more people from all levels of their organization in the decision-making process:

▶ Safety and environmental managers participate in buying decisions, shaping the choice to minimize future problems instead of waiting for disaster and then rushing in for reactive clean-ups and reviews.

▶ Financial and legal people are involved in setting up contracts and considering which terms are best suited to the company's financial needs at the time—and how to build in flexibility for future needs.

▶ HR people become involved to assess the training needs associated with a capital purchase or an innovation that affects day-to-day operations, so the company can consider the direct and opportunity costs of training as part of determining the value being delivered by a supplier.

▶ Manufacturing people work with quality issues that arise in the customers' operations and set up arrangements to provide just-in-time inventory to the customers.

▶ R&D people work on their company's future needs. Finding out where the customer wants to go is a critical point that needs to be explored and developed if your organization wants to stay viable.

In the end, more and more people are contributing to customer decisions, and the supplier's direct sales representatives simply can't meet with all of them in the quest for the sale. That is why it is important for any supplier, and the people working in that supplier, to get involved in influencing the decision-making process at all levels within their customers' organizations. They speak the same language as their customer counterparts, can understand the issues and needs, and can visualize and contribute solutions that are meaningful to various levels of the customer organization.

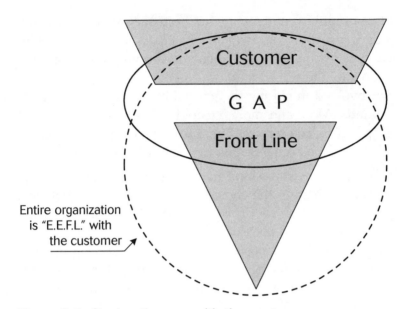

Figure 9.2. Closing the gap with the customer

But the key to this is having a communication structure and culture in your company that is open to contributions from all levels of the organization—and expects their participation. Figure 9.2 illustrates this by showing everyone in the organization involved in the process of closing the gap with the customer, "effectively engaged on the front line."

Building relationships of continuity and trust with customers is what it is all about. This continuity and trust has to be built by people. Those with account responsibility are automatically involved with the customer by the nature of their positions. But applications experts and industry specialists can be involved in this process as well, provided they are *engaged on the front line*. In fact, this goes for everyone in the organization. The proportion of people in your organization working on customer relationships relative to the total organization will determine your momentum in the market.

The quality of the people that an organization can bring to its customer relationships will determine the level at which it can operate in these relationships. The higher the quality of the individuals involved, the higher the quality of the knowledge that can be brought to bear on any problem that your customers present.

Effective Engagement on the Front Line

> Effective engagement is when an associate takes responsibility for and is actively involved with satisfying the needs and expectations of our customers so that Buckman Laboratories becomes the preferred choice.
>
> —Mike Anstey, Buckman 4th Wave Meeting, 1994

Of all the descriptions that I have heard as to what "effective engagement on the front line" means in practice, Mike Anstey's is the best. Mike was a division manager based in Singapore when he wrote this; today, he's corporate vice president in charge of R&D. He posted it to one of our Forums and went on as follows:

> In my opinion the underlying thrust of the *80% effectively engaged on the front line* goal is not to make sure that 80% of our people actually talk to a paying customer for a measurable frequency and duration, or to be sure that 80% of our people actively use the Forums and E-Mail, or to be sure that we get the accounting right so that our department measures up to this new corporate goal. I think rather it is a matter of "how do we get as many people as possible creating and transferring as much knowledge as possible in the best way possible in order to have a positive impact on the customer." It's about bringing the full weight of the knowledge that exists in the hardware, software and wetware [by which he meant people], in a relevant and useful manner, to bear upon the requirements of the customer.
>
> We are doing a lot of these things now, but if we can get all of our people doing this all of the time, just think of the power that will be unleashed. It's not about definitions, numbers, or procedures or things. It's about involvement, commitment, creativity, passion, and ultimately the freedom to do everything we can, and to use all of the knowledge we have, to make sure that we have done our utmost to satisfy our customers in all areas.

Until we can fully and effectively engage all of our own people, with a technological fix and within a cultural milieu wherein they can all be comfortable, then we haven't sufficiently addressed the question of engagement as a company.

In other words, reality is a concept; engagement is a mindset.

It is about teaching each other and learning from each other. It is about nurture of the individual.

Making Knowledge Sharing Customer-Centric

It's essential to connect that collection of minds that exists within the company across company barriers, geographic barriers, and cultural and language barriers. That's the only way to transfer knowledge effectively across time and space to meet the needs of the customers.

Since the individuals on the front line cannot do their work with the customer if they're sitting in the office, they need a robust system for communication of the type described in Chapter 8, one that will support them wherever they happen to be. This is where the latest and greatest knowledge on how to move the organization forward resides.

But it's not enough to support the sales reps as they chat together about customer needs. Everyone else in the organization needs to be hooked into the same system and participating in the same discussions. They have to be attuned to the ever-changing needs of the customer so that the organization can respond rapidly to any need at any time, anywhere in the world. To do this, you have to think in terms of radically shifting the span of communication of every member of the organization.

How do you increase the span of communication so all your associates can go wherever they need to go for information and knowledge? That is where the concept I call the *Community of One* comes into play (see Figure 9.3). People need the capacity to function independently, and also to hook up with anyone else as needed. That takes systems that are simple to use and robust in their output.

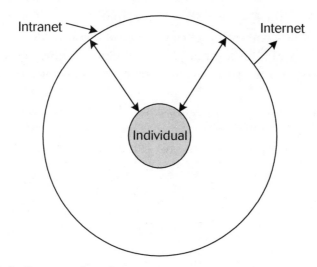

Figure 9.3. Community of one

Community of One and How It Expands

In a knowledge-sharing environment, the critical skills are identifying needed knowledge, locating it, and developing relationships strong enough to persuade its holders to share it. This involves a facility with dispersed work that may come naturally to the next generation, people who are growing up as familiar with computers as their parents were with television, but is a difficult stretch for many of the current employees.

It turns out that play is one of the best ways for people to learn these important skills. Buckman Labs associates are connected to one another by the company intranet, which is hooked into the Internet to give them access to the outside world as well. You can bring a dispersed workforce up to speed quickly and easily if you give people free access to the Internet and encourage them to explore this new world at company expense. It is much cheaper to pay some network charges than to bring people together to teach them in a classroom setting. In addition, the individuals all learn best by exploring those areas that are of interest to them.

We have found this approach much more efficient in imparting knowledge about how to get value from the Internet and our own intranet than any other method we have tried. As people develop skills in remote exploration and relationship building, they learn to function as a Community of One that is part of a variety of greater wholes: communities of practice and communities of learning, some within the company and some outside the company. All will be important to the expansion of each individual's span of communication.

I believe that the new organizational model for business will be an expansion of the Community of One that is formed around the individual and will look something like the diagram in Figure 9.4.

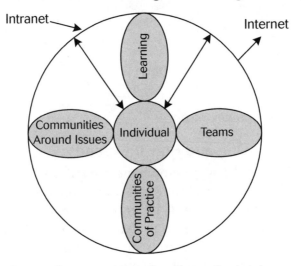

Figure 9.4. Expanding a community of one for business

This is just an elaboration of the Community of One illustrated in Figure 9.3. Participation and involvement in these communities will depend directly on the amount of freedom people have to choose where to devote their attention—and the success of these communities will depend on the level of participation they achieve.

One way to encourage such participation is by connecting everyone to as many of the electronic databases and knowledge bases of the organization as possible, so they will have more opportunities to share. In an electronic version of the old maxim, "Many hands make light work," many informed minds vastly improve the chance that someone will see and remember a key detail needed to advance the discussion toward an effective solution.

But business-oriented access isn't enough on its own. To get people committed to the larger communities, rather than merely involved on an ad hoc basis when they want something, the communities must become a part of life. And that requires the organization to take the step—counterintuitive though it's apt to seem to anyone steeped in the command-and-control style of business—of providing and encouraging the use of a global electronic break room, where people can share trivia and nonbusiness insights to their hearts' content. The more ways people have to interact with each other across time and space, the more comfortable they become in this new world. In the Buckman Labs electronic break room, associates can share anything as long as it does not violate the Code of Ethics.

This policy recognizes that it is the sharing of trivial matters that allows people to get to know each other and begin to build patterns of trust. It happens all the time in the face-to-face world. As acquaintances eat together, play games together, and tell jokes to one another, they bond into a group and set the foundation for sharing substantive matters when the need arises. By allowing this same kind of bridging activity to take place across time and space, a company can begin building a culture that genuinely encompasses its world.

Rather than simply allowing people to play online, you could take it a step further and propagate the online equivalent of chess, bowling, and softball leagues or amateur theatricals. It's possible to build games played across time and space that are designed to teach your people how to work across time and space in your business. At Buckman Labs, for example, we run online quiz shows modeled on Michael Feldman's *Whad'Ya Know?* We also use the virtual conference tool to play a guessing game based on corporate logos: someone puts up a PowerPoint show made up of letters cut out of logos—say, the "I" out of "IBM" or "Intel Inside"—and the team members then try to figure out the source of each letter. The main thing is to make it fun to be involved in meeting the needs of your business.

The greater the span of communication for each associate— that is, the more people they customarily interact with for work and play—the more important to the whole organization each will feel and the more occasions each will find to contribute to meeting the needs of your customers wherever they may be. So my advice

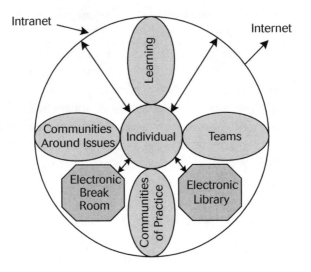

Figure 9.5. A Community of one in business

is to take this expansion of the span of communication as far as you can. Make it possible for everyone to assume responsibility for as much as they are willing to pick up. It will improve your day-to-day operations and it will reveal the leadership potential that exists in every corner of your organization.

All this culture building needs to be done in those areas that will help the business move in new directions, not just where the business is today. Focus on where you are trying to go for the future, not where you've been in the past. Keep on the lookout for new ways to take advantage of the radical increase in the span of communication that technology permits by learning how to help individuals extend their span of influence into new areas. Once you build a cultural framework where individuals feel free to move forward on their own initiative and assume responsibility for making things happen, you don't have to worry about control. Within that framework, people will control themselves.

Making It All Work

The best-performing systems are those that are aligned with the strategy of the organization and satisfy a need that the organization is trying to meet. In addition, the individual participants have to find something in the system for themselves or they'll sit on their hands. It doesn't matter how much the system has to offer the organization as a whole if it doesn't make it personally worthwhile for the associates to use it and learn new habits to do their work. People just do not have the extra time to fool around with a new way of doing things if it doesn't help them redefine their own time equation of work—let them do things better and do better things, not just a little more efficiently than before, but dramatically faster and more effectively. Without that individual benefit for the individual, you can forget it; no one will be willing to spend time learning a new system. It's essential to remember that each participant is a Community of One—you can use threats and incentives to get them to go through the motions, but you can't inspire the wholehearted participation you need for long-distance communities of practice unless the desire comes from within.

Finding a Real Need

Typically, systems do not work because their designers weren't focusing on a real need of the organization. And that's an easy mistake to make, as organizations have many perceived needs—while their real needs are few and far apart. The broader the focus of your effort around the needs of the customer, the better the system's chance to redefine the time equation of work.

At Buckman Labs, we got off the ground when we focused on enhancing our ability to bring the knowledge of the entire organization to bear on any problem that a customer might bring to us. We knew our driving need was to do that much faster and to do it better on a global basis. We had the knowledge in the global company, but we did not have it in each operating unit. It was a question of moving knowledge to where it was needed, when it was needed, at speeds we had not considered before. We knew that if we could do this, we could change the customers' perception of our ability to meet their needs. And we knew that the outcome of this effort would determine whether we survived and grew or stagnated as an organization. We knew that we had to change and we were determined to make the system work.

We have continued to modify the system over the years as we have learned new ways to make it work better. This is not a static system. It is dynamic: it changes and evolves as the needs of our customers change.

It is important that your system grows over time and continues to increase the value added to the organization and to the individuals involved. Think about how you would redefine the time equation of work so that increased productivity can be achieved over time. That is where additional payback can occur from your efforts.

But the important parameter to watch is a need of the organization that you want to meet in a new and better way. Keep it tied to the strategy of the organization. It is much easier for people to stay focused on making the system work if you are really helping the organization move forward with a coordinated strategy and meet its real needs. In fact, if you manage that, people will help you come up with modifications to the system to make it better. Involve your users in this process of evolution.

Convincing the Sales Force to Share Customer Feedback

It is not enough to support the front line with knowledge from the rest of the organization. In return, the front line has to provide feedback to tell the rest of the organization where the customers are going and how they want to get there. The more widespread that knowledge is, the faster the organization can respond to new trends and directions.

These new trends start with one customer in one part of the world; then another one, frequently in another part of the world, will start down the same path. By staying focused on a global perspective, your people can pick up these trends earlier than they could when they looked at things on country by country. If you want to be a fast-moving supplier focused on the ever-changing needs of your customers, then you have to pay attention to the trends that are developing among them. It behooves the people with direct customer contact to keep the rest of the organization informed about the trends that they see, and it behooves the rest of the organization to stay attuned to what they are seeing as new issues as they interact with customers.

This all may sound unrealistic at first, because detailed customer info is something sales reps generally conserve for their own benefit.

In practice, however, it turns out that basic human psychology kicks in: people like to reciprocate. Once the sales reps are talking directly to associates in R&D and getting solutions and advice from them, they find it only natural to open up with more of the background information about their customers and what they want. In fact, they will use this opportunity to get R&D's attention for their pet project for their best customers. This kind of interchange creates a culture of sharing, which has turned out to be vital at Buckman Labs in increasing the speed of innovation in the organization. As a result, our front-line associates are able to help the customers move faster and faster in the directions they want to go. This has resulted in correspondingly higher returns to the organization—and those involved.

If you are marketing by global virtual teams working with global customers, then it becomes very easy to stay attuned to the trends that are developing with each customer group. In fact, it is much easier to keep track of trends if you are organized this way than if you stick to the old way of having a marketing department in each country. Movement to a networked organization that is organized across geographical boundaries based on the customers' needs on a global basis is a way of speeding up your response to the needs of the customer.

Where Do You Stand?

Think about your customers. Do you know what knowledge assets your customers value most? Do you know what knowledge assets the organization needs to develop now for maximum return in the future? Can you redefine your customers' expectations into something that your competition cannot deliver? What outcomes do they desire today and how might this change in the future?

Think about the way your people interact with one another. What is the expected span of communication and span of influence for those who deal directly with customers? For research and other support personnel? How can you increase the span of communication of your associates so they can connect with someone wherever they need to go for information and knowledge? How can you help your associates increase their span of influence across the organization and beyond?

Think about the time equation of work—the general assumption about how long things take to get done in your business. Can you redefine that equation? Can you redefine how work is done? Can you redefine what the product of the organization is in the eyes of the customer? How can knowledge become a larger part of the value proposition you deliver to the customer? Can you build a true knowledge-driven organization? How would you define what a knowledge-driven organization is?

Becoming a Knowledge-Driven Organization

If you're ridin' ahead of the herd, take a look back every
now and then to make sure it's still there.

—Will Rogers

The value of knowledge in an organization increases as it moves faster and further in response to the organization's needs. At the same time, awareness of organizational needs points up places where the knowledge base has to expand to be ready for the future. This expansion can be an individual effort—via on-the-job training and experience or in formal learning activities. Alternatively, it can involve expanding an organizational knowledge base that requires a collective effort to develop. In any event, productive knowledge growth is focused on the immediate needs of the customer and where the customer is going rather than on any subjective approach to learning.

These knowledge needs are real and have an immediate impact on the success of the organization. This focus on the knowledge needs of the organization and the individuals involved as a driver of action is critical to being a knowledge-driven organization. It all gets back to cash flow. The generation of cash flow on the front line with the customer is the greatest need of most organizations. It is why a business is in business. The cash inflow over and above the associated costs is what determines whether the business succeeds or fails. The degree to which you can involve the entire organization in this endeavor will determine how much momentum you will develop as an organization.

The end result of all of this effort is to make any combination of parts of the entire organization available at any time, anywhere in the world. People who see a need should not have to wait until management makes up its mind to do something. For today's volatile markets, success and even survival demand an organic organization capable of responding instantly when conditions demand it.

The faster you can come up with a real, workable solution to a customer's needs, the better. Speed of response is critical to differentiating yourself from the competition. If you want prospective customers to turn to you first, you need to redefine their expectations about speed and quality. That means redefining your decision cycle as an organization so that you're moving faster than your competition without sacrificing quality. This can be done only by continually working on ways to get closure faster. Think speed—and all the old reservations about the need for command-and-control will fall by the wayside.

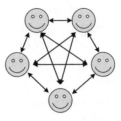

CHAPTER 10

Reward Associates for Sharing What They Know

We are each of us angels with only one wing, and we can only fly by embracing one another.

—Luciano de Crescenzo

A command-and-control business tends to take competition as a guiding principle, not just in its dealings with rivals in the business world, but also in the way its own parts deal with one another. Units compete for resources, people compete for position and influence, and out of all that rivalry the best interest of the company as a whole is expected to emerge. Very often, the results are good—good enough at any rate to confirm the expectation that this is the way things naturally work and should work. In the process, however, much that is valuable—both in resources and in human ingenuity—is ground up and wasted in efforts that do nothing to help the company deal with the outside world.

The goal of establishing a knowledge-sharing organization is nothing less than to break up this pattern of internal competition and bring the advantages of cooperation home to the participants so clearly that the group's interest and the individuals' "rational self-interests" merge. When people share what they know, as opposed to simply passing along the output of what they do, their whole outlook toward work changes radically. Here's a case in point.

Back when Buckman Labs was just beginning to make some headway with online knowledge sharing, one of our chief researchers and I sat down and talked about the impact this new method of communication would have on the way his department worked. He started with the assumption that they would go on much as before, creating new compounds on their own initiative and handing them off to the rest of the organization, which would take them gratefully and do wonderful things with them.

I said I thought the process would change over time. The Research Department would find itself needing to stay in touch with the marketplace on a daily basis by monitoring the online dialogues and participating in discussions of real business problems. There would be a much closer couple between R&D and the real problems in the marketplace, with the researchers moving toward understanding and attacking the trends developing on product needs, rather than doing so much fundamental research.

He was concerned about where he was going to find the time to do all this communication, with all the important research that he was doing. That is, he saw the communication as a distraction from his real work; I thought it would become an essential part of his real work, because he was going to need to focus more on solving immediate customer problems and less on longer-term fundamental research.

It turned out that the answer was somewhere in between. The R&D staff did begin participating in the solution of immediate customer problems and opportunities, making their work more relevant to the needs of the organization. But they didn't abandon their own lines of thought entirely. What we learned was that by having the R&D people focus part of their time on the real problems of the business through this communication with the front line, we improved their insight as to the direction research should be taking in the future. Some researchers proved to be particularly good at bridging the gap between R&D and the front line; they evolved into the primary communicators who provided the connections or links to the R&D effort. Needless to say, their stature rose within the organization, because they filled a vital role of determining future direction of the R&D effort. This transformation to a new role in the organization was typical of what we were seeing across the company.

My senior researcher never quite became a true bridge—he couldn't quite wrap his mind around the idea of completely rearranging his priorities—but he did move significantly off his initial position of opposing the extra work. Eventually, he became a key supporter of the transition we went through. In his own quiet way, he went through as big a culture change as some of the more visible members of the research community who actually did make themselves into bridges across the organization. By understanding and accepting the new order of determining directions, he learned how to move faster into the future, finding his own secure place in the new culture.

Success is its own reward for those who succeed. To get real mileage out of it for the organization, however, you need to pile on rewards that others will see and want for themselves. But those rewards needn't—probably shouldn't—be wholly or even mostly financial, as financial rewards rapidly turn into entitlements and lose their motivating power.

Autonomy is one of the most durable rewards available; if you allow those who first begin using the system to shape its development to suit their own work patterns, they will enjoy their increasing control over their work lives, and others will be drawn to the excitement. That will form a buzz of favorable publicity, and you can add to that publicity by sharing the news of successes achieved with the new way of doing things. Make heroes out of those who lead the organization in effective engagement on the front line and others will seek to emulate them.

A lot of this leadership will come from those on the front line itself. The ones who start getting faster results for their customers will quickly see the benefits. They will want more. Let them show the way so that others will have success also. The organization will follow.

Help People Build Their Own Networks

Installing new systems for communication in new ways is a messy process at best. No matter how much tweaking you do before the rollout, you will never get things completely right. So don't try.

My advice is to get your new system to the point where enough questions are answered for it to be feasible to use and then open the gates. Next, find out who is using the new system and getting value from it. Pick those early adopters, the ones who understand what the system is supposed to do, and involve them in making it better. You will find that they are usually the best knowledge sharers in the organization.

The building of good people-centric systems is an evolutionary process. Rarely will software straight from the box have everything you need; you almost always have to get some modifications to make it suit your needs. In addition, your experts' predictions about the training people will need on the new system are rarely correct in the beginning. As you roll out the system, make sure someone is keeping an eye on questions like these:

- ▶ What areas of the software are causing most people to have problems?
- ▶ Does the software do what its vendor claimed it would do?
- ▶ Do the users have the collaborative skills to take advantage of it?
- ▶ Do you have enough information technology support staff available to help out when people have problems using the software?
- ▶ Do the support staff understand the software well enough to help with the problems people actually have?

Feedback from the early adopters is critical in making a great system out of good software. By involving your associates in this process of continuous improvement, you are giving them the message that they are important. When you say, "We value your judgment and we want your assistance in making this system better"—and you make it clear that you mean it literally—the psychic income will go a long way toward keeping your initial group of converts on the cutting edge of developments. In addition, they will be good sources of new directions that will help you improve your systems over time, so the payback from involving these individuals in your process for improvement of existing systems and as part of your planning for the future is well worth almost any investment in their comfort and engagement in the process.

First Choice of Toys

Because your early adopters are also the most prolific knowledge sharers in the organization, it makes sense to give them the latest in equipment and software. In fact, you need to think in terms of keeping this leadership group at the forefront of your equipment acquisitions so they can continue to play their leadership role in the organization. And look beyond the home office—you need to work with early adopters who are geographically dispersed around the world so that you can pick up the kind of problems you will have in different areas. For example, at Buckman Labs we are continually amazed at how differently software functions with different connection protocols. The timing can be enough off to create problems that never appear with the protocols it was designed for. The early adopter group is a good test bed for anything you will want to make a part of your systems.

Early adopters tend to be your company's most successful people. A recent study by Xerox found that successful employees are more likely to share knowledge than unsuccessful ones (cited in Moorcroft, 2003). In addition, the report also pointed out that that people who used the word *knowledge* rather than *information* were more inclined to share freely. It does make a difference in what words people use to describe what they are doing. Keep your early adopters on board by involving them in your new directions. Give them the opportunity to maintain their status. It will pay big dividends.

Take People to the Fourth Wave

At Buckman Labs we made our first big jump into full-bore knowledge sharing in 1993. In addition to new software and connectivity, we had expanded the distribution of computers to our associates so they could all get into the system. Most had laptops at that time. The online Forums were up and running and the results were beginning to roll in. All of us involved in the introduction of these systems were very excited at the prospect of really redefining the company's competitive equation as we brought our associates up to speed.

It was obviously time to celebrate our successes. That year, we really were changing our culture to one of sharing knowledge to achieve success across time and space. We'd been able to radically shift our speed of response to the needs expressed by our customers from days and weeks to hours or, at the most, a few days, on a global basis. This had a significant impact on our competitive ability.

So, in early 1994, we began laying plans to have a meeting later that year, combined with our Fall Planning Meeting, that would both honor and reward the people who had done the best job of sharing knowledge across time and space in 1993. We called it the Fourth Wave Meeting, using a term I heard Tom Peters coin to describe what follows Alvin Toffler's first three waves: the age of the Creative Use of Knowledge.

The key question was how to determine who qualified to come to the meeting. I finally went to see Alison Tucker, the system operator who was facilitating the discussions in the Forum, and asked her if she could name the top 50 associates who had shared knowledge within our fledgling system for the benefit of the company in 1993. She said: "No problem, I can give you that list in rank order."

After I picked myself up off the floor and went back and checked how much I could spend on this celebration, I went back and asked her if she could name the top 100 knowledge sharers for the year. Again, she said: "No problem, I can give you the second 50 in rank order also."

By this time, my curiosity was up and I wanted to see how far she could go. So, after checking the budget again, I asked about the next 50 associates. She said, "I know who they are, but I can't give them to you in rank order."

That was good enough for me, so I used that number when I set the parameters of the meeting. We would take to the Fourth Wave Meeting the Planning Team and the top 150 individuals from around the world that had thus far done the best job of sharing knowledge. As word of the list leaked out, it became obvious that some important people in the company were going to be left behind and some secretaries were going to go in their place. People were coming from all over the world. Some had never traveled very far from home. As you can tell, this was developing into an interesting meeting.

We brought these early adopters together and asked them what other trends they were seeing in how the company needed to evolve. They were invited to sit down with the Planning Team to give their input on issues needing to be addressed by the company. The message was simple:

> You are the people who have embraced the investment in new technologies we have made as a company, and we are interested in hearing what you have to say about other things going on in the company and what directions we need to move in. You are the ones who have taken up the challenge to move the company forward. This trip (and the assorted gifts and mementos you'll be taking home) is a reward for what you have done. But there is more—more opportunities will open up for you as you successfully and productively move the organization forward on this new model.

That was their message and the message to all other associates.

So we went to Scottsdale, Arizona, in November 1994 for three days of celebration, fun, and work. We established what we meant by "Effective Engagement on the Front Line." We explored 10 different areas of "Open Space" activity. We developed the basis for the Foro Latino—the Spanish- and Portuguese-language Forum. We completed a reorganization of customer service in the United States. When the early adopters gathered for the second day of meetings, they found a new IBM ThinkPad notebook computer and a leather computer bag waiting at each place. We wanted to send a message that they were special people and we wanted them to continue doing what they had been doing.

We got to meet people face to face that we had been sharing knowledge with for the past few years. It was amazing how many times someone would look up when they heard someone talking and they would say, "You are George Halligan!" (Or whoever it happened to be.) And they would be right. I think what they were

across time and space together in one part of the world, so they can talk with each other directly, as Buckman Labs did with the Fourth Wave Meeting. While such a gathering is recognition for sharing over some period of time, it is also a way to bring together those individuals who have opinions about your future and a predisposition to share those opinions and turn them loose on the next round of problems.

Travel as a reward can be particularly useful for those who are working on long-distance projects with major customers. If you can get brave enough, allow those involved with the customers to make their own decisions as to when to travel, rather than leaving their immediate superiors to make the call. You will get a much bigger bang for the money expended. You will also reward those who are taking you in new directions and helping to redefine the time equation of work.

The best players deserve the best toys. Make sure that those who do the best job of knowledge sharing are upgraded to the latest hardware and software on a faster track than those who do not. Publish that fact so that everyone will know what the requirements are to be on the fast track for upgrades. Actively encourage knowledge sharing through the distribution of your hardware and software.

The users know what the system needs. Involve those who do the best job of sharing across time and space in the pilot activities where new directions are explored and new ways of doing work are developed. Involve them very early in the planning stages of these new directions. You can establish criteria for this involvement that are adjusted periodically so that fresh ideas are inserted into the developmental process. You might consider a service limit, or the top 10 people who share, or some criterion of service time—say, serve for three years and then have a break of a year before being considered again for service.

Visible signs and symbols fuel participation. The leather computer bags from the Fourth Wave Meeting did as much as anything to create a useful level of envy and desire to emulate the knowledge-sharing leaders among the rest of the workers. It keeps things moving to use something concrete and desirable like a computer bag as an annual reward and identifier for the people who do the best job of sharing. Keep the reward simple and consistent, but keep it focused on a new group each year. It's best to make the winners sit out for three years before being eligible to compete again—the intrinsic rewards of participation will make sure they don't run out of steam in the interim and the constant possibility of winning will help draw new blood into the active group. You want to reward a significant number of people each year—at least 25—and you want them to be dispersed geographically across the organization so as to encourage knowledge sharing globally.

Games and contests draw people in. Have a contest to see who can predict when the 10,000th message will be sent on your collaborative systems. Or the millionth message. These periodic rewards keep everybody interested in what is going on and looking at what is happening in your collaborative systems. You can have similar awards for section leaders, sysops, or cybrarians who are focused on making the system go. But, above all, do not make it a pay-for-messages scheme. You want to reward meaningful contributions, not manic keystrokes! Remember: you need outcomes, not just activity.

Pay still matters. Intrinsic rewards are the most durable, but they don't do the job on their own. Make sure that you recognize those who do the best job of sharing knowledge across the organization with meaningful pay increases, tied to actions that benefit the organization and not to position on the organization chart. Knowledge sharing should be one of the principal components of any pay system, as it is a key activity in moving an organization forward. This means that you have to have concrete ways of determining the value delivered by knowledge sharing. All parties have to understand these. I can assure you that you will not get this completely right the first time you try it, but if you have a culture of continually revising the system to make it better, you will evolve your way there.

Those who don't play go nowhere. The people who engage in active and effective knowledge sharing across the organization should be the only ones considered for promotion. I do not mean by this that all of them should be promoted on any kind of regular schedule or even necessarily considered for promotion. But the level and quality of participation should be the critical criterion for putting people on the list of those being considered for promotion—or for leaving them off. Making knowledge sharing an essential component of advancement sends a strong message about where you want the organization to go.

Nothing's perfect. Leonard Cohen writes, "Ring the bells that still can ring. Forget your perfect offering. There is a crack in everything. That's how the light gets in." As you set out to reward your people for the good stuff they do, it is best to avoid forcing them to follow a rigid approach to achieve success. Rather, create conditions that will increase the probability of getting where you want to go and then have faith in your people to carry you there.

Where Do You Stand?

Think about your incentive systems. What behavior are you rewarding? Is it the behavior you want to see?

Think about knowledge sharing in your organization now. What are 10 ways you might reward your associates for their knowledge-sharing activity? How do you reward the best of the best differently from the rest? How do you create some excitement in your organization about where you want to go? How do you make people feel good about what they are doing? How do you make it fun for your people to go in the direction that you want the organization to go? Do you trust your people to take your company forward?

The Power of Reward

You need to encourage change in the direction that you want to go. Culture change cannot be demanded; it can only be encouraged by opening the windows of opportunity for change. At Buckman Labs, the key turned out to be knowledge sharing. If this is a direction you want your organization to go, then reward those who move in this direction by increasing their opportunity to advance. Make involvement in knowledge sharing part of the review process on measurement of results. Consider for promotion only those who act to share knowledge across the organization. Then promote the best of the best.

Let your creativity run free to generate some enthusiasm for your efforts. Do not be afraid to dream up games or contests to get your people interested in moving in a new direction. Just be sure the new direction is tied in with your strategy, so that you do not have your people chasing something that will not take them—or you—in the direction you want to go.

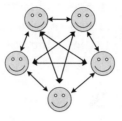

CHAPTER 11

Build Critical Mass in the Use of Your Knowledge System

Even when you're on the right track, if you stand still, you'll get run over.

—Will Rogers

Time. It's the world's most valuable resource. Everyone needs it, everyone wants it, and no one can ever obtain more of it—you can only use your allotted 24 hours a day more or less wisely. The more you can get done in the time available to you, the more productive you will be.

That applies to organizations as well as individuals, though an organization can often cut elapsed time on a job by bringing more hands and minds to bear on it, increasing production if not productivity. And organizations can handle many tasks at once.

But organizations are made up of people, and people make their own choices regarding what to do with their time. If you want the kind of productivity that comes from knowledge sharing backed by the wholehearted and willing support of all your associates, you have to set things up so the effort is personally valuable to them. And then you have to keep building the system so that the effort becomes more and more valuable as time passes—it won't stay static. Either it is going to grow in importance in the minds of the users or it will slowly die as they find more rewarding things to do with their time.

Making the First Big Jump

> Deep change requires us to take into account the diversity, opinions, consensus, and conflict present in relationships. Dialogue is the process by which a community's broad-reaching needs can be met.
>
> —Suzanne Maxwell

Cultural change follows a predictable process, and the steps can't be rushed or skipped—though they will take different amounts of time depending on what you are trying to do and how big the group is. For some reason, the process always seems to involve three different and distinct action periods, each separated from the others by at least one night's sleep.

Thus the shortest span of time to introduce significant change is three days. If you can get everyone involved in your target cultural system together in the same room, you can make a real and lasting change that fast. At the other end of the scale, if you are trying to move a far-flung organization, it can take three years for the message to penetrate and the new patterns to establish themselves.

But it's always useful to think in terms of three complete cycles to achieve any fundamental change. These cycles can be described as follows.

Cycle 1: *You've gotta be crazy!* The first day or period is marked by incredulity. Asked to change, most people begin by thinking, *What are those idiots going on about? They want us to do what?!? Where did this fad come from?* You will hear all the reasons why it cannot be done. Every excuse in the book will come out of the woodwork. Some weirdly assorted groups will band together because they view the proposed change as a threat. Stay calm and continue to make your case. Be persistent and consistent about your direction. Answer all the questions seriously and consider all the objections as legitimate, while maintaining your position.

Cycle 2: *It ain't gonna go away after all.* After they've had a chance to sleep on it (or see it repeated in the next monthly newsletter or annual report), people will begin to believe that this change is not going to go away, that it is for real. This second day or period is marked by a realization that the organization is really going to move in the stated direction and that it's necessary to start figuring out what to do to make the change happen with the least trauma. The objections will still be there, but reality is starting to set in. Help people sort through the initial storm of reactions and uncover the real issues that they will have to deal with as you move forward. Remember that they are still scared about where you are leading them. Help them to separate the wheat from the chaff and begin dealing with the wheat in good faith.

Cycle 3: *Y'know, that's not such a bad idea.* Two nights down the road, most people are ready to get on board. This third day or period is marked by both acceptance and commitment to action to make the move forward a success. It is during this period that you can solidify where you want the organization to go and deal with any remaining stumbling blocks. There will always be some, so look for them—they are important and cannot be neglected. Sometimes these issues will make it obvious that the initial proposal genuinely needs a change in direction and that this is the time to make that change. People have come around far enough to give the new proposals a real try, but they're still willing to conclude that their initial predictions of disaster were correct. When you work with them to smooth out the real obstacles that they see and you didn't think of in advance, they will understand that your new direction is practical as well as deliberate and desirable.

I have never figured out why it takes three cycles to achieve this kind of commitment to a new direction or way of doing things. However, every time I tried to do it in two, the resulting degree of commitment fell far short of the times I gave it all three. It seems to take that second break and new beginning—on a new day; lunch isn't enough to help things come together when you have a meeting. Someday, I will learn from a psychologist or social scientist why this is so. In the meantime, I accept it as fact and put it into my time equation for achieving fundamental change. And change is essential if you're looking at developing real knowledge sharing in an organization that retains any trace of its roots in the command-and-control past.

Bringing the Whole Group on Board

There is no such thing as merely surviving or maintaining the status quo in business. As in the organic world, there is only growth and decay, and growth is the business of business.

—Isay Stemp, *Corporate Growth Strategies*

Any reasonably well-designed system for the improvement of the organization will attract a group of early adopters. People become pathfinders because of curiosity or a desire to be first or some combination of the two. Even in a dynamic and forward-looking organization, however, the first announcements will draw in only about 20% of the population that you would wish to engage. But you need most of the other 80% if you are going to have a viable system that will return value to the organization. The pioneers—like the people who attended the Buckman Labs Fourth Wave Meeting I described in Chapter 10—will help you begin to fine-tune your system so as to attract enough users to approach critical mass in the organization.

The probability that you will get 100% of the population using any new system is relatively low; but if you can get a sufficient number on board to make people assume that they ought to be able to find everyone they need to reach there, then you have reached critical mass. It's a little like the situation with the Internet—back in 1994 or 1995, when businesses were starting to put up Web sites, it was something to talk about but not something everyone did. Nowadays, it's hard for a business to get by without one; people say of the holdouts, "They don't have a Web site, so you'll have to phone ...." You want your holdouts to begin overhearing things like "I don't think he checks the Forums much, but you can reach him at thus-and-such if you think it's worthwhile ...."

So how do you reach critical mass? It takes a series of efforts by many different people. I know of no one right answer, but I can give you some examples of what has worked in the past—which has a reasonable chance to work in the future.

Appealing to Individuals

Keep in mind that you are dealing with people, with all the variety they can bring to the scene. Even alone in a room, every individual is a mass of skills and intentions and conflicting desires—a literal Community of One who may react to a given message very differently depending on the conditions and demands of the moment. Everyone will have baggage from the past and prejudices about the future. Everyone will feel busy, pressed for time to take care of all their current responsibilities. Only those for whom novelty has an absolute value will take on anything new just because it's there—and you won't have nearly enough of those for critical mass.

To encourage people to move in a new direction, you have to deal with this baggage and you have to deal with this time problem. It's essential to help them get rid of enough baggage to take on new directions and to redefine their time equation of work so that they can be more productive than in the past.

People have to want to use the system. They have to be able to use the system. They have to have good reasons to do so. And those reasons have to involve real needs of your business—it is not enough to sit back and create systems that do wonderful things but have no connection to where the business is trying to go, or to find engaging places to play with the system and never do anything else with it. The degree to which everyone is focused on and absorbed with executing the strategy of the organization will determine how well you will succeed in the marketplace.

The steps outlined in this chapter will be just a beginning for you. Use your imagination to think of additional things that you might do to help your people to become knowledge workers. But, as you continue your efforts to build critical mass, stay focused on where you are trying to go with your strategy.

Notes from the CEO

Whenever you introduce a new system that will change the way work is done and take the organization in a new direction, you will be dealing with culture change—and culture change of this type needs to be led by management, including top management. It cannot be left to the information technology specialists. You are on a journey of continual culture change. It is not the role of the IT department to lead culture change in the organization. That is the role of management—the responsible executive needs to take an active role, as I did when Buckman Labs introduced its new system in the early 1990s.

In my experience, you get people to move in a significant way in new directions one person at a time. Think about opening windows of opportunity for them to redefine their personal time equation of work while dealing with the real needs of the business. Describe what the opportunity is. Sell the program.

Typing and Other Skills

You've got to think about big things while you're doing small things, so that all the small things go in the right direction.

—Alvin Toffler

One of the first skills that a Community of One needs to stay in touch with a larger virtual community is the skill of typing. Archaic as this form of communication may seem in the electronic world, the keyboard is still the fastest and most reliable input device that is generally available. Until someone comes up with a cheap and sturdy neurological interface or subvocalization microphone and saturates the market with it, every knowledge worker will have to be to some extent a keyboard worker. And that means knowing how to type; hunt and peck just isn't fast enough to leave time for anything else in the day.

But not all that long ago, typing was regarded as a clerical skill, somehow beneath the dignity of a knowledge worker or manager. You will have people in your organization who chose not to learn to type or who learned for schoolwork and then set the skill aside. When it becomes a requirement, many of them will be embarrassed to say that they do not know how to type.

So one of the simplest things you can do is to load a simple typing program as part of the standard software package on every PC you distribute. It costs very little and it will let everybody improve their knowledge work productivity quietly and without embarrassment. Just think of what the payback would be for your organization if you could achieve a 10% increase in throughput among your knowledge workers. I suspect that most organizations could get at least that much from simple increases in typing speed. You can't command it—but people will reach for it if you make it available and desirable.

Another skill that your people should acquire is the best way to communicate in networked organizations. Considerations of status tend to recede from people's awareness as they reach across the network and communicate more as equals. Participants soon find that the knowledge and persuasive arguments they bring to the scene are more influential than their job title in the organization. Unsurprisingly, some instantly love this aspect of open communications systems, while others—those who have learned to rely on positional power or at least to enjoy its trappings—find it distinctly unsettling. At Buckman Labs we constantly remind people that the reduced emphasis on status is right and appropriate by making it the basis of the first two provisions of our Code of Ethics:

▶ That the company is made up of individuals—each of whom has different capabilities and potentials—all of which are necessary to the success of the company.

▶ That we acknowledge that individuality by treating each other with dignity and respect—striving to maintain continuous and positive communications among all of us.

This is something that you can teach best by modeling. You have to have the courage to communicate openly and objectively about the opportunity at hand. Do not use your rank or position to establish the validity of your thought if you want the open participation of all your associates. Any exercise of positional power on your part will cut off the dialogue that you have spent so much effort to encourage.

The higher up the organizational chart you are, the more important it is for you to encourage dialogue within the boundaries of your organization. Within Buckman Labs, our boundary is our Code of Ethics. It is vital that you manage the discussions from the "values" perspective and not from the content perspective. If you already have a code of ethics that doesn't address this point, you don't need to revise it. Instead, as noted in Chapter 8, set up something new—call it a Statement of Values for Effective

Communication—to achieve the same result. If you demonstrate, as a leader of your organization, that everyone's participation is wanted, you will send the clearest signal that the normal obstacles to participation no longer apply.

Effective networked communications open the door to another vital skill—working smoothly with people you rarely see. The path to get past barriers in the use of new systems may not be as obvious as you first think. Involve those with the problem in its solution, and you will frequently be surprised at the solutions they come up with.

The following sections describe some the specific situations we encountered at Buckman Labs and our responses to them. Your experience will differ in detail, but the same general principles will apply.

Foro Latino. We ran into a problem in Latin America when we put in our Forums for the sharing of tacit knowledge across the organization. We found we were not getting the same percentage of that part of the organization using the system as we were in North America and Europe. Not even close. Because Latin America was (and still is) an important part of our total operation, we addressed this problem in our Fourth Wave Meeting and established an Open Space Meeting—titled "Palm Beach"—to deal with it, with Andres Gonzales as section leader. Here is the assignment as given:

Missão (Portuguese) = "Remover as barreiras existentes para transferência de conhecimento global."

Mission (German) = "Bestehende Barrieren zu beseitigen, um einen weltweiten Wissensaustausch zu ermöglichen!"

Misión (Spanish) = "Remover las barreras en la transferencia de conocimientos alrededor del mundo."

Missione (Italian) = "Rimuovere le esistenti barriere nel trasferimento delle informazioni nel mondo."

Mission (French) = "Eliminer les barrières existantes au transfert d'idées de part le monde."

Missie (Flemish) = "Het verwijderen van de bestaande barrières voor een wereldwijde overdracht aan kennis."

Mission (English) = "To remove existing barriers to a worldwide knowledge transfer."

This includes training, language support, and help with Fast-path.

What we learned was that we had a cultural issue to deal with. In seems that in the Latin cultures it is not acceptable for an engineer to ask a question, as engineers are expected to know the answers. However, engineers often make the most effective front-line customer representatives precisely because they are the ones who can solve problems, so we use a lot of them in that role. So, our Latin engineers were finding the Forums awkward because the system was built on the assumption that someone would trigger a general discussion by asking a question. That posed serious difficulties in getting our systems up to speed in that part of the world.

The group concluded that there were actually two problems to consider. Besides the general reluctance to ask questions, we had to deal with the language issue. English was not the first language for our Latin American associates; they could speak it well, but they did not feel comfortable writing it. They felt that they could not be precise enough to be understood. Between the two issues, we were dead.

Our solution was to create the Foro Latino, a completely separate Forum for our associates that would be conducted in Spanish and Portuguese, the two languages of the region. Eliminating the language barrier made it feasible for Foro Latino participants to interact comfortably, which allowed them to find ways to work around their cultural barriers and get information when they needed it. Although we set this up for our Latin American associates, it is used by our people around the world who are comfortable functioning in these languages.

The Foro Latino is still a part of our total system, and it is open to all. Indeed, since the introduction of these changes, Latin America has become one of the most active centers of forum participation in the company.

Many individuals find it interesting to go into the Foro Latino and test their Spanish and Portuguese comprehension. As a global organization with individuals shifting around the world, we have no residency requirement to access this particular Forum or any other. We have also hired a translator for our Knowledge Resource Center (our company library) to monitor the Foro Latino and move messages and answers back and forth between it and our English-language discussions, helping associates reach each other who would otherwise find it difficult or impossible to do so.

Break Room. The goal of a knowledge-sharing system is to make online communication a natural part of the working environment—to extend the walls of the immediate office space around the world. As I've mentioned before, it turns out that natural communication can't be purely serious—people who interact only formally never really learn to trust one another.

By providing an electronic break room for trivial interactions in the same format as the business-oriented systems, we were able to get our people comfortable with the thought of sharing knowledge across time and space. We set aside a section in our Forums where associates can come together and socialize, using exactly the same system in the same way as they do for work-related discussions. Only the content is different. They sell cats and dogs, they tell jokes, and they discuss national and global issues and root for their World Cup representatives. They search out the best restaurants or things to see in new towns. The only restriction is that all postings must be consistent with our Code of Ethics. We will pull something off our Forums only if it is inconsistent with our Code of Ethics. Otherwise, it is OK, even if it criticizes company policy or practice.

Access to the Internet. The Internet is one of the most important communities for any company—it's where company intranets come together, where customers meet suppliers and other resources and the whole world opens up on every desktop. I suspect that we will see more and more application of Web technology in the solution of business problems as we try and connect all of our individual Communities of One together in new ways.

Giving your associates access to the Internet, and all it brings, is one of the best ways to teach them how to operate in this new world of online interaction and to shift your organization in the direction you will probably be going. Let them play, explore, and learn.

Buckman Labs pays the network charges for individual exploration and relationship building on the Internet because we view that activity as fundamental training for how we will be operating in the future. Sherman Woo did something similar at US West in the early '90s and called it the Global Village. It was very successful in bringing a large, diverse organization together for the solution of business-specific problems across time and space.

Where Do You Stand?

Think about participation in your current systems for online interaction. What proportion of your workforce is using them? Do you have critical mass? What is keeping the holdouts out? What can you do to help the rest of the organization see that these systems are useful?

Think about the systems themselves. Are they personally rewarding to use? Do people have the skills to take advantage of them? How will you make your systems so valuable to the users that there is no question where they will go for information and knowledge?

Value for Time

"Critical mass" is a useful concept when you're figuring out how to get a knowledge-sharing system into productive operation, but—like any metaphor—it doesn't altogether capture the reality of what you're dealing with here. People aren't atoms. Each and every Community of One can be part of the reaction today, roaring along with the system and making good use of it, and then out of it tomorrow, either by deliberate choice or by pressure of other obligations.

The kind of productivity improvements required to keep up with today's accelerating markets requires redefining the time equation of work for everybody. And not just once; it has to be a continual effort, moving faster and faster just to avoid sliding back.

You can't drive people to do this. They have to want it for themselves and not just for what it means for the company, and that means you have to build in personal enjoyment and other intrinsic rewards—continual play and learning as well as chances to build respect and influence, along with a genuine sense of global community that supports a fluid, horizontal organizational business model.

The Internet exploration opportunities and the electronic break rooms are thus a permanent part of the process; although I've introduced them as a way to draw people in and introduce the basic techniques, you can't think of them as temporary expedients.

The cultural change involved in making knowledge sharing part of your everyday work processes is real and deep—and essential. If you don't become a knowledge-driven organization and somebody else in your field does, they will pass you and become your worst nightmare. If you do, your organization's ability to multiply the power of work—to apply real leverage—will grow dramatically.

The next chapter describes the way communities form and reform around issues and areas of practice. It then introduces the first and most basic technique Buckman Labs adopted for work in the new environment, the Open Space meeting.

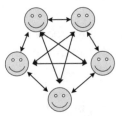

CHAPTER 12

Strategies for Building Communities That Span the World

A public corporation should now be regarded not as a piece of property but as a community—although a community created by common purpose rather than by common place. No one owns a community. ... The core members of communities are more properly regarded as citizens rather than as employees or "human resources"—citizens with responsibilities as well as rights.

—Charles Handy

Once upon a time, having a telephone was a big deal. A business phone of your own—or better still, lots of phones so you could reach lots of other important people at the same time—meant you were really somebody. Nowadays, phones are ubiquitous, and it's a relatively rare worker who even has to share the use of one and a rare company that makes more than a token effort to control phone access. And even though getting through to someone by phone is still a matter for fairly tight control in many organizations, where diligent gatekeepers protect the time (and status) of those regarded as more valuable than the rest, the scope of phone communications has lent vast power to our social networks.

Online communications are reaching a similar point far earlier in their history. It's not yet true that everybody is connected, but it is relatively easy to get there—provided the political powers of the organization will allow it.

The computer is nothing more than a glorified communication device, after all, and the key to knowledge sharing is to forget about status affording access and open it up to everybody in the organization. You have to give everybody the tools to be knowledge workers if you want a knowledge-driven organization, because every member of the organization has something to contribute. The whole organization loses if anyone is excluded as a result of technology or politics or is limited by anything but his or her own ability to influence others across time and space. And the whole organization gains as people settle in and begin to work with each other in the realm of ideas.

Harnessing the Power of Online Interaction

Whatever system you use to allow people to interact spontaneously across time and space, the effect is the same. You've built a very powerful tool for dealing with fast-changing situations by bringing people together in flexible groups called Issue-Driven Communities to focus on the needs of your customers and your organization. This is what will lead the organization into the territory where it needs to go.

These communities are where the future of the organization will evolve, because they focus on helping the organization move in the right direction rather than on raw speed. In addition, they also reinforce their members' loyalty to the organization that makes them possible.

Issue-Driven Communities

Results are obtained by exploiting opportunities, not by solving problems. All one can hope to get by solving a problem is to restore normalcy.

—Peter Drucker, *Managing for Results*

An Issue-Driven Community is just that—a group designed to take action on a pressing issue, that is, a problem that needs immediate attention or an opportunity likely to evaporate if not seized at once. The focus is on responding as rapidly as possible. This is not where deep studies are done. This is where action is required right now!

These are the communities that will allow you to deal with dynamic situations on a day-to-day basis and do business across the silos of the global organization. This process of crossing the boundaries among organizational silos to meet current needs rapidly, as they develop, will redefine the organization's structure as a network rather than a hierarchy. The importance of Issue-Driven Communities cannot be overemphasized.

Because they will be dealing with real issues of the organization that require fast action, these communities need to be open to everyone who could conceivably contribute to addressing the problems or opportunities that might come up. In our experience at Buckman Labs, the more associates with access to a Forum, the better it functions. We have found that we cannot predict where the essential bits of knowledge will come from. Therefore, for the Forums that we are looking to for fast action around the needs of the business, we provide complete access to everybody in the organization.

As Peter Drucker says, the greatest possibility for the organization is to exploit the opportunities that arise. Since the need is for fast action, it is best to have these communities continually monitored by a system operator so that knowledge that is not readily available can be brought in on a moment's notice. Our system operators at Buckman Labs are in our Knowledge Resource Center and are more appropriately called *cybrarians* rather than librarians. They have two broad roles. The first is to bring the knowledge in our knowledge bases to bear on the issue and to search the Internet for additional knowledge that might be germane to the issue at hand. The second is to alert others in the organization that they know could be instrumental in dealing with the issue at hand to get involved in the dialogue.

As problems or opportunities are dealt with in an open Forum that everybody has access to, the organization's new knowledge grows and develops in front of everybody. This allows people across the organization to learn about new things as they are happening, just by reading along as events unfold around the world. This dynamic learning is critical to keeping a global knowledge workforce up to date on the latest developments.

In addition, this new knowledge can be captured and put into a knowledge base for reuse in the future when someone else has a similar problem. That turns out to be far simpler than it looks at first glance.

At Buckman Labs, we spent a fair amount of time tinkering with systems of knowledge base codification, trying to work out the best way to document all this new knowledge. In the end we just gave up. Whatever we did to code our knowledge bases, it always seemed too slow to meet the needs of a fast-changing organization. We could not wait the months that it always seemed to take to get something codified.

So instead, we put the key discussion threads into a full-text search database and opened it up to Verity, a huge search engine. Verity lets us do full-text searches very fast, which turns out to be much more efficient than spending a lot of time coding each message for retrieval. The next time someone comes up with a similar problem, the community doesn't have to start from scratch, even if the associate who raises a question and the ones who first respond have no idea the topic has come up before. This is how we manage to retain and harness the valuable knowledge in the organization.

You will find that Issue-Driven Communities will become one of the most powerful systems that you can develop for improving the ability of the organization to redefine the time equation of work. Speed is essential when you are dealing with opportunities and problems. But you will have to push your associates to move fast.

As I noted earlier in the book, it's entirely possible to maintain the quality of the response as you speed it up, but you have to keep reminding people that speed is the first requirement. You can do this by highlighting stories that show just how fast a particular issue was dealt with. Or how much faster your people reacted than your competition did when you snagged an opportunity. Stories of success in actual situations are what get people excited about moving in a new direction even though it involves some initial effort on their part. Focus on moving fast as an organization so that you can take advantage of your opportunities and deal with your problems as they arise.

Have the courage to go where the opportunities that your customers present take you. You might be surprised where they will lead. Have the courage to be a fast-changing organization around the needs of the customer. I suspect that, if you do not, your competitors will.

Communities of Practice

Etienne Wenger and William Snyder used the term "Communities of Practice" to describe "groups of people informally bound together by shared expertise and passion for a joint enterprise" (2000, p. 139). (The term was first used by Wenger and Jean Lave in 1991 in their book, *Situated Learning*.) Communities of Practice tend to be bands of individuals who come together for some reason and stay together because of the value added that the members obtain by associating with one another and sharing common experiences and knowledge together.

Given that definition, what I'm calling an Issue-Driven Community would be considered a Community of Practice. I prefer to differentiate between the two, however, because of the significant difference in the sense of urgency and the diverse population required to create the dynamic character I regard as the essential feature of an Issue-Driven Community. Generally speaking, Communities of Practice contain fewer members and do not have the same sense of urgency as Issue-Driven Communities usually do. They take a longer, slower look at developments in their field, which can also be valuable to an organization—but on a different basis.

A Society of Chemical Engineers chapter could be a Community of Practice, as could the Dental Society, the researchers in a company, the marketing people: these are all groups of people with similar interests. At Buckman Labs, our research group is tied together using special software into a Community of Practice where access is limited to those in R&D. This software helps them discuss new compounds and share knowledge about research efforts. We also have a Community of Practice for people who install and use our accounting software across the organization, for those who work with recycled fiber, for those in the financial areas of the company, for those in manufacturing, and so on. In addition, we have set up special Communities of Practice around particular customer groups, so that deep knowledge sharing relative to those groups can occur. Access to some of these communities is restricted so that confidential information can be shared among those who have a real need to know it. As you build your Communities of Practice across the organization, do not hesitate to try unconventional groupings that might allow your organization to go in new directions.

Communities of Practice can be particularly useful in helping to build a global organization out of a lot of individual operating companies in separate countries. You can share process improvement information among the silos in your manufacturing area. You can share marketing skills that have been learned in different places. Any grouping of people whom you want to have in closer contact with each other is a candidate for a Community of Practice. So be creative in building your Communities of Practice. Actively support them and promote their use throughout the organization. We allow anyone at Buckman Labs who wishes to create a Community of Practice to do so. We will set it up and then it is up to those who want to get involved to carry it forward.

We have also found that some Communities of Practice need both a private space to interact among themselves and a public space where they share with the rest of the organization. It's essential to be sensitive to such issues, as each of your Communities of Practice will turn out to have different requirements for privacy and outside interaction.

Communities of Learning

All your online communities can also be Communities of Learning. Anytime people interact in the course of doing the business of the organization, learning can take place. The more opportunity people have to participate in such communities, the greater the learning—especially when learning is an intentional part of the organization's motivation for putting these communities together. A Community of Practice builds the general effectiveness of all the practitioners who take part in it, even if they only observe its discussions; an Issue-Driven Community doesn't exist just to deal with the issue at hand but to help participants grow over their lifetime. As you put your communities together, don't overlook the opportunities for learning across the organization.

As Peter Senge says, "Increasingly, successful organizations are building competitive advantage through less controlling and more learning—that is, through continually creating and sharing new knowledge. ... Yet only genuine commitment can bring about the courage, imagination, patience, and perseverance necessary in a knowledge-creating organization" (Senge, 1997, pp. 30-32). As the spans of influence of individual members of the organization expand, knowledge moves across the organization at speeds that were not possible before, and learning doubles and redoubles. This rapidly growing knowledge creates value for the organization and simultaneously creates continual opportunities for learning as more individuals are drawn into the process.

The challenge, as I've said repeatedly, is to create the environment and culture in which each individual Community of One will feel comfortable sharing knowledge as far as possible, openly and freely. This is where an open commitment to learning for its own sake as well as for the sake of the business will really come in handy, as it will help people establish the habits of teaching and learning that promote development of a truly knowledge-driven organization.

Basic Online Interaction: The Open Space Meeting

> If you bring the appropriate people together in constructive ways with good information, they will create authentic visions and strategies for addressing the shared concerns of the community.
>
> —David Chrislip, Center for Creative Leadership,
> *Collaborative Leadership*

At Buckman Labs we refer to the deliberations of our communities—especially the issue-driven variety—as "Open Space" meetings. These differ from the face-to-face Open Space meetings described in the management literature, because they're not face-to-face at all: they're virtual—ongoing discussions of customer needs and solutions that range back and forth around the world and work their way to solutions almost as quickly as the problems can be framed. They are far more efficient than normal face-to-face meetings because no one has to wait around for things to start, pick up, organize; it all happens organically and everyone participates when they wish to do so, rather than being dragged away from more immediate work.

As leadership consultant and professor Meg Wheatley would say, order is all around us: we only have to embrace it and let the order come out of using the open space. This concept, in my opinion, is one of the ways that organizations will be able to maintain continuity on the key drivers for their business going forward.

Open Space Basics

An Open Space meeting operates on four basic principles:

- ▶ Whenever it starts is the right time.
- ▶ Whoever comes is right for the group.
- ▶ Whatever happens is the only thing that could have happened.
- ▶ When it's over, it's over.

Timing. *Whenever it starts is the right time.* At Buckman Labs, an Open Space meeting starts when someone launches a threaded discussion under Outlook Express, posting a message to ask a question or present a problem or alert us to an opportunity or make a statement in our Forums. Whenever someone wants to raise an issue, whether it's Tuesday at 10 in the morning or Saturday at 10 at night, things can get under way.

Participants. *Whoever comes is right for the group.* When someone tosses out a topic, people come together around that issue. Not everyone in the company, of course—it isn't necessary for everyone to make an effort to respond to every issue. No one has useful knowledge to contribute in response to all questions. It's only necessary to draw in a few people who are attracted to a particular issue and have knowledge to contribute to it. They are the right people to start the ball rolling. They have the power to drag others into the discussion and call for research in any direction necessary to provide answers. At the same time, they can all follow "the law of two feet": anyone who is bored, not learning anything, or finding nothing to contribute is honor-bound to walk away from the discussion and let the others get on with it.

Outcome. *Whatever happens is the only thing that could have happened.* The people drawn into the discussion begin their dialogue around the need of the organization that has been presented. When an issue is introduced as a problem requiring a solution, participants share their knowledge of possible answers, but they're also primed to look for an opportunity hiding within the problem. Frequently, that is where the greatest possibilities for innovation to take an organization forward can be found.

As people come and go, the process of self-selection quickly stirs the pot until all the elements of needed knowledge are thrown together and a usable solution emerges. When I say it's "the only thing that could have happened," I'm exaggerating, of course—many problems have more than one solution. But it's the only thing the company needs *right now*: a specific, effective approach that will get the job done and let people move on to something else or a lead that we can develop into a new product or service.

Ending. *When it's over, it's over.* The dialogue continues until whoever raised the issue in the beginning is satisfied that his or her needs (and thus the needs of the organization) have been met. At that point, the dialogue stops and the Open Space meeting is over. Frequently, side issues have emerged from the dialogue and new Open Space meetings are spiraling off from it. New individuals are attracted to these new issues and the process continues unabated.

Implications for the Organization

> Lettin' the cat outta the bag is a whole lot easier 'n puttin' it back in.
>
> —Will Rogers

Open Space meetings are not for the faint of heart. People take ownership. They come up with solutions. The chance to range over the issues brings out dormant possibilities in people. They raise embarrassing questions. You can ask people to focus on work-related issues, but once you invite them to tackle serious questions in a no-holds-barred way, you can have repercussions far beyond the particular Open Space meeting that initiated the thought.

Participation in Open Space meetings creates the expectation that things will be different in the future. People assume they will see more empowerment, less bureaucracy, and greater cooperation. If this is not to be, then you will only create cynicism in the organization if you open the door partway and then try to slam it shut. So don't begin to explore the concept of Open Space unless you are prepared to entertain suggestions for significant changes in organizational structure and procedures. You cannot control the process once it starts. You have to be prepared to go where it takes you and at the pace that your people will dictate.

Where Do You Stand?

Think about your workforce. What kinds of communities does it include? What kinds would be useful to develop? Do you trust your associates? Are you successfully overcoming the barriers you encounter in running a global business?

Think about Open Space meetings. Is your company ready for them? Is it OK for your associates to walk out of one of your meetings if it is not creating value for them? Which wave are you riding? Can you embrace company-wide awareness? What do you want to do today?

Think about your organization's time equation of work. Are you willing to give up command-and-control to get speed of response to the opportunities and problems that your company faces? Are you willing to change your organization and its approaches to the marketplace as fast as your customers are willing to change? Do you want to get out in front of where your customers are going? Do you want to successfully perforate the silos in your organization and define new communities that will allow you to share knowledge on a global basis?

Life with Community

To enjoy the benefits of knowledge sharing, it's essential to find ways to extend each individual's span of influence beyond the face-to-face circle to the new global world, across time and space. It takes courage to turn loose of command-and-control and allow people to organize themselves into communities that address issues and to build knowledge on their own. It takes both courage and imagination to allow and participate in Open Space meetings and use the results for the advantage of the organization. It takes patience to be able to help people with the culture change necessary for them to function in new ways. Old dogs (and most of us who reach a point in an organization where we can begin to implement this sort of change are getting to be fairly old dogs) really can learn new tricks—and then discover the satisfaction of teaching them to others.

If you are prepared to radically redefine the time equation of work with all its consequences, both profitable and unsettling, then online community building is a great tool to unleash the power of the organization. It will help you speed up your ability to innovate around the needs of the customer. It will help you come up with new products faster and get them introduced faster. It will help you solve problems faster with your customers and it will help you get closer to the instant solution that your customers desire. It will also help you reorganize your company around the flow of knowledge rather than geography.

Recognize that when you turn that switch on for Open Space meetings across time and space, you are starting a revolution in your business. You cannot avoid it. Enjoy the ride! If you keep looking for the opportunities that present themselves and have the courage to go where they take you, they can take you and your customers into expanded relationships capable of attaining new heights of profit and return on investment.

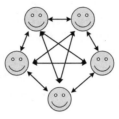

CHAPTER 13

Create Virtual Teams

The computer will smash the organizational pyramid. We created the hierarchical, pyramidal managerial system because we needed it to keep track of people and things people did; with the computer to keep track, we can restructure our institutions horizontally.

—John Naisbitt, *Megatrends*

Spontaneous communities that form around the needs of the organization are fine for dealing with occasional or unusual problems or opportunities that arise. But for definite assignments with a beginning and an end or for work on an assignment with a global customer group, you need teams. And when those assignments involve individuals scattered across the world, you need virtual teams.

For the techniques of forming virtual teams discussed in this chapter, I have drawn upon material learned through association with Applied Knowledge Group, Inc. of Reston, Virginia. For more information, you can reach that organization directly through www.akgroup.com or at 2100 Reston Parkway, Suite 400, Reston VA 20191.

Virtual teams resemble online communities in many ways, but with some key differences. Communities are typically formed by those who select themselves to be involved, whereas teams are usually formed by management to accomplish a specific task. Also, communities tend to be transient, defining themselves and dissolving as their members' interests change. Teams, by contrast, can last as long as you desire. When they are formed around a project—and projects always need to be completed in the shortest possible time—you want intense, effective action by the teams. That makes it necessary to pick the team members carefully, to help them develop simple protocols for interacting with each other, and to make sure they have the skills to be effective knowledge workers.

When you form teams around long-term needs of the organization, say, to work with a global customer, then you begin to redefine your operations at a very basic level. Unlike short-term teams, long-term teams radically alter an organization's internal relationships. Their members are more or less permanently assigned to the team activity and their commitment to it is total or nearly so. That changes their reporting patterns, pulling the organization into new forms that can pose problems because they challenge the legal structures the company has adopted to fit into the requirements of the countries where it has established itself. We will need new forms that are protected and legitimized by transnational institutions so that employees can be employed and have their rights protected on a global basis rather than on a national basis. We are already seeing the beginnings of this fundamental change today.

Perhaps after a decade or two of constant use, the culture of online community work will become pervasive. At that point, it may be possible to address all or nearly all of a company's specific goals and targets as organically and naturally as Buckman associates now respond to a sales rep's sudden need for knowledge to meet a customer request. For the present, however, if something is in the company plans, it needs a selected and well-primed team to deal with it.

What Is a Team?

A *team* in this context is a group of people mutually accountable for creating a product, delivering a service, or carrying out a mission. A *virtual team* is made up of geographically, functionally, or organizationally dispersed people who rely almost completely on technology as their primary means to communicate, coordinate, and collaborate with each other. The importance of virtual teams is growing as organizations recognize how many of their key processes are functioning across time and space. Through such teams, an organization can redefine itself horizontally to function on a global basis, but it requires a substantial adaptation of the concept of span of control to do so.

When teams are virtual, it changes the dynamics of how team members learn to work with each other, to build trust, to manage expectations, and to deliver on commitments. Even small distances can make a huge difference. For example, in 1977, MIT professor Thomas Allen calculated that people are not likely to collaborate very often if they are more than 50 feet apart. The greater the physical separation among team members, the more important it is to reinforce purpose (shared vision) as the ongoing reason for continuing conversation, cooperation, and knowledge sharing. You have to have a clear purpose for what you are about if you wish to maintain the dialogue and knowledge sharing necessary to have a functioning team at a distance. This is just the beginning of what it takes to become a successful virtual team.

Some of the techniques that you can use to move to greater spans of control across time and space were described by Frank Ostroff and Douglas Smith in their article, "The Horizontal Organization" (1992). A horizontal organization is defined by business processes and work flows directed to the needs of an ultimate user: customer, supplier, or distributor. It's made up of teams, and team performance is the most important thing for managers to track and support. Not every operation lends itself to horizontal organization, but the form should always be considered when the ultimate user is clearly identifiable. The authors recommend the following:

► Organize around a process, not around a task. Identify the main four or five core processes in your business. Organize to perform everything that's necessary, in sequence, to satisfy the ultimate user, the customer. Best performance is achieved by teams working together, passing the baton, to gain the desired measure of customer satisfaction.

► Flatten the hierarchy by combining related tasks. Emphasize flow and try to reduce to a bare minimum the number of activities that divide the core process.

► Assign ownership of processes and process performance to a team. The team (not exceeding 15 to 20 people) manages, directs, and supervises up to thousands of people involved in the delivery of the product or service.

► Align performance and evaluation to the satisfaction of the ultimate user. There can be a big difference between performance that looks superior because it meets internal standards and performance that looks superior to the customer.

► Make sure that teams have the ability, responsibility, and authority to make decisions. Avoid separation of decision making from implementation. Provide the team with access to any company information and databases its members deem necessary to achieve best performance.

► Concentrate on team building: multitask, multicompetence, cross-training, use of complementary skills. Training, education, and updating must become a continuous process, an integral part of any job.

► Maximize contact with the outside world. Engage customers, suppliers, and members of the public affected by your operations by asking for advice, suggestions, and criticism. Team members should engage in continuous, meaningful dialogue with end users.

► Reward team performance, not individual performance. Superior team performance depends on individual team members' ability to work together toward one main goal: satisfying the needs of the end user.

To operate horizontally means operating virtually—a company that wishes to be a viable player today has no other option.

Collaboration Challenges

This shift to the virtual organization is driven first and foremost by the natural dispersion of your workforce. If you are scattered in more than 80 countries—as we are at Buckman Labs—it is easy to see the value delivered by being able to function virtually. It allows you bring people together to meet the needs of the organization and take advantage of opportunities as they present themselves without worrying about logistics.

It's essential to assemble talent wherever it exists in the world. When you rely on a physical network of face-to-face departments and teams, you will often find that the distribution of skills and the distribution of need for those skills just don't match up. Intellectual muscle has to be brought to bear on the needs of the organization wherever they come up. A physical organization has to move people around to do this or to find and hire new resources on the spot when the need arises. A virtual organization has a huge advantage here, because it can simply open the channels to allow people to apply their skills from wherever they are to wherever they are needed.

The complexity of modern work often outstrips the talents, expertise, and experience of any one functional or technical group. If the talent is anywhere in the organization, then functioning virtually is a viable way to go forward. To use the intellectual capital of the organization effectively and fully, it's essential to think in terms of hybrid teams that reach across the organization to meet the demands of the day. These hybrid teams may contain members of more than one discipline or operating company.

Meanwhile, global customers are increasingly demanding global solutions. What they want is the best global response to their needs—executed effectively and in a coordinated fashion at the local level wherever they and the supplier interact. Consistency of response on a global basis supports your customers in the global directions of their organizations. To keep up with the customers, your people need the capacity to determine the best global solution and then either implement it or customize it as required to get the intended effect at each location.

The speed at which you can innovate as an organization will

determine your competitive position over time. Shrinking product development life cycles are putting enormous pressure on all industries to be first to market. This need for speed is forcing organizations to reconsider how they allocate talent and move know-how more flexibly around the organization.

Virtual teams can use technology to speed up the process of understanding the "who, what, where, why, and when" of a situation, so they are well equipped to coordinate activities and respond rapidly to issues as they arise across time and space. Groupware will provide the means for innovation, but it does not provide the motivation or the method to collaborate. Innovation in virtual teams requires that team members have a good working knowledge of the collaborative tools and the facilitation skills to generate and refine ideas that will work. The skills involved in a knowledge work have to be developed just like any other skill set.

Real-time meetings, essential as they often are, don't get much actual work done. All organizations are discovering the importance of being able to move forward between real-time meetings, whether they're face-to-face or virtual. This need for continuous progress is increasingly driving organizations to reexamine their work practices and the methods by which they coordinate and collaborate. Much of the demand for collaborative workspace is being fueled by the need of groups to create a shared view of work in which they can operate without being limited by time zones or geographic proximity to their colleagues.

Virtual teams generally need to be built on the fly, as needed and where needed. It's an increasingly unaffordable luxury to build such teams in the standard way of having the members meet face to face initially. The time required to take all the members out of service long enough to get together and learn one another's strengths and capacities will cost too much—over and above the sheer cost of travel, which is climbing faster than the rate of inflation. So virtual teams need to establish themselves virtually.

Teamwork at a Distance

In reengineering, one questions traditional assumptions and procedures, and then starts over. But this requires breaking down fiefdoms—in marketing, engineering, manufacturing, finance, for instance—and redeploying workers in inter-disciplinary teams.

—"The Technology Payoff" (*Business Week*, June 14, 1993)

Most people and most companies have developed enough ingrained knowledge of teams and teamwork that you can put any moderately well-selected group into a room and outline the general problem with a reasonable expectation that the new team will grasp its purpose and get started on the task without much wasted motion. A virtual team takes more groundwork.

You need to make sure that everyone involved really does understand the purpose of the effort and the basic assumptions on which the group will be operating, because much of the work will be done in isolation and people won't necessarily notice if someone goes off on a tangent. You also have to be extra careful that the people drawn into the team have the skills to work in a virtual environment as well as the specific skill sets that make them desirable choices for the team—or develop those skills very rapidly as the team's work begins—and then you have to encourage them to develop a shared sense of the team as an entity with a life of its own. In many situations, the team will contain a subgroup of people who share a physical location and can work with each other face to face as well as scattered individuals who rarely or never set eyes on any of their fellow team members. That situation poses special problems for the organization; it may be essential because of the distribution of individuals with the required skills, but it's bound to make it harder for the team to gel as a unit.

Charters

To bring everyone onto the same page—literally—it is best to begin by taking the time to develop a charter for the team. That is, the team leader or project leader responsible for translating business goals and strategy into specific plans, performance objectives, deliverables, and schedules should work with the team to develop a written statement of what the team is to accomplish. Once accepted by both management and members of the team, the resulting charter will help keep everyone on track throughout the effort.

A charter defines the deliverables expected from each team member and clarifies how each can contribute to the success of the team, allowing the team to prioritize its work and focus on the elements required for success. This allows the members of the virtual team to operate independently, without continually having to ask someone for decisions about what they choose to do. And besides spelling out what the team members need to get done, the charter helps them fend off the continuous stream of extraneous to-do items they're likely to receive from business associates and others concerned about the outcome of the team's work.

A charter takes individual assumptions about goals, deliverables, and roles and merges them into a clear reference point for everyone on the team or counting on its output. And the development process itself is important—it's the activity of hammering out an agreement that produces a shared understanding strong enough to guide the far-flung members of a virtual team. A charter imposed from outside will get lip service, but the hours or days saved by providing a set of answers up front will almost certainly be lost many times over as people act on their diverging views of what it really means.

Skills

The charter develops shared assumptions about what the team is to do, what takes priority, and what each person is responsible for contributing to the end product. Writing it also begins the process of welding the group into a genuine virtual team. As the members develop the charter, they will begin to demonstrate that they have the skills to work well together—and to discover the areas that need improvement. There are bound to be some such areas.

You would think that if a group of people all agree on where they are going and you've tied them together with technology and provided them with a collaborative platform, they could proceed smoothly. Unfortunately, the probability of success is still very low if they simply assume that they can get on with the job at that point. The team has to work out how it will align its assets for effective action and it has to make sure everyone involved has or develops the skills necessary to be effective team members across time and space. The technology that permits online interaction is more than a set of tools; it's an opportunity to realign work practices so as to streamline the whole process and redefine the time equation of work.

These are the skills essential for online collaboration:

- ▶ Revealing and resolving conflicting assumptions.
- ▶ Stating performance expectations among team members as well as between the team and its leadership in terms that generate support rather than resistance.
- ▶ Differentiating between what fits within the charter and what does not.
- ▶ Identifying the knowledge needs of the team and figuring out how to gain access to knowledge the team doesn't currently possess.
- ▶ Recognizing the political issues that need to be resolved within the team and between the team and its potential supporters and detractors.
- ▶ Determining the relationships the team needs for success, both among members and with outside groups and individuals.
- ▶ Selecting and communicating the kinds of information to pass back and forth to maintain effective working relationships and keep everyone up to date but not overwhelmed in trivia.

Group Identity

Another challenge that has to be met while aligning purpose is to build a sense of shared identity among team members who are dispersed in different parts of the organization. Whether the members are dispersed organizationally or geographically or some combination of the two, the basic question is "Who is 'us'?"

Teams come in different sizes, shapes, and configurations that affect how they communicate and collaborate. By understanding how the team is put together, the members can deal with many of the issues most likely to occur. When you're setting up a virtual team, you need to consider all the elements that will affect how everyone on the team can be an effective member.

Management must set the stage for effective team activities and give everyone on the team the time and priority allocations needed to achieve the objectives of the team. The surest way to doom a team to failure is for management to say that the members of the team will have the time and authority to do what is necessary for success and then create conditions that make that impossible.

Depending on the complexity of the team assignment, management may commit only a small percentage of a given member's time to the team—or it may make the team an individual's sole assignment. The smaller that percentage is, the smaller it had better need to be; no one can work effectively when two authorities are demanding the same patch of time. Likewise, management may set up a team to report to someone either higher or lower in the organization than the level where most of its members normally work; that can make a big difference to the reaction of the members' managers to the activities of the team. If team members and/or their managers perceive the team as less important (by virtue of having a less influential reporting relationship) than its members' "regular" jobs, the team can't afford to make any substantial demands on their time and attention. It's essential to deal with all these protocol issues if team activities are to be successful.

If several team members work in the same place, it can be even more complex than with a fully virtual team to make sure that all the members see the group in the same terms. The people who can work face to face have to take care that the information needs, technical challenges, and concerns of dispersed team members are met. You have to make sure that everybody has an equal opportunity— and technical ability—to contribute. Conversely, those team members who are dispersed have to make sure that their questions get answered in terms that meet their requirements; if someone suffers in silence, the rest of the group can be forgiven for assuming their suffering teammate is happy with the current state of affairs. Team members need to establish their identity. Working together, both types of team members—geographically close and dispersed—benefit from explicit discussions about the assumptions they are operating under. It is crucial for them to take the time to negotiate "rules of the road" for their collaborative relationship.

The Special Problems of Part-Virtual Teams

One way to think about the two types of members in a part-virtual team is to give the groups names that in a general way describe what they are like. I like to call the team segment that shares a physical location a *planet*, as its members will tend to operate in a similar fashion. The dispersed members I think of as *moons*, because they tend to revolve around the planet politically and functionally.

Planets. The following lists some statements that describe conditions and attitudes frequently held by people in the planet contingent. Which sound familiar to you?

- ► What's good for the majority is good for the minority.
- ► We only need to tell moons what they need to do their immediate jobs.
- ► Moons have the same priorities we do.
- ► Of course moons welcome the opportunity to travel!
- ► When in doubt, get on the phone.
- ► Face-to-face meetings are really the best way to get anything accomplished.
- ► Surely we can come up with a policy that will address any important contingencies that might arise.
- ► We don't really need a shared calendar—we'll just task the moons as necessary.
- ► Life must be a lot easier for moons; they're working at a distance from all the day-to-day pressures around here.

Moons. And here are statements that describe conditions and attitudes frequently held by people working as isolated moons. Which sound familiar to you?

- ► Anytime there is a meeting, I'm the one who has to do the traveling.
- ► People on the planet never bother to clue me in on key conversations among themselves.
- ► People on the planet assume that I have no responsibilities other than to respond to them. The deadlines they give me are totally unrealistic.
- ► People on the planet—and the team leader—feel free to

dump tasks on me without checking my calendar or current responsibilities. My boss just gave me another assignment. Who do I satisfy first?

▶ No one bothers to fill me in on the gossip—the context and background of what's happening. I get only the formal communications and none of the informal information that would help me to make sense of it.

▶ I always have to schedule conference calls at the convenience of the larger group.

▶ It's hard to develop a sense of identity and community with other moons when you don't really know who they are.

▶ I may have an equally valid or better way to get something done, but the majority always seems to rule.

▶ I never know what is going on with other members' calendars or how what I am doing will affect them.

▶ No one stops to ask if I would prefer to collaborate asynchronously rather than synchronously.

Generally speaking, people who are part of a planet group prefer synchronous communication, while those who are dispersed as moons prefer to communicate asynchronously. This simple difference can have a big impact on whether someone can participate effectively or not. If you are dealing with a global dispersion, then insistence on communicating synchronously can break a team.

The Astronomy of Teams. Regardless of what a team is designed to do, its configuration will affect its internal interaction patterns and the issues that its members will face. By paying attention to the way their team is configured, people can anticipate many of the common problems and plan how they will work together more effectively. Taking the astronomical analogy a bit further, it's possible to identify several types of configuration, each posing other challenges that need consideration. Table 13.1 suggests some of the differences characteristic of different types of partially dispersed teams.

Turning a Group into a Team

A team needs a settled purpose, but that's not enough. Besides knowing their collective task, all the people on the team need to

Type	Configuration/Description	Special Challenges
Mars	A large group of co-located people with a few dispersed teammates in distant locations. Like a planet surrounded by a few lesser moons, this configuration tends to distort all interactions in favor of the largest group.	Teams in a Mars configuration need to ask themselves, "What do we expect all members to know and what have we done to make sure that they know it?" Unless specific steps are taken to include the dispersed elements of the team (the moons) in regular interactions, to give everyone equal access to information, and to solicit and widely share team input, dispersed members are apt to feel marginalized and out of the loop.
Binary Star	Two large co-located groups, roughly the same size. The dynamics between two dispersed groups of equal size are apt to involve heavy competition simply because of the easy division between "us" and "them."	Whatever the merits of any given dispute, "they" will become a convenient scapegoat for everything that is not clear, not working, or perceived as a waste of time. Binary star teams are apt to unduly restrict access to information by members of the other star and to evolve separate and distinct cultures based on geographic location.
Saturn	A large group of co-located people with several dispersed teammates in distant locations. In this configuration the satellites may equal or outnumber the members of the co-located group.	The satellites are apt to be considerably impatient with the co-located people when the "planet" wants to default to face-to-face meetings. For the satellites, even online synchronous meetings are inconvenient when compared with communicating and collaborating asynchronously. As in any federation, all members will pay closer attention when the views of all prevail in determining procedure and norms of behavior and the development of governing decisions.

Table 13.1. Types of teams described as heavenly bodies (continued on next page)

Type	Configuration/Description	Special Challenges
Galaxy	Teammates dispersed geographically across time zones and other organizational structures.	This configuration will stretch a team to its capacity in terms of its ability to define unifying purpose, understand and play to one another's strengths, develop methods to organize and integrate work, and build consensus on collaborative work practices. The most common demand of this configuration is that people need a great deal of interaction to feel as if they are part of a group.

Source: Applied Knowledge Group, Inc., copyright 2003. Adapted with permission.

Table 13.1. Types of teams described as heavenly bodies (continued)

know their own personal roles and purposes. Whether or not they say so, every member arrives with questions like these: "Why am I here?" "Who are all these other people?" "What talents can we tap into?" "How do I know I can trust these folks?"

One of the most critical questions for the dispersed members of the team is "Why am I here?" For people to be effective team members, they need to know how they will fit into the overall context of what is the team is about. They need to know why their contributions matter and what they are expected to do in working with other members of the team.

You can often safely let such issues go without saying in face-to-face interactions, but you must spell things out for people on dispersed teams. It is very important to discuss these issues openly so that all members of the team know why they are there and how everyone else on the team fits in. As a recent participant in a virtual team launch commented, "You can make all the speeches you want about sharing information, leveraging knowledge, and tapping team talents, but when you get right down to it, why should I trust you?" If you want to be able to move fast, then you must pay attention to developing that trust. The team needs to develop answers to the following questions:

▶ What does each of us bring to the joint effort?

▶ What are the relationships we need to create and sustain in order to work together effectively?

▶ How will we create and keep a sense of community and connectedness while we are separated by time and space?

▶ How do we tap the talents in the team in the best possible way and know when to reach outside the team for additional talent as needed?

▶ Given the task that we have been assigned, how do we reconcile our work style preferences?

▶ What are our expectations about how we will work together and respond to each other?

▶ How does our individual ability to collaborate impact our ability to function together as a team?

▶ Where are the gaps in ability and how do we close them?

It All Comes Back to Trust

Building trust across time and space is a critical element in the functioning of virtual teams, and the level of trust is a good indicator of their ultimate success. The faith that any member of the team has in the goodwill, intentions, honesty, and reliability of his or her teammates will have a dramatic impact on how effective he or she is as a member of that team. If team members have never laid eyes on each other, talked face to face, or broken bread together, the group will be doubly challenged. The greater the differences among members of the team, the greater the challenge they will find it is to work together. Working for the same company is not the same as speaking the same language, having the same cultural background, being part of the same generation, carrying equal levels of responsibility, or sharing an organizational affiliation—and a virtual team is bound to have differences in some or all of these areas.

To cross these barriers and develop trust in one another, team members need to be assured of each other's legitimacy—they need to know that each member of the team really has the authority and the desire to make commitments and live up to them. They need a shared purpose. They need to know that they have the backing of the larger organization—that they won't be disowned when they come up with results. They also need an ongoing sense of achievement: as results begin to develop, all the team members need to know what has happened and what needs to happen next.

At Buckman Labs, we've found these four factors critical to building trust:

► Forming mental images of one another
► Agreeing on common goals
► Identifying shared values
► Negotiating basic protocols

Mental Images. When two people meet for the first time, each is curious about the other's name, appearance, history, purpose, and expectations. Until you know something about an associate, your communication is apt to be superficial; coordination is going to be difficult and collaboration impossible. A face-to-face introduction covers the basics very quickly; unless someone is deliberately concealing something, you pick up what their name is, what they look like, and at least a sense of where they come from, why they are there, and what they expect.

An online introduction, by contrast, is much shakier—people can say absolutely anything and, in some of the odder byways of the Internet, those you encounter will make false claims about their species, let alone such basics as age and sex. Part of that uncertainty carries over into the business environment, casting a shadow on long-distance relationships.

For a virtual team, the solution is to explicitly address identity issues up front and in writing when the team is formed. This includes formally introducing people to one another and explaining why each was chosen for the team. Everyone should then be invited to share enough of his or her background and personal information so that all members of the team can get a feel for who they are and what they have to offer. More information is better than less at this point.

One of the most useful things dispersed teams can do is to take digital photos of each team member and post them to a team map that shows geographic location (and time zone!), recaps their roles and responsibilities, and lists some of the things that each one does very, very well. You might even include whether the team member is a night person or a morning person—that is, the hours this person will be at peak performance and other team members might get the best interaction on something important to the team.

Common Goals. Most teams start out with one goal that rapidly metamorphoses into something else. Scope statements change, requirements evolve, management gets distracted, and original goals may be overtaken by events. A major element of faith in virtual teams is that the members are all pulling toward the same goal or vision, not just similar or parallel goals. Each individual member of the team wants to know that they all share an agreement on what the destination should be. A quick and powerful way to bring this issue to a head is to ask all team members to describe the team goal personally, in his or her own words, and then to compare versions. The idea is to build at least a 90% consensus on the goal and what it will require of the team both individually and collectively. Threaded discussions are a good way to help virtual teams arrive at this level of consensus.

Shared Values. The Code of Ethics will give virtual team members a sense of coming from the same place in terms of values. If your company has not developed a Code of Ethics that defines your shared values as we have at Buckman Labs, then you might consider this approach at a team level. As noted earlier, if you have a Code of Ethics that doesn't address the relevant points, take the time to develop a Statement of Values for Effective Communication across the team. Virtual team members don't need to be clones of one another, but it is helpful if they can agree on the practical implications of the following values and translate these values into day-to-day behaviors:

- ▶ Honor commitments.
- ▶ Share information promptly.
- ▶ Express support.
- ▶ Applaud contributions.
- ▶ Play to strengths.

It helps for the team to start a conversation with a message along the following lines:

What does "honoring commitments" really mean? How

would we know if someone fell short? How do we make commitments in the first place? What's the difference between "I'll try to get to it this week" and a commitment? How do we know as a team when we have a firm commitment?

The practical reason for discussing shared values is that values are the foundation for ground rules on how the team will interact and operate. After you have built several virtual teams and gone through this exercise each time, you will find that many of the core values that are articulated are the same from team to team. At this point, you should be able to establish some core values for teams that are organization-wide.

Basic Protocols. For team members to be able to trust one another, they have to be explicit about exactly what it is that they all expect from each other. This ranges from how often each member will check e-mail and the shared calendar to how consistently they follow agreed-on naming conventions and procedures for version control and reporting. Generally speaking, the simpler you can keep your systems and approaches, the easier it is to get up to speed quickly.

Pay attention to these questions and see how you might simplify your systems for collaboration. What information are team members expected to routinely share with each other? What sorts of protocols will govern how they interact in teleconferences, e-mail, instant messaging, threaded discussions, shared folders, and online workspaces? How quickly can they expect others to get back to them with answers to questions?

All these expectations represent legitimate questions based on assumptions about how people will work together. Unless these assumptions are spelled out and negotiated, virtual team members may disappoint one another as often as they succeed in working together smoothly. Minimal rules of the road for virtual teams should address the following points:

▶ What information is to be shared by the team and how are we going to do it?
▶ What does it mean to participate in this team on a day-to-day basis?

► How will the team manage its workflow?

► How much time has each individual member—and each member's boss—allotted for team participation? (Those who accept the responsibility of team membership must make sure they have time allocated to team activity.)

► What naming conventions should we should use as a team so that we can organize and find the material we share with each other?

► What notification procedures should we use so that we all stay on the same page with current information?

► What are the acceptable ways for us to resolve conflict or disagreement and what are the unacceptable ways?

Work Practices

It would be great if people could intuitively grasp how to use new technology in the best, most productive way. But most people master only the program features they use on a day-to-day basis. Most of the technology available today is far more complicated than the average user will take advantage of. The rule of thumb most people follow is "If I need to do something I haven't done before, I'll learn the feature at that time."

And there's the rub. People adopt technology when they positively, absolutely must use it on a daily basis to get their work done. Simple conservation of energy makes everyone a great practitioner of just-in-time learning. When there's no need to change— or when too much is changing at once—then they revert to old ways of working. It's more comfortable that way.

Unfortunately, the basic collaborative skills involved in working smoothly with other humans are not skills that come naturally and, by and large, they're not taught in schools. Working face to face, it's generally possible to muddle through without them and almost always without using the technological tools that allow them to be exercised at a distance. As a result, people come to online collaboration with good intentions, but they're using technology they understand only partially.

So, they tend to revert to older, even if less efficient means to do the work. Online conferences with application sharing give way to overnight FedEx envelopes and long, ear-tiring conference calls. When people get frustrated with each other, technology is usually the first thing they jettison. This tendency is exacerbated by the fact that the technological solutions offer varying levels of support for what virtual teams are trying to do, and the team may be trying to use a system that doesn't actually work for its immediate purpose.

Here are some of the options for helping bring people and technology together.

Wave One solutions (e-mail systems, list servers, and multiparty phone conferences) are designed to meet different needs. E-mail works well for one-to-one communications, but can overload people's in-boxes when applied to many-to-many interactions. List servers work well for one-to-many broadcasts, but do not support in-depth discussions whose goal is to arrive at a decision and to take action. Multiparty conference calls can certainly reinforce a sense of community, but they are unsatisfactory when used to brainstorm, develop consensus, and work through the pros and cons of specific options. While each is individually useful, none of the Wave One solutions provide what is needed by teams with complex and evolving tasks.

Wave Two solutions (threaded discussions, synchronous online conferencing, and interactive presentation tools such as whiteboards) contribute to more effective communication and coordination, but they do not provide for a collaborative workspace that would support a team throughout a project. Threaded discussions enable dispersed team members to see what the others have to say about a subject across time and space. But it can be awkward to preserve and store this information for effective use at a later time. Again, none of these solutions provide a functioning virtual equivalent of a physical workspace.

Wave Three solutions (applications such as Documentum eRoom, IBM's QuickPlace, or Microsoft's SharePoint Team Services) have focused on the need for collaborative workspaces. Yet these technologies are inadequate in themselves. It's in the team members' discussions of and agreements about how they are going to work together via technology that the challenges of virtual collaboration can be addressed. Paradoxically, these "soft skills" of collaboration are the hardest part of learning to work virtually.

When people work across time and space, the fact that they are doing so through technology changes the dynamics of their working relationships. Team members who work side by side share a common physical experience of work. Dispersed teams need to consciously recreate that "common ground" in virtual rather than physical workspace. Co-located teams assume that if you are there at work that day, you know what's going on. Dispersed teams need to consciously ask and answer these questions:

▶ Who knows what?
▶ Who's doing what?
▶ Who's in motion?
▶ What's on the horizon?

Working together via technology forces team members to become more conscious about teamwork and what it means on a day-to-day basis. Technology is not intuitive. The members and the whole team will all function better when all parties understand how a particular feature is going to help them do what they need to do better, faster, and cheaper.

Where Do You Stand?

Think about your organization's structure. How are you going to move toward a more horizontal organization? Do you feel that this would be useful in your company? What problems do you see in doing this?

Think about teamwork. What are the key issues in your company that you would want to form teams around? What resources are best brought together that might not be co-located? What are your costs (opportunity and travel) to bring people together for a face-to-face meeting? Are your systems aligned to support collaboration? Are you process-oriented or are you task-oriented? Can you get comfortable with a team's taking responsibility and having authority for key decisions on an important issue in your company? What are the issues that your organization will have to face to be able to function across time and space using teams?

Building Virtual Teams—Virtually!

The quickest way to double your money is to fold it over and put it back in your pocket.

—Will Rogers

You will need to address the issue of virtual teamwork if you want to radically redefine the time equation of work in your organization. This can be an intimidating concept, but it is the only way to move forward individually and as an organization in this fast-changing world. Turning away from it, on the grounds that it involves more change than you want to deal with in your company, is tantamount to using Will Rogers as your financial advisor—which will do nothing for your power in the marketplace.

It will make the process easier if you bear in mind that simply connecting people with technology doesn't guarantee that they automatically know how to communicate, coordinate, or collaborate to get the job done. Growing agile virtual teams and solid, long-lasting online communities takes not only technical know-how but also the ability to build strong working relationships at a distance and to negotiate explicit protocols and practices needed to work together successfully.

Teams and communities must be able to align around purpose, people, practices, and the technical platform chosen. They need skills not only in managing information but in managing relationships and managing their tools. The goal is to be able to build virtual teams virtually. But to do that, everyone needs to learn some skills as individuals. As these skills are acquired, the potential increases for moving much faster on a global field to meet any

---

Exhibit 13.1. Virtual Team Recap

Purpose

▶ What are we trying to achieve?

▶ What is the task's relationship to the bigger picture?

▶ What priorities will determine whether we succeed?

- ▶ What are our boundaries?
- ▶ Why will it make a difference?
- ▶ Why is it critical that we share knowledge?
- ▶ Why must we develop collaborative skills?

People
- ▶ What talent, expertise, and knowledge do we need?
- ▶ What kinds of working relationships are critical?
- ▶ What is in this for me?
- ▶ Why do we need each other?
- ▶ Why is trust important?
- ▶ Why do we need input from outside people?
- ▶ How will we negotiate expectations?
- ▶ How will we establish mutual accountability for success?
- ▶ How will we play to each other's strengths?

Protocols and Practices
- ▶ What practices will streamline our communications?
- ▶ What protocols will keep our workspace workable?
- ▶ What will link core and dispersed team members?
- ▶ Why are protocols important for good interaction?
- ▶ Why does workspace discipline matter?
- ▶ Why do we need a cybrarian?
- ▶ Why will protocols help us make best use of time?
- ▶ How will we communicate, coordinate, and collaborate to get the job done?
- ▶ How will we capture lessons learned?
- ▶ How will we avoid info glut?
- ▶ How will we stay on track and avoid distractions?
- ▶ How will we inform others of our purpose?
- ▶ How will we deal with the impact of working via technology?

Platform
- ▶ What tools are available?
- ▶ What do we need to accomplish using these tools?
- ▶ What requires real-time exchanges? When will asynchronous exchanges serve as well or better?

> ▶ Why do we need to adapt tools for both project management and knowledge sharing?
> ▶ Why do version control, naming conventions, and access rules matter?
> ▶ How will we pick the right tool for the task?
> ▶ How will we decide who to include or exclude?
> ▶ How do we avoid reinventing the wheel?

need of the organization at any time. Exhibit 13.1 summarizes the key questions to apply to the problems of building virtual teams.

Although the skills I've described here are essential to building the level of expertise needed for a knowledge-driven organization, I can assure you that they are not show stoppers. This is not rocket science. It is learning how to function in a new world that is not face to face. In many cases, today's children have already learned how to do this. It is now time for their elders to catch up with them. The objective is to build virtual teams virtually, because it is much cheaper and much faster to move ideas and knowledge around than it is to move people. This is how you can redefine the time equation of work.

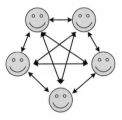

CHAPTER 14

New Products and Services Based on Knowledge

Life consists not in holding good cards but in playing those
we do hold well.

—Josh Billings

Thus far I've been singing the praises of knowledge sharing
and talking about it as essential to success and even survival in a fast-moving marketplace, but the details have
almost all been about the effort involved in setting it up and the
amount of cultural change and other forms of disruption it may
involve. Is it really worth the effort? It is indeed. Here's a true story
of what it meant for Buckman Labs.

Redefining the Value Equation

Don't be afraid to take a big step if one is indicated. You
can't cross a chasm in two small jumps.

—David Lloyd George

Once upon a time—from its founding to the mid-1940s—Buckman
Labs was a product-driven organization. We created chemical

compounds for the control of microorganisms, corrosion, and scale in industrial processes, designing them to be the best of their kind and selling them wherever they had a use. One of our principal customer groups was the paper industry, where we were known as the "bug men" because we supplied specialty chemicals used for slime control on the wet end of a paper machine.

We weren't exactly a one-trick pony, because we were well known for a variety of products, but we did not begin to supply all the chemicals and additives used on a paper machine. Of course, no one else did either, at that point. A typical mill had 30 to 50 suppliers whose products were used on the wet end of a paper machine, and we were satisfied with our place in the pack.

The value equation for Buckman Labs was More = Better. Our sales force kept up a drive for volume based on the products the customers used. The more drums of chemicals we sold to our customers, the more money we made.

But then the crisis hit. Increasingly, our customers began moving toward fewer suppliers on the machine, in an effort to cut costs by reducing the work required to maintain their stocks of chemicals and by arranging for volume discounts. They called it moving toward a "sole supplier" relationship. They would give all their business to the one or two or three suppliers that looked likeliest to do the best job of providing them with the required products and services and provide the most substantial reductions in cost to the mill.

Buckman Labs was at an immediate disadvantage in this environment. Although we supplied some critical chemicals, we did not control enough of the total value purchased by the mills to be a significant player. We had to team up with other companies just to stay in the game. This consolidation of suppliers occurred over several years; we ended up with a high percentage of our sales coming from "purchase for resale" products—things we had to buy so we could offer a broad enough product line to survive on this new playing field.

Costly and awkward as this arrangement was, it did give us an opportunity to become familiar with a broad range of chemicals and additives for our customers. We added to our knowledge base both as individuals and as an organization. As we learned how to use these new products, we began to look at how we could make them ourselves and improve our profit margins. Our increasing familiarity with the new product lines allowed us to come up with more effective and efficient ways to apply them. This ultimately led us to come up with products and results that were better than the industry standards. We leveraged our evolving global awareness of products that were common in one part of the world but unknown in another, and we also leveraged our global base of manufacturing know-how. The movement to a global knowledge-sharing system was starting to pay dividends by turning a crisis into an opportunity to move in new directions from a product perspective.

This evolutionary process transformed us into a significant supplier to the paper industry and set the stage for the next development there. Increasingly, over the 1980s and 1990s, our customers moved from two or three suppliers per mill to a sole supplier in a mill, and then began looking for a sole supplier that could serve several mills. They also began demanding consignment inventory at each mill—we had to keep supplies on site that our customers didn't pay for until they used them. So, while we had more business at any given mill, the cost of doing business there was going up at the same time. At each iteration of the process, the customers wanted more and more for less and less on a per-unit basis—but the overall value of customer relationships grew to staggering heights. We kept putting more and more eggs into each basket, and the potential risks of losing a customer kept going up at the same time.

It was at that point that we began to think in terms of partnering with customers in their business and helping pursue their goals. We would take over the chemical additive side of an operation and perform that function for the customer—for a fee based on the production of the mill or on some other overall basis, not the number of drums of chemicals shipped to the mill. Although there is a persuasive correlation between the chemical needs of the mill and the production rate, this pricing system caused a significant shift in the value equation. Instead of making more money by shipping more chemical to the mill and convincing the owner of the value delivered by each product, we now had to deliver a result for a fee. The customers did not care what chemicals we used or how much we used. All they were interested in was a result that allowed them to produce paper at a given cost for this activity.

For Buckman Labs to make more profit in this value equation, we had to become more knowledgeable in the application of the chemicals so that we would use them more effectively. The value equation had been turned upside down: suddenly, Better = Less. The smaller the quantity and variety of chemicals we used in achieving the desired result, the better for us. Knowledge was more important to the result of the company than shipping more products.

This continual pressure to do more with less has taken our knowledge base in new directions as we have learned how to dance to the new tune. Now, we can think in terms of completely new value equations for the company as well as new products to make and use. If we can provide a complete chemical service to a mill for a fee, why can't we take this concept a little further?

We did. We now are working with customers where we have assumed responsibility for all the chemicals in their operation and taken over the equipping and staffing of their technical department for all the chemical and biological analysis that they require. This concept is now spreading across completely different customer groups with significantly different needs. We've moved on from the paper industry where the trend started and introduced it to our water treatment and leather production customers. What started out as a simple global knowledge-sharing exercise around the immediate needs of one set of customers has led us into a complete transformation of the value equation for both our customers and ourselves.

More New Products from the Knowledge-Sharing Process

You cannot solve the problem with the same kind of thinking that has created the problem.

—Albert Einstein

Chemical management isn't the only new knowledge product at Buckman Labs. We've come up with many others over the years. Some of them may seem obvious and some maybe not so obvious, and some of them may well be transferable into your business, whatever it may be. This is where you need to let your imagination roam into what is possible and have the courage to try many things to find out what will really take you in new directions. It's what the future of business is all about.

A transformation process like the one that took Buckman Labs into a new value equation is just one possibility. While you may well find something along those lines as the ultimate result of the effort, there's no need to focus on going for the big win all the time. Look for the small and moderate advances that will keep you in the game and make the journey worthwhile, helping you learn what is possible and what is not possible.

Here are some examples of knowledge products and other initiatives that emerged at Buckman Labs over the years—some new things we found to sell and some new ways of working that made us more valuable to our customers and thus made maintaining a relationship with us more attractive. This list is not complete; there are many more examples in our company. There are also doubtless many variations that could work in other industries but not for us. Just talk to others in your industry and Communities of Practice and keep your ears open for tidbits that spark new thoughts. As you review this list, let your imagination roam over what you might do with such an idea in your own company.

▶ **Best Practices Database.** At Buckman Labs, learning to create best practices on the fly instead of distilling them through endless hours of hard work let us respond to the multiple variations in the marketplace at a speed significantly faster than before. As you begin sharing knowledge across your organization, watch for similar opportunities. You will find it simple to identify and accumulate best practices worth saving for future reference.

▶ **Learning Modules.** The Buckman Labs Learning Center has begun developing learning modules as a byproduct of the creation of best practices. We've found that it shortens the cycle of learning dramatically for us, helping us become a genuine learning organization. If you pay attention to the best practices that emerge from your online discussions, you'll find they will lead you to the creation of modules of learning that will help you teach some new ability obtained or developed in place to your people elsewhere—and perhaps to people employed by your customers.

▶ **Lessons Learned.** Insight into how to share knowledge effectively within an organization is valuable information in its own right. Buckman Labs customers have accepted the knowledge we offer them on this topic, improving their operations while making them eager to develop deeper relationships with us. As you develop knowledge on how to leverage knowledge, share it with your good customers so that they can achieve the same advantages that you have, making them more prosperous and you more valuable to them.

▶ **Applications Database.** Buckman Labs took advantage of its global knowledge when it developed its technology management services, and still more when it began exporting them to customers outside the paper industry. As you begin to share knowledge around the needs of your customers, you will see similar patterns of needs surfacing from the threads of conversation. Use that knowledge to develop special programs for dealing with these needs in the future. Packaging this knowledge for immediate distribution to customers who have yet to implement the new technology is a good way to build credibility with those customers.

▶ **New Product Development Style.** By bringing R&D into the ongoing front-line discussions of customer needs, Buckman Labs has been able to anticipate what customers will want next and provide it as soon as the need is felt. It may take the researchers a while to get used to the idea, but having the R&D group monitor the threads and look for trends and opportunities is probably the fastest way to get feedback to the R&D group. You could assign someone else the task of accumulating needs for new products and sending them along to R&D, but we have found this process to be much slower.

▶ **Redefined Time Equations.** We have found at Buckman Labs that the sharing of knowledge around an issue or need or opportunity will trigger thoughts on ways to accomplish something better and faster than before—often not just a little better and faster, but a radical redefinition of the whole time equation of work. As you share knowledge more broadly and deeply in the organization, stay alert for these opportunities—they open up at unexpected moments and can provide you with some of your best possibilities for productivity improvements. Besides changing your own processes over time, these insights can often be exported to your customers. For example, we've taken the lessons learned in redefining the pedagogical approach of our Learning Center and used them to help build new approaches to learning at some of the "Paper Schools" at public universities across the country.

▶ **Corporate Repositioning.** It was knowledge sharing that inverted the value equation at Buckman Labs, so that we now often make more profit from a given customer by shipping less product than before—and have a happier customer into the bargain. Be alert to those transforming epiphanies that will come from time to time as you follow the needs of your customers to where they want to go. Try and learn what it will take to get in front of where they are going. Reposition your company so that you will be where your customers are going. If you can, get in front of the curve of change over time, so that you can project to your customers directions that they might want to consider going in the future. This will put you in the position of helping your customers determine their best future directions: in a direction that you are already familiar with.

▶ **New Organization Models.** Don't be afraid to look at completely new models for your organization or focus (for instance, moving from products to services). What are some of the needs your customers are talking about besides the ones that can be satisfied with a physical product? It was just such thinking that led Buckman Labs to form global teams to work with global customers so that we could provide global solutions in the meeting of their needs.

▶ **Speaking and Consulting.** At Buckman Labs, we found that our customers were interested in our insights into knowledge sharing and distributed learning across the organization—and happy to pay us to come and help them develop similar programs for themselves. Keep an eye on your operations for areas that you might be able to use as a basis for consulting with your current customers or even with others that don't have an immediate use for your traditional product or service.

All these new initiatives can be the result of sharing knowledge across time and space around the issues that customers raise. I am sure that you can think of many more that are particularly germane to your industry. Knowledge sharing involves much more than just solving the problem or seizing an opportunity that is in front of you at the moment. The challenge is to redefine the organization from a product-driven organization to a market-driven organization to a knowledge-driven organization.

Product-Driven to Market-Driven to Knowledge-Driven

As you travel along this continuum, making knowledge a bigger and bigger component of your product, you need to be continually alert to opportunities to redefine your relationship with your customers. For example, out of our experience in helping many customers make the move to Buckman products and services over the years, we have developed the Transition Workshop, a face-to-face session that runs for one to three days and provides a successful process for implementing our programs up front, making sure all parties know what everyone needs before we assume responsibility for the operation. The workshop has become the basis for defining our mutual relationship and the initial move toward helping the customer define where we should go in the future.

The opportunities that come out of a process like this can lead in unexpected directions. Do not be afraid to go where such opportunities take you. You may be pleasantly surprised.

As you watch for opportunities in the chaff of everyday activities, it helps to keep some simple questions in mind. Buckman Labs has been using a set of idea-stimulating one-word questions for this purpose for a very long time, producing results completely out of proportion to the tool's size and complexity. "Creativity for Our Customers" is our ongoing promise to ourselves and the world; this list is the foundation that allows us to put muscle behind it. (This checklist originated with Alex Osborn, who presented it in his book, *Applied Imagination*, in 1953.)

- ▶ Adapt?
- ▶ Combine?
- ▶ Magnify?
- ▶ Minify?
- ▶ Modify?
- ▶ Rearrange?
- ▶ Reverse?
- ▶ Substitute?

One or more of those questions will almost always open the way from problem to solution and from solution to opportunity.

Where Do You Stand?

> To know that we know what we know, and that we do not know what we do not know, that is true knowledge.
>
> —Confucius

Think about your products and services. What is it that your customers are willing to pay for today? What about tomorrow? Are you encountering pressure toward commoditization? What will that mean for your value equation?

Think about your customers. Who are they? What do they really want? What combination of capital assets and knowledge assets will allow you to develop and be dominant in some new core competency that has a higher added value for the customer? How would you change the value proposition for your customers? What investments in knowledge assets will allow you to move in this new direction? How should you define it for your customers?

Knowledge and Value

> It is not the same to talk of bulls as to be in the bullring.
>
> —Spanish proverb

The important point to take away from this chapter is that it never pays to limit your imagination on what might be possible. The speed at which you can shift your culture and become a fast-changing organization around the needs of your customers will have a big impact on how far you can go in this transformation process.

It is almost impossible to predict the path that you should take before it opens up for you. You have to get into the process and begin experiencing the problems that go along with the change that you are trying to achieve.

So develop a general idea of the direction that you want to go and begin moving. Do not wait until you have the perfect plan of action. You will never have the perfect plan of action. Start moving today. Try some things that you have been wondering about and keep moving forward toward your goals. Seize opportunities as they come along.

Step back from time to time and think about where you are going and how you redefine it to your advantage. Do not be afraid to redefine your goals as your learning increases. You will find that knowledge will ultimately be a major component of your new product offerings—or end up being the product itself.

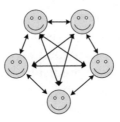

CHAPTER 15

Practical Education:
Let Your Associates Grow

Increasing the capability and capacity of our associates to deliver superior value to our customers, capture market wealth and customer share by delivering the right knowledge and learning to the right person at the right time in the right place.

—Mission of the Buckman Laboratories Learning Center

K nowledge sharing will only take you so far. It makes your organization more efficient and effective at deploying and applying what its people already know. But how does new knowledge get into your systems? As Peter Senge points out, lasting institutional learning develops in only three ways—research, practice, and capacity building. That is, some knowledge grows in your technical and research centers and in the course of work with your customers, but there's a whole world of knowledge being generated beyond your immediate view that you need to acquire and build into your operation.

Tapping into the external knowledge generated by universities, trade associations, and other research organizations—groups that are in the business of creating and capitalizing on knowledge—can make all the difference to an organization's ongoing strength. How can you incorporate these sources into your systems effectively?

Of course, you can hire some of their output. Everyone who joins an organization brings in a body of knowledge that then has a chance to enter into its knowledge-sharing channels. But that's not enough. If you rely on new hires for all your knowledge needs, you wind up undervaluing your existing associates and risk losing their vital insight into how your business and your customers work—all of which would be a welcome addition to your competitors' knowledge bases.

For individuals as well as organizations, knowledge either grows or becomes obsolete. If you want your organization to grow and flourish over time, then you have work on capacity building—that is, to set things up so your people keep growing, by giving them both informal and formal opportunities to learn new things. Senge defines capacity building as "the enhancement of people's capabilities and knowledge to achieve results in line with their deepest personal and professional aspirations," which may sound high-flown but is deadly practical in today's marketplace.

The desirability of learning at all levels has at least lip service almost everywhere today, but what people should be taught and how it should be taught are much more controversial topics. Arguments turn on whether it is better to work on remedial competencies or areas of strength and whether teaching should be face to face or at a distance. The right answers may vary depending on the circumstances and the purpose of the learning experience, but for business the key element to remember is that the goal is to protect and promote the competitive ability of the organization. You need to look toward the knowledge base of your organization five, 10, or 20 years down the road and do what you can to help it grow.

Competencies Versus Strengths

Sharing knowledge is not about giving people something, or getting something from them. That is only valid for information sharing. Sharing knowledge occurs when people are genuinely interested in helping one another develop new capacities for action; it is about creating learning processes.

—Peter Senge, "Sharing Knowledge"

The decision to work on competencies or strengths will have a major impact on an organization's success. Marcus Buckingham, global leader for the Gallup Organization's Strengths Management practice and author of Gallup's best-selling management books *First, Break All the Rules* and *Now, Discover Your Strengths*, argues that the critical question is "What is the best way to increase each employee's performance?" Is it better to use the approach of building up competencies? Or is it better to help individuals grow to be the best that they can be? It's useful to explore these two approaches and see why one is really preferable to the other.

Building Competencies

Competency building started out in the military as an effort to create the perfect officer. The idea was to rate individuals on what they could do, have them work on specific competencies that they lacked, and then rate them again the following year to see how they'd developed. Both the U.S. and the British military have long since abandoned this approach to leadership development; they found that no matter how they measured it, the results always showed that it simply did not produce better officers. Nonetheless, it has migrated into the business world, which continues to cling to it as a disciplined process to select, measure, evaluate, develop, and promote employees.

Competency-based performance management systems usually begin with an organized attempt to define the behavioral competencies expected of each key role. Then the human resource department designs an interviewing system to guide the hiring process toward potential employees likely to have the requisite competencies, and a performance rating system that scores current employees against the same list. They may use 360-degree feedback or assessment by the employee or the employee's manager or a combination of techniques, and they may have other performance metrics as well, but the net result is a performance rating for each employee coupled with a list of competencies regarded as missing or in need of development.

That list—labeled something like "Areas for Improvement"—forms the basis for an "Individual Development Plan" designed by the manager and the employee to outline steps toward personal development. The process is repeated the following year. An employee who can demonstrate improvement against the plan will get a higher performance rating than one who cannot and the performance ratings flow into the organization's "Succession Planning System" and thus help determine who is promotable and how high.

Human resource departments like this method a lot because it gives them a key role in business development. They assert that they can identify the people whose competencies will give the company a competitive advantage as they progress through the ranks. This sounds like a good idea and it's doubtless a great comfort both to HR personnel and to managers who would otherwise face some awkward decisions, but there isn't a scrap of evidence that competency-based performance management systems actually improve productivity, customer satisfaction, employee engagement, retention, safety records, or any other measure of real performance. Quite the reverse, in fact. They generate endless paperwork and wheel-spinning, and often lead people to attempt things they cannot do.

These are the assumptions that undergird all competency-based performance management systems:

- People who do well in a given role all use the same behaviors to succeed.
- Anyone can learn to use these successful behaviors.
- It is useful to try to learn all these behaviors, because building up areas of weakness is what leads to success.

Time and again, however, business researchers have found that all three assumptions of competency building are flawed in a fundamental way. For example, in *First, Break All the Rules,* Buckingham reports discovering that the best managers share none of these assumptions. Instead, they tend to hold by the exact opposite:

- **Many roads lead to success.** That is, people who do well in a role all get the same kind of results—but they do very different things in the process. Trying to get everyone to perfect the same set of competencies is as useless as trying to teach cats to fly; what's needed is to teach them to get where they need to go when they need to be there, using whatever style best fits their own strengths.

▶ **No one can learn everything, and some things are almost impossible for any adult to learn.** Some behaviors stem from natural talents or very early experience, which makes them difficult to acquire later in life and effectively impossible to impose from outside. Others can be developed in a fairly straightforward manner. Buckingham cites empathy, assertiveness, focus, and adaptability as examples of the former, and things like product features or self-awareness as examples of the latter. Competency-based systems conflate the two categories into broad topics such as "Handles Change" or "Inspirational Vision" and claim they can be mastered with training and practice, leading to hours of wasted effort.

▶ **Success comes from building on strength.** Fixing a weakness is damage control. It can help prevent failure, but it won't get anyone past average. Building on strength, on the other hand, allows people to figure out how to use what they do well to get the results required for success and make their areas of weakness irrelevant.

In my own experience at Buckman Labs, it's the second set of assumptions that win, every time. Damage control is inherently limited and limiting. To help all your people to be the best they can be—to find their own paths to success and learn the skills that will allow them to use their own natural talents to best advantage—you need to focus on building their strengths.

Building Strengths

Buckingham recommends turning the competency-based approach on its head. To increase each person's total performance, the following measures are what work:

▶ For each role, identify outcomes rather than competencies.
▶ Select people for a role based on their natural talents, choosing individuals who have similar talent sets to those already successful in the role in question.

▶ Measure each person on the outcomes required for the role.

▶ Seek to identify each person's areas of talent and relative weakness.

▶ Encourage each person to strengthen talents with skills and knowledge, then find ways to manage around areas of weakness.

▶ Reserve the label "Areas for Improvement" for strengths that can be developed; it's wasted on weaknesses.

▶ Rate each person from year to year on improvement in outcomes—that's the performance you want and need, so that's what you should track.

The goal of building on strength is to capitalize on the unique talents and abilities of everyone in the organization. And people are all unique. Everyone brings an individual mix of talents to the job, along with an individual style of thought and way relating to others. These differences represent resources that can and should be conserved and developed for the benefit of both the organization and the people in it. At Buckman Labs we recognize the importance of individual differences with three provisions in our Code of Ethics:

▶ That the company is made up of individuals, each of whom has different capabilities and potentials—all of which are necessary to the success of the company.

▶ That we acknowledge that individuality by treating each other with dignity and respect—striving to maintain continuous and positive communications among all of us.

▶ That we will recognize and reward the contributions and accomplishments of each individual.

In line with these provisions, we've chosen strengths over competencies across the board. We believe that it is essential to help all our associates identify what they are good at and then focus on turning their talents into real strengths.

Locus of Learning

Building strengths is a continuous process—a matter of true lifelong learning. But lifelong learning can't be a matter of lifelong class attendance; after all, the perpetual student never gets around to doing a job. It's essential to set things up so people can learn where they are rather than forever having to attend a class somewhere.

The traditional pedagogical approach, where students sit in groups at the foot of the master, will not achieve this goal. Face-to-face education has many strengths and its many devotees still assert that it has no equal for effectiveness and general rightness. Nonetheless, it won't move a business forward. When there's an ongoing job to get done, you have to look at a different pedagogical model. *Rather than sending students to a classroom, you need to deliver the classroom to each student—at any time desired and anywhere in the world.* The same technology that permits knowledge sharing within an organization also allows it to make education leap across time and space.

This approach is beginning to take hold even in the formal education establishment, where both traditional universities and new for-profit learning companies offer "distance education." Distance education can take many forms. Students receive coursework sent out on paper, via television, or as multimedia deliveries over a computer system; they interact with the instructors and often with each other both asynchronously and in real time, depending on the needs of the course. For an organization interested in improving learning opportunities for its people, distance education is ideal.

At Buckman Labs, our associates are already connected electronically to our global network, so we have chosen to deliver the classroom to them over our intranet rather than requiring them to travel to a classroom. It's simple economics—of the five cost elements in continuing education (travel, housing, space, loss of service, and instruction), three essentially disappear when the course is put onto a network and the fourth is greatly reduced. And with the logistical costs of education all going up faster than the rate of inflation, getting control of these costs is critical to being able to open up windows of opportunity. Here's how it works:

Travel cost to the classroom. Travel time and transportation expense are both significant when you start moving people around. If the prospective students are all in the same building, these factors won't amount to much, but if they are scattered around the world—as our associates are at Buckman Labs—then they add up fast. You need to make sure that you are considering this cost on a global basis when looking at your organization. Do not just look at this cost in one operating company. Think globally.

Housing cost while taking a course. People attending a class have to live somewhere. If they're at home, it's not a problem, but a far-flung organization often tries to bring people together in the corporate headquarters or in some other distant city that requires a stay in a hotel. The price of meals and lodging is not an insignificant part of the total cost of educating your associates.

Cost of the classroom. Whether the classroom is in the office, a learning center, or a hotel, it is not free. Construction, always expensive, is rapidly becoming exorbitant. This cost is frequently buried in the price of the hotel rooms where students are staying, the administrative depreciation of the facility if you own it, or somewhere else. But it is still there.

Loss of service cost. Every time you send any of your staff to a class, your organization eats the opportunity cost of having the students do something besides their regular jobs. At minimum, you incur the salary and benefit cost of each individual, plus whatever nonrecoverable income the students would have generated and whatever additional costs may be involved in delaying the output they would normally have produced. For example, if a student is a sales rep with responsibility for a territory or a group of clients, then this cost includes the sales that he or she could have made during the period of classroom training but that went to competitors instead. This lost service is the single biggest cost of providing education to associates, but it is rarely calculated by business today. By contrast, distance education generally takes up only a part of the business day, so the students can often do much of their ongoing work without interruption.

Cost of the content. The cost of the teacher or content provider is the last thing you ought to worry about when considering the education of your associates. This is where the good stuff comes from. Yet the tendency over the years has been to see what could be done to keep the salaries of the teachers down as a way to reduce costs. This is counterproductive; to get people where you want them to be, it's important to offer them the best content you can find, regardless of the cost of the content provider. The more you can save in other areas, the more you can make available here.

And there's a sixth cost element, as well. When an employee takes classes on the job, the employer normally takes care of the economic costs involved—but that doesn't mean that the training is truly free for the participant. With face-to-face training events, participants have to deal with the social cost of being away from their families for extended periods of time. When employees are on the road a lot, these social costs can become very significant in the life of a family. Distance education makes it easier for people to maintain their own lives as well as their ongoing work—and that helps maintain their morale and thus their regard for their employer and their value to it.

One Comprehensive Solution

At Buckman Labs, we set out to reduce the logistical and social costs of continuing education to a minimum, while maximizing the benefits to the organization and the workforce. In 1994, we put together a team to explore how we could provide training over our network. The team included associates (and even retirees!) from a range of disciplines, so that we could capture what we had done in the past, were presently doing, and could do in the future in the area of education.

We hired the Lotus Institute to support this effort and produce the requisite administrative and delivery software. Lotus responded by developing Learning Space, one of the first and most comprehensive learning management systems, which went on to provide the benchmark for a fledgling e-learning industry and continues to play a significant role in today's market as part of the Lotus product line.

Buckman Labs learned a great deal from the effort. We used the basic concepts in the construction of our own e-learning depart-ment, which we call the Learning Center, but we eventually wrote off the investment in the software. It turned out that we could not use Learning Space effectively because our network didn't have sufficient bandwidth everywhere we needed it. As I mentioned in Chapter 6, a very high percentage of our people have to dial in to reach the system, and in the mid-1990s this meant that we could not depend on a baud rate of more than 14,400. It was not practical to radically increase the bandwidth in our network at that point, so we proceeded to redesign our Learning Center concept, using Web technology that gave us adequate loading and response times over dial-up lines. This was completed in May 1997 and the Learning Center was born.

The Learning Center's Task

In addition to its sweeping mission statement (quoted at the beginning of the chapter), the Learning Center is charged with providing the following services and features:

- ▶ **Initiative-Driven Programming.** The Learning Center has the job of promoting company-wide globalization efforts, productivity improvement programs, process improvement programs, and other projects that have strong support from the CEO or senior management. Learning Center staff assist with and in some cases drive activities designed to get widespread participation in such initiatives.
- ▶ **Change Management.** The Learning Center serves as a change agent, driving change or providing facilitation of a complete transformation process, using programs such as those based on Spencer Johnson's *Who Moved My Cheese?* or other team-based selling systems. This is particularly useful when the company embarks on a new strategy or is in the process of an acquisition.
- ▶ **Leadership Development.** In collaboration with Human Resources, our Learning Center develops leadership skills at Buckman. This focus on leadership development is designed to produce internal management bench strength. The Learning Center coordinates its activities with the Center for Creative Leadership and other programs designed to increase the value-added role of management within the company.
- ▶ **Career Development.** Buckman's Learning Center focuses

on individual skill development and on managing the process of career development in the company. This activity requires the tight collaboration of the entire company, but in particular senior management and corporate Human Resources, Marketing, Manufacturing, and R&D. It involves assisting with the ongoing development of the performance management system and with the development of aggressive education strategies to help with associate retention. This initiative includes management, leadership, and human relations as well as technical skills training and development.

▶ **Customer-Supplier Relationship Management:** The Learning Center helps associates learn to work effectively with customers and suppliers. This activity is in direct support of Marketing activities and initiatives. It includes building skills in negotiation and relationship management. The Learning Center also works with people in the supply chain (vendors and customers), offering customer-supplier workshops, customer satisfaction surveys, safety training, industry training, and other programs designed to build value into the whole relationship and avert problems between Buckman and its suppliers and customers.

Thus the Learning Center isn't just a training department with a new name and some pious but soon-forgotten hopes. Instead, it takes advantage of the cost savings that have become available as technology develops to redefine the whole Buckman Labs approach to education. It plays a significant role in the ongoing development of the company's staff and their counterparts in customer and supplier organizations, and every day it accomplishes something toward building the company's capabilities for the future.

The Learning Center uses a blended approach to distance education. To maximize the impact of the learning on the organization, its staff engages with associates via a wide variety of tools before, during, and after each course. Coursework may be face to face, online synchronous, asynchronous, or self-paced. Most of the just-in-time education is based on self-paced education using predefined modules and almost all our strength training from our cooperating universities is via various forms of distance education, either paper courses or through digital delivery.

The important thing is to have a seamless transition among the different forms to achieve the best transfer of knowledge to the student. Sometimes, that does still involve bringing people together for at least part of the program. For example, the two-week course on facilitation includes preliminary work by the participating associates and their supervisors, a face-to-face course, online Web conferencing to leverage the experiences of our global facilitator pool, and online discussion groups and knowledge bases that former students can continue to use. The course has established an online global Community of Practice that is charged with stewarding facilitation skills and capacity for Buckman Labs.

By using Web technology to build the interface, the Learning Center can adjust its approach to meet the ever-changing needs of the company and to take advantage of technological developments. Currently the effective bandwidth used for design purposes is a baud rate of 28,800. The eventual move to wireless communications on a global basis, with the bandwidth that technology offers, will lead to another significant revision of methods of delivery of education.

Specific Accomplishments

Since the beginning, Buckman's Learning Center staff have revised, improved, and expanded their pedagogical methods many times. They currently make more than a thousand courses available to our associates. Course content comes from a variety of internal and external sources, including about 20 universities around the world. Course offerings are in Spanish, Portuguese, French, German, Italian, Flemish, and Mandarin as well as in English.

Multilingual coursework is just the beginning. Recognizing that everyone learns best in his or her native language, whatever it is, Buckman Labs has made the Learning Center the focal point of translation efforts in the company. During the first quarter of 2003, Learning Center staff translated more than 280,000 words of material for the company. Collectively, the associates of the Learning

Center have lived or worked throughout the world. They speak a dozen languages and have at one time sold all of Buckman's product lines. In other words, the Learning Center is as diverse as the company is. This knowledge base within the Learning Center helps to ensure a tie to the business and culture of the company.

By brokering course material from regional and recognized university sources, the Learning Center allows Buckman Labs to offer associates around the world courses for credit and degree programs ranging from assorted certificates through the Ph.D. level. The savings accrued from distance education cover the cost so well that the company can provide most of these courses free of charge. (But there's a kicker in the free offerings: associates pay nothing as long as they get a passing grade; if they do not, then they have to reimburse the company for the price of the course.) There are no restrictions as to the courses that employees might take. While there is a policy bias for work-related offerings, everyone is encouraged to explore whatever subjects appeal to them and offer a potential for growth, and to develop their natural talents to be the best that they can be.

As distance education activity has increased at Buckman, the cost per hour of learning delivered has dropped significantly because of the absorption of the fixed costs of the program. (See Figure 15.1.) Total costs of the Learning Center are now below $40

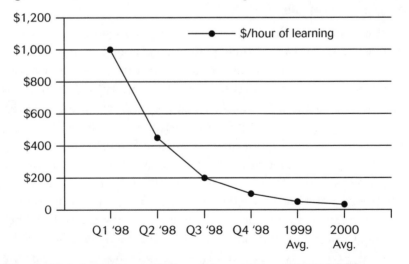

Figure 15.1. Learning activity cost, per hour, 1998-2000

per hour of learning delivered. This includes the cost of all courses, whether internally generated or purchased from outside, plus the cost of translation services. The cost to produce new e-learning content has also decreased as new and more powerful tools become available. Compared with 1997, the Learning Center can now produce twice the quality of learning experience in one-third the time.

What a Learning Center Can Do for You

The ideal learning center is a broker of content. It can generate company-specific coursework internally or bring it in from the outside—from anywhere. As you take funds away from the logistical problem of moving people around and apply these funds to the content side of the equation, the potential for expanding opportunities for your associates become unlimited. You can reach anywhere in the world to find the partner that will help you provide the best learning experience for your people. You can interface with fine universities anywhere in the world. You are no longer limited by geography, only by your imagination.

You can chunk this content into modules—perhaps as short as 15 to 20 minutes in length—that fit the need for just-in-time learning on a particular issue or point. You can reassemble these modules in different combinations to address particular needs or courses. You can bring together content from outside and combine it with some internal content to meet a particular need. Once again, the opportunities are limited only by your imagination.

You can open up opportunities for your people to take courses for credit and in degree programs from many universities around the world. The United States has a great university system, but the vast bulk of it is still based on the old face-to-face model. Once you break the mold and look at content at a distance, then the opportunities can be anywhere. For example, when Buckman Labs researched this area in the early 1990s, we found that most of the best universities for content that would fit learning at a distance were outside the United States, though the University of Phoenix Online offers content that fits the model of learning at a distance very well. The University of Phoenix is a for-profit U.S. university with more than 80,000 students and its success is an example for the whole learning industry.

Variety is more important than finding the one best source for distance education. The content providers are all changing over time, some getting better and others getting worse. Don't lock yourself in with one supplier—none of them can be counted upon to offer consistent quality in perpetuity. In any case, you do not want all your people to come from the same mold. You will want diversity in your educational mix. And choice is a very important element to keep in the picture: people often like to take courses and degrees from universities relatively near their homes—places they (and their families and friends) recognize and trust. For a global company, providing a wide range of geographic, linguistic, and subject-matter opportunities makes it easier to draw all of your employees into the program and make their use of it more satisfactory, both for the company and the participants.

Obstacles to Success

Fears of change will pose the greatest obstacles to success with a new learning center. The problem will not be technology. Instead, you will have to deal with constant objections from the very people whose support you need most. *Face-to-face education is the best pedagogical model that there is,* they will argue, *so why would you want to change? Why do you want to reduce the quality? How are you going to teach organic chemistry lab work?*

It's true that with today's practical bandwidth of 28,800 baud, some courses are difficult to teach at a distance. But with imagination and creativity (allowing the technology to deliver the lecture and recitation while using local facilities for laboratory space or other physical equipment needed for a course), it's already possible to bridge these gaps. The economics of the situation are forcing the change in delivery method, and wireless connections will eventually make worry over bandwidth obsolete. Of course, people will always need to *do* things as part of learning—as Will Rogers said, a few learn by reading, a few more by observation, and most "have to pee on the electric fence for themselves." But once simulations become sufficiently efficient and convincing, many courses that currently require a hands-on component will be much more cheaply and safely presented online. Someday, I firmly believe, the opportunity for learning at any time and anywhere as a Community of One will expand until it fills the market. The existing pedagogical model will become a relic for the history books, alongside penmanship exercises and group recitation from a printed text.

Another significant challenge to the growth of the distributed learning model stems from the changing role of the middle manager. What managers struggle with is the change from command-and-control to stewardship. When people have free access to development activities and training, many managers feel as though they are losing control of their associates' development. What they need to learn is that, although individual associates are now making the day-to-day decisions about their personal development, managers still retain responsibility for the overall development direction for associates to fulfill their job requirements. With the advent of a distributed model, it no longer makes sense for the manager to find, approve, and deliver all training. Paperwork proliferation can make the cost associated with getting approval to take a course exceed the cost to deliver the course. As training methods change, the underlying culture of responsibility for training will change also.

Where Do You Stand?

Think of your organization's capacity-building process. Where is your new knowledge coming from? Are you growing it, hiring it, or infusing it into your current employees by way of education? How do you plan to stay abreast of developments in your industry or field? How are you going to increase the knowledge base in your organization?

Think about the time equation of education—and the cost equation. Are you carting people to knowledge or bringing knowledge to people? What could you do to move toward the latter approach? What kind of resources could you free up in the process?

Think about what it is that you are trying to build. Are you working to maximize the strengths of your people or are you focused on closing the gap on competencies? How do you plan to stay abreast of developments in your company? Are you interested in your people growing to be the best that they can be? How might you help them get there?

Learning Today and Tomorrow

Every company—and especially every global company—has a workforce that includes many people who had no chance to get an education early in life. Economic necessity often requires people to go straight to work as soon as possible. They do not have a choice. It is not a question of brains; it is a question of economics or social position or both. As you recognize the need to move faster as an organization and adapt to the shifts in technology, the composition of your knowledge base will change. Redefining the educational process to build bench strength throughout the company will radically shift your people's opportunities to grow—and radically enhance their value to your company.

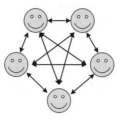

CHAPTER 16

Metrics: Outcomes from the Flow of Knowledge

You can't depend on your eyes when your imagination is
out of focus.

—Mark Twain

You get what you measure—as in the proverbial Russian
rope factory, where the manager ordered the machines set
for hawser (very thick) when his quota came in terms of
weight of output and set for twine (very thin) when it was in terms
of length. And easy as it is to chuckle at simple-minded commis-
sars, that's the natural human reaction. People do adjust their
behavior based on the way their efforts will be judged.

That constant pattern has major implications for any organizational change effort. Knowledge sharing is no exception. When
you look to see what you have done, make sure you're looking at
the right things. You need measures of customer effectiveness that
track what your customers really want and you need measures of
knowledge sharing that track what it is contributing to your organization's success.

What to Measure

> Vision without Action is fruitless. Action without Vision is
> pointless. Action and Vision together can change the world.
>
> —E.O. Wilson

When the desired outcomes are less than clear, it's tempting to overmeasure—to collect data on everything that can be measured and end up with such a collection of results that it's hard to tell what matters. That's obviously inefficient, so it then seems logical to concentrate on easily measured aspects of the situation and hope that move will simplify the picture and provide a reliable index of success. That rarely works out well either.

It's easy to measure activity levels—numbers of events, volumes of transactions—but that kind of data has no necessary relationship to results. The educational establishment, for example, often used "seat time"—the aggregate hours students spent in class—as a proxy for educational value, but both test results and the experience of employers working with the educational system's output have called that measure into question. Likewise in business, it's easy to develop a false sense of security by focusing on a collection of numbers that measure activity and not achievement. That's not just inefficient; it's counterproductive—tantamount to pulling the tree out of the ground just to see if the roots are growing. And it can lead to true aberrations, as one company found when it measured on-time performance by tracking when a certain product left the factory building en route to the customer. It made sense to do so, as shipping time depended on many uncontrollable factors, but an analysis of complaints led to the discovery that workers were "shipping" product to a freight car on a siding beside the plant, then spending another week or so finishing it before sending it off.

I believe that it's essential to set activity measures aside and focus on organizational goals. The only way to tell if you are moving in the right direction is to have goals and a strategy for reaching them, and then to assess the techniques used to execute the strategy by the way things work out in relation to the goals.

Measure What You Want

Focusing on outcomes is the way to go. But what kinds of outcomes make the most difference? Which areas will have the most impact on the company's future?

To me, the ultimate outcome is being able to stay in business and grow as fast as possible while keeping the customers happy. But I haven't found a way to measure that directly, so the trick is to develop metrics—things that can be measured—that vary with that result. By identifying at least two such metrics and combining them into an overall index, you get a clear idea of where your program is going.

One important metric is *speed*. The speed at which an organization can function effectively will determine how fast it can achieve closure on an issue by providing a solution. But what matters is *focused* speed, not wheel-spinning: measures of transactions per time unit may look like speed metrics, but they're tied to activity rather than to outcomes. The goal must be to reach conclusions faster than the competition. Wavering organizations are rarely effective in the marketplace.

Another important metric is *innovation*. The quality of an organization's innovation will determine how much distance it can put between itself and its competition. Innovation is critical to three separate aspects of the organization's operations:

- ▶ **Product.** Selling a commodity is a losing strategy. If that's what you're doing, then you need to do some thinking about how to differentiate yourself from your competition. Use your imagination. Innovation isn't just a matter of creating a different product that will provide some breakthrough benefit. Most innovation in products comes as small steps along a path that takes you in the direction you want to go.

- ▶ **Marketing.** Marketing has gone far beyond the simple "see customer, deliver product, collect money" that I started with some 40 years ago. The customer relationship is a key element in whether you will be around in the future or not. Look for partnership arrangements that allow you and the customer to redefine the value equation for both of you. The more you can move in that direction, the better off you will be. Innovation in the marketplace is a key element to moving a company forward.

▶ **Manufacturing.** 19th-century manufacturing is tough in a 21st-century world. Adjusting your production processes and locations can help you differentiate yourself from the competition and give you an edge in the market. You can go for continual improvement through small evolutionary changes, as we frequently do in the chemical industry, or for breakthroughs that will take big chunks of time out of the manufacturing process. Whatever your approach, all productive innovation is useful to the organization.

Whether you are dealing with a physical product or a service, the need is the same: to measure innovation as part of the outcome that is generated. And the best place to measure the outcome is as it is accepted and paid for by the customer. That is the ultimate test of whether the innovation is a real contribution or just a puff of smoke to make everyone involved look and feel good.

Combining speed and innovation in a metric provides a measurement of how fast the organization is able change in each of these areas. That is the ultimate test of your competitive ability. Are you raising the bar on how fast you can reinvent yourself as an organization? Is the customer accepting this and paying for it or are you just churning the water? Think in terms of ratcheting innovation up to the point where it makes a significant difference in the perception that your customers have of you.

Metrics to Consider

The metrics listed here are those that we have found useful at Buckman Labs, plus some that I think would be useful in tracking the process of building a knowledge-driven organization. You can doubtless think of others, but these will give you a good start at understanding what is happening with your organization over time as you develop and execute your strategy. The key element in all cases is the effort to measure outcomes rather than activity.

Speed of Response to Customer Needs. The speed at which your organization can achieve closure around the needs of your customers is a relatively simple metric that will begin to orient your people's efforts in the right direction. I am not talking about how fast someone can come up with an answer to a question or inquiry, but about how fast you can get to the point where the customer agrees that the solution is working—or, at the very least, to the point where the person on the front line with account responsibility for the customer expresses satisfaction with it. That is the reason that at Buckman Labs the threaded discussions continue until the person who raised the issue in the beginning announces that the answer is sufficiently complete to satisfy the customer. Only then is closure achieved and the discussion can terminate.

So measure how long it takes to get working responses to the needs or problems your customers raise. Note that the key word here is *working*; if you don't keep up the pressure on that point, people will revert to what's easy to measure—simple speed of any kind of response—and lose track of the need for real solutions. The issue must remain open until the individual who raised it is satisfied; nothing short of that means anything at all.

The effort to keep speeding up *effective* customer response time will reveal things in your own operation that you will have to address to become more nimble as an organization. At Buckman Labs we have reduced customer response time from days and weeks to a few hours or, at the most, a day or two. That's a clear and measurable improvement in speed of response and it translates directly into improved sales. This is particularly true at the furthest reaches of the company. K'Netix—our intranet plus the network—enables us to achieve the same response time anywhere in the world. We have effectively moved the entire organization to wherever it is needed at any point in time.

Speed of Response to Customer Opportunities. Opportunities are those rare events where the window opens wide. If your organization is prepared to deal with them, it can make major moves forward; if it's not, someone else will.

Customers are continually pushing their suppliers to improve performance. When a customer finally gets to the point of opening a window of opportunity, you do not want to squander the potential. You will find that, by learning how to improve your speed of response to customer needs, you will put your organization into position to deal with opportunities with equal speed as they arise. This metric is just an extension of the preceding one. Though they don't come up as often as problems and needs, opportunities are very important to the long-term success of your company.

Speed of Innovation. The percentage of revenue coming from sales of relatively new products will provide a useful index of whether you are opening up new markets or simply mining old ones. At Buckman Labs, we track the percentage of revenue coming from sales of products less than five years old, as shown in Figure 16.1. This metric tracks total company performance on speed of innovation around products. Sales has to define the need by listening to or watching customers, R&D has to create or find the products, Manufacturing has to produce them or arrange for their production, and Sales must complete the circle with the customers on the front line.

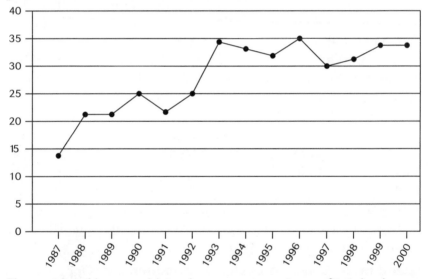

Figure 16.1. New product sales as a percentage of total sales

Nobody can be complacent; it requires total company involvement. It takes relationships of continuity and trust throughout the company and with the customer. The higher the result, the faster we are able to move as a company to satisfy our customers' needs for products. Thus this metric tracks innovation that the customer accepts and pays for.

New product sales contribution turns out to be a very effective total company metric of the results of knowledge sharing. For example, at Buckman Labs the figure used to average between 13% and 18%. In 1987, we distributed PCs to our people and went with IBM's global network for e-mail and access to some databases. Our speed of innovation jumped at once and new product sales immediately went to the 20%-25% range. The figure stayed there for about five years—until we switched to CompuServe, which was easier to use and opened up more effective discussion systems. Interactions among our associates increased significantly at that point, because the Forums were set up to deal with real business problems. We got a significant step-up in our speed of innovation at the same time, bringing new product sales contribution to the 30%-35% range.

While new product sales contribution is a very good metric for a product-driven world, it doesn't provide everything a knowledge-driven company needs. For example, it will not pick up benefits from the changes that the marketing department initiates in your customer relationships. If marketing is now taking over part of the customers' business and getting paid for a complete service of which products are just part of the value added, then you will not see results from that initiative in this metric. Neither will you see the benefits of a change in manufacturing, no matter how much the profit margin on a product increases as a result. However, it is possible to tailor the metric to address marketing innovation and manufacturing innovation.

Marketing Innovation. Marketing innovations usually involve some redefinition of the value equation with the customer—perhaps by becoming a sole supplier, perhaps by taking over a function rather than simply providing the things needed to run it. Whatever you do, the result is a flow of revenue from the customer to the supplier. It is only a question of definition. By gathering together all the revenue generated by being a relatively new sole supplier—say, sole supplier in relationships lasting five years or less—and dividing that by your total sales, you will get a metric that deals with innovation relative to being a sole supplier. By tracking this metric over time, you can determine whether you are going up or going down in your ability to become a sole supplier.

Depending on what you include in your metric, you can develop innovation-speed metrics for any marketing area. The challenge is to come up with a definition that will stand the test of time. If you keep changing the definition to fit the desired action of the moment, then you cannot measure the speed of innovation over time. Remember: if the resulting information is to tie into the product innovation metric, it has to last many years. It is important to give careful thought to what definition you will use.

Manufacturing Innovation. Manufacturing innovation involves some part of the production process—which is a very wide field indeed. Adjustments in procedures and tools for anything from raw materials inventory handling to final assembly and packaging can reduce your cost of goods sold and increase your profit on a product. Sometimes the impact of a change will be small, sometimes it will be huge, but it all helps you move in the right direction.

The challenge again is to have a definition of innovation in this area that will stand the test of time. As with marketing, it's essential to pick a definition and stick with it, so the year-to-year figures stay comparable. You can monitor improved production processes and their output, and use another rolling five-year metric to track the proportion of revenues derived from products whose manufacturing processes have been upgraded. Alternatively, you could measure changes in gross margin, tracking the contribution of products whose gross profit margin has improved in the past five years relative to the contribution of products whose gross margin has fallen or held steady. Such a total can be derived from existing financial data, so it would be easier to compute than a process upgrade metric— but it would also be harder to interpret, because other factors (such as costs of raw materials) could produce similar types of changes.

Growth of Your People. As I pointed out in Chapter 15, people need to keep growing and learning or they will gradually become less important to the organization and will be marginalized. Allowing this to happen would be a horrible waste of the resources spent on hiring and training them. But once you establish the goal of helping people maximize their strengths to the point that they overshadow their weaknesses, you need a metric that will let you see how well you're doing.

The common way to measure whether you are staying abreast of knowledge development needs is through a listing of the courses that your people take and pass. However, while this gives a measure of activity levels, it doesn't really track the outcomes of the educational process.

A better metric would be the expansion of individuals' span of influence across the organization. Those capable of influencing others across time and space have a greater audience and their efforts will become more and more important to achieving success as an organization. As individuals with increasing spans of influence become obvious, they can be picked by the organization for advancement and promotion.

Being able to identify these talented individuals allows you to focus your efforts and put them on a faster growth track within the organization. Those who are not capable of influencing others across time and space can be intelligently eliminated from the company or put in positions where they can contribute in relative isolation. While this may sound harsh, we have found that it is the people who expand their span of influence who really matter. Their value to the organization is significantly higher than that of anyone, no matter how brilliant, who insists on working alone. If you can increase the percentage of your people with an expanded span of influence in the company, you will be able to move faster as an organization.

Identify those of your people who are comfortable sharing knowledge across time and space and influencing others. You can do this with a simple rank-order approach, as we did at Buckman Labs for the Fourth Wave Meeting, or by participating in enough of the discussions to observe firsthand who has developed the requisite skills. Or you can get into more sophisticated methods of measurement integrated with your performance review program. But however you locate these people, help them to become more effective and make heroes out of them. Since they are pioneers in your organization in the use of new systems, you should involve them in helping the organization determine directions for new systems in the future.

Mentors. The number of middle and upper managers who satisfactorily act as mentors to their juniors—as reported by those juniors—provides a useful metric for how well you are doing at building leadership bench strength across the organization. As discussed in Chapter 5, with the abandonment of command-and-control practices, the middle manager's role has changed from being the gatekeeper of information to being the mentor and developer, helping people succeed in the fast-changing world in front of them. Everybody can now focus on closing the gap with the customer rather than shuffling paper—and it's important to your organization's future to see that they do so.

Productivity. Another excellent measure of organizational success is an index of per-person accomplishments. Whether in sales or service or manufacturing, producing more value per unit of time is an essential mark of progress. At Buckman Labs, we have found it very useful to measure the sales revenue achieved per person over time and the operating profit achieved per person over time. These metrics can be broken down into finer and finer components, such as sales revenue per representative and the like, where (as described in Chapter 2) they make a useful basis for incentive awards that provide a real incentive for enhanced performance. Metrics like this can also be developed for the manufacturing areas of the business.

Using Measurement

> The fellow that can only see a week ahead is always the popular fellow, for he is looking with the crowd. But the one that can see years ahead, he has a telescope but he can't make anybody believe he has it.
>
> —Will Rogers

When you choose the same time period for each metric, you can add the different metrics together to get a total company index of innovation. Speed is what matters here—it doesn't matter if you seem to be comparing apples and oranges if what you care about is how fast they roll.

Innovation, from any source, is a constant factor in the ongoing success of a business in today's market, so it's useful to get a high-level look by combining metrics for the speed of innovation around products, marketing, and manufacturing to get a total company metric of the speed of innovation. The key thing is to make sure that you are consistent over time so that you can determine your progress.

One way you can get a quicker picture of what is happening on the speed of innovation is to shorten the time period that you use before an innovative development rolls off the count. Think in terms of three years rather than five years. You will introduce more variability into the numbers by shortening the time component, but that can be smoothed by the application of statistical techniques, if necessary.

As you consider metrics to adopt for your organization, look for the outcomes that reflect efforts to change the company over time to better serve the customers. You want metrics that will illustrate this activity. Here are some of the key questions:

▶ What is your strategy?
▶ What are you trying to accomplish with your customer?
▶ How do you measure your effectiveness with many customers?
▶ How do you measure the effects of knowledge sharing and collaboration?
▶ What kind of outcomes change directly with your chosen strategy?
▶ Which areas will have the maximum impact on your future?
▶ How will you measure the different forms of innovation?
▶ How might you combine the different forms of innovation so that you can achieve a total company metric of the speed of innovation that you are achieving?

You need to think in terms of metrics that will allow you to see years ahead of where you are today by focusing on the outcomes of your actions. That effort may not make you the most popular person around, because you will be looking a lot further ahead than the majority of your associates. Don't worry about that. Think about how you might communicate what is being achieved in your outcomes so that others will begin to be able to see as far as you can. It will be through the outcomes that you will get a picture of the future state of your company.

Where Do You Stand?

Think about your strategy. Do you know where you are trying to go? Do you know what you are trying to accomplish with your customers? How individual is your product? How can you make it unique?

Think about your results. How do you measure your effectiveness with a given customer? How do you measure your effectiveness with different classes of customers? With all customers? Are you different from your competitors or are you slogging down the exact same path? How do you want to be different?

Think about innovation. Is it something you want to achieve? If so, how do you measure it in all of its different forms? Do you measure the activity itself in each area or do you measure the effect on the outcome?

Think about your knowledge-sharing efforts to date. How do you measure their effects? Are you focusing on the activity itself or on the outcomes? Are you doing everything you can to enhance your people's knowledge and effectiveness? Do you know who among your associates are the best at knowledge sharing? At mentoring others in the organization?

Measurement Drives Success

If you keep track of the right things, you'll find you can achieve faster change over time in the directions you want to go by moving knowledge further and faster than before. Work to achieve closure around your needs as fast as possible. As you learn how to push the speed of achieving closure faster and faster, you will find that you are also achieving a faster rate of innovation as an organization.

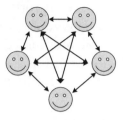

CHAPTER 17

The Things No One Can Copy: Speculation for the Future

Only as high as I can reach can I grow.
Only as far as I seek can I go.
Only as deep as I look can I see.
Only as much as I dream can I be.

—Karen Ravn, 1903-1970

This small poem—which I found on the wall of a Mr. Pride car wash in Memphis, Tennessee, with no author credit— captures an essential truth for knowledge sharing (as for many other aspects of life)—seeing what might be possible takes a mental stretch, and you have to see a possibility before you can build toward it. It's necessary to step out of your comfort zone to reach for the stars.

At Buckman Labs, the process started with the shift in our associates' span of communication through the use of computers and computer networks. With the advent of the Internet, people could easily communicate with anybody in the world without the necessity of going through anybody else first. This ability began to put pressure on our existing command-and-control structures, pushing the company toward a network. Instead of operating in a face-to-face world, we had entered a world that knows no physical boundaries, where people are limited only by imagination. It soon became clear that success in this new world required everyone involved to learn how to increase their span of influence across time and space.

The cultural change necessary to take advantage of this new order of things is rarely an easy transition. People of my generation find ourselves learning by watching our children rather than teaching them how to achieve success in this new world. For example, I serve on the boards of two institutions of higher learning and it is interesting to watch how far in front of the professors the students are. At times, it seems as though we need to reverse the educational process and let the professors learn from the students. The world is turned upside down. Yet the change does not stop there.

David Weinberger (1998) captures one of the other main currents of change in an article aptly titled "The Death of Documents and the End of Doneness." This is how the article ends:

> The cards are stacked against documents. We are seeing a massive cultural shift away from the concept of *done-ness.* The Web allows for constant process and enables open-ended groups of people to be invited into the process. Things on the Web are never done, and the damn "under construction" sign is implicit at every site. Why should anything be declared "done" when that means taking responsibility and arbitrarily picking a place to freeze a process in a context that is always, always, always changing? Documents are things that are done. That is why the Web will kill them.

Does that mean that we will not have documents anymore? I suspect not. As long as we have lawyers, we will have documents. What I think will happen is that their need in society will go down and the importance of them will diminish. We will learn to move forward on the basis of trust and relationship building across time and space rather than on the contents of rigid documents. In some ways we will be going back to the habits of a time before the spread of literacy, when the ability to build relationships was the mark of a leader and the ability to create and interpret documents was the province of specialists—if it existed at all.

Documents will still have importance as symbols of relationships, but they will not govern their success or failure. That will be determined by people's ability to build trusting relationships across time and space on the basis of values rather than documents.

Everyone who hopes to engage in knowledge work will need to learn how to build these trust-based relationships. And people will not trust those who do not readily offer trust of others. Sometimes the expression of trust is explicit—a handshake or exchange of eye contact—but sometimes it is tacit and the participants simply understand that trust is there.

Look Outward to Look In

If you work in a company, whatever its characteristics, the chances are good that you would like to have a more flexible and innovative organization. You would like an organization that is comfortable taking risks and is entrepreneurial in its orientation. You want it to be creative, adaptable, and responsive to change. But the quest for these desirable goals tends to lead to ever more soul-searching into the structure of the organization.

If you really want these attributes in your organization, the way to get them is to focus on your business—not on your organization. The best place to look for the basis of change is in the future of your business. Look where your customers are going. What do they want right now? What will they want five years from now? Ten years from now?

If you look to your current organization for insight and planning, what you learn will tend to keep you from developing the kind of structure you need for the future. Like any creature, an organization has a vested interest in continuing to exist. The best way to solve your problems is to focus on your business opportunities—on what your customers want. Let the organizational model flow to where you have what you need to meet the needs of the customers as you go into the future.

There are a thousand right ways to organize your business.

What are your customers saying they want you to focus on? How do you do what they desire? How should you change over time? How do you do it faster and better than anybody else? Because of the attributes of the networked model, I believe the world of business will see a shift toward that model of organization.

As Sheila Moorcroft noted in the *Gurteen Knowledge-Letter* (2003), recent research by Xerox found that successful employees are more likely to share knowledge than unsuccessful ones. It turns out that the use of the word *knowledge* rather than *information* makes a distinct difference in the way people think and behave. That means it may be desirable to pay more attention to the words that prospective employees or prospective suppliers use—and to take care to use the word *knowledge* correctly in describing your own actions and those of your staff. Determine those who share knowledge openly in your organization and make sure that they are on your short list to consider for promotion to increased responsibility. Involve them in the new directions of the organization.

Skills of Knowledge Workers

Knowledge work—as Peter Drucker points out cogently—is the key to economic growth now and for the foreseeable future. Neither resources nor capital can create an ongoing competitive advantage in the face of superior knowledge. He adds,

> The only comparative advantage of the developed countries is in the supply of knowledge workers. It is not a qualitative advantage: the educated people in the emerging countries are every whit as knowledgeable as their counterparts in the developed world. But quantitatively, the developed countries have an enormous lead. ... The productivity of knowledge and knowledge workers will not be the only competitive factor in the world economy. It is, however, likely to become the decisive factor, at least for most industries in the developed countries (Drucker, 1997, p. 22).

The current movement of white-collar jobs from the developed world to the developing world is just a trickle that will accelerate in the years ahead. Every business will be playing on the world stage. Will yours know how to play?

Unfortunately, although colleges and universities do a good job of teaching raw facts and analysis skills, they do a lousy job of teaching the skills required for knowledge work. More, they teach the wrong skills, emphasizing competition rather than cooperation and collaboration. Outside the sports arena, few students have a chance to learn to work as part of a group whose results are based on team effort or to share what they know openly and completely with others, even face to face, let alone with people they have never met. And that's something knowledge workers need to know. It would take much more training during the formative years for people to reach the workforce capable of anything like their full potential as effective knowledge workers. And those who do not get it then will have to spend productive time later in life learning these skills to avoid being shunted into isolated, low-value jobs in the new environment.

If Drucker is correct that knowledge is the new driver of economic progress and that increasing outcomes depends on increasing productivity and innovation, then what can companies do to increase the productivity and innovation of knowledge workers? This breaks up into two questions. The first is "What should you be doing?" The effort to answer returns to the theme of Chapter 16: you have to know what you want and be able to tell whether your actions are producing more or less of it. The second is "How do you make results more important than process?" As discussed in Chapter 5, people must be able to concentrate on results that promote your overall purpose—without being distracted by endless approvals and procedures.

Because a company must be able to put knowledge to work, even on knowledge itself, it needs to be organized for constant change. The company must be organized for innovation. Innovation is essential to survival in a fast-changing world. That means we have to work on the assumption that perpetual destruction of existing approaches is the norm.

Time and the Knowledge Worker

The challenge for most organizations is to get the speed of innovation high enough so that it really makes a difference in efforts to

outdo the competition. Building speed of innovation requires shaving time off every step of the process. But as I noted in Chapter 11, time is that unique attribute in which people are all equal. Everyone has 24 hours a day, every day, and no more, and no one can allocate all 24 of them to work.

Key Point: *People will use only those systems that add value to their effort relative to the time they expend.*

Technology has allowed the expansion of each individual's span of communication and has allowed the expansion of the work-oriented hours that someone can put in without feeling unduly burdened. People are now working on planes, in hotels, and at home. They can get in a little work on vacation, at the race-course, even while fishing. Anytime someone wants to get connected to the office, it's available.

As a result, organizations can be functional at any time of the day or night even without staffing for full round-the-clock operations. And anyone interested in being a global player must be able to function day and night to synchronize with global customers. The "office" is now on the network—a place as much virtual as physical, or more. This raises some serious questions for the future.

The first approach that companies have used to take advantage of the new flexibility is to encourage (or require) people to improve their output by working more hours, making productive use of time formerly required for traveling to and from work and of intervals taken from time formerly allocated to leisure. This has resulted in improved productivity statistics, because it makes it possible to do more with a given workforce. But this approach is self-limiting; it rapidly reaches a point where people feel they're doing enough and further productivity improvements are not forthcoming. Many organizations have already reaped the maximum benefit available from this application of technology.

Another way to increase productivity per hour is to take advantage of the increased span of influence that networking allows to the most advanced and articulate associates. By connecting people with problems to those with answers, the electronic network reduces the amount of wheel-spinning and lets people make better use of their time. Unlike the demand for more time, this

approach is open-ended: it can continue to expand more or less indefinitely. However, it requires a significant change of culture within the organization, which comes slowly over time—people need time to get used to this kind of give-and-take and to realize that what Scott Adams calls the "the Way of the Weasel" (sidestepping work and refusing to give wholehearted advice) is not the road to success or even survival in the new environment.

Rather than requesting more time, what companies need to do is redefine the workday so as to eliminate the time wasted in the normal course of the business day. Recapturing this time would allow a radical improvement in the productivity of knowledge workers. But how much will knowledge workers be willing to change lifelong habits of working and socializing with other people to achieve this next productivity improvement? It will take the redefinition of the culture of work to achieve that next level of improvements. If you think organizations have seen change in the past four or five decades, just wait until the next generation takes over. We are in for a long period of change in the time equation of work and how it will be done.

Recapturing lost time isn't a matter of figuring out how to turn knowledge workers into machines, switched on and running at full power for every minute of the full workday they're getting paid for. Quite the contrary—it's a matter of arranging their working interactions so they can make their full contribution at whatever time of the day or night they're best able to work. Here are some of the things we learned at Buckman Laboratories about these remarkable people who are creating our future for us:

- ▶ Knowledge work can occur anytime and anywhere, whenever people want to engage their brains. They do not have to be at the office to do knowledge work.
- ▶ People work best at different times of the day or night. Some are morning people and some are night people. Encouraging knowledge work to be done at that time of best production can improve productivity relative to the time expended.
- ▶ People using laptops are two to four times more productive than those using desktops, because desktops can function only when their users are physically in the office, which is less

than 25% of their time. Distributing laptops instead of desktop computers frees knowledge workers from the physical office and permits redefinition of the time equation of work.

▶ Many people are using the office as we know it as a social gathering place; their work is getting done elsewhere. Meanwhile, the cost of construction is still going up faster than the rate of inflation. And the sheer time it takes to get to the office is growing more and more burdensome, as highways clog with cars and people move deeper and deeper into the countryside in search of an agreeable living environment. If the funds now used for building and furnishing offices were freed up to build systems for effective communication, an organization could increase its return on investment many times over. And if the time people now spend on the road, fraying their tempers and putting their lives (and your investment) at risk, were freed up to devote even in part to the issues of your business, you would gain an immediate boost in energy and productivity.

Thus, I would encourage you to focus on the time that is being wasted in your organization by moving people around and start thinking about how you might redefine the time equation of work by moving ideas and knowledge around. It is much cheaper and much faster to move ideas and knowledge than it is to move people. I believe that technology has advanced to the point where radical changes in productivity are becoming possible—and where the shape of still more radical future improvements is beginning to become visible.

The Technological Edge

The ideal communications device isn't quite here yet, but it isn't necessary to wait for it. Although, as Stanley Davis and William Davidson write in *2020 Vision* (1991, p. 33), "Until the technological blending of telephones, televisions, and computers is accomplished, the infrastructure is not complete, and the economic core, therefore, is not mature enough to develop the truly new models for management and organization," I don't think it's necessary to keep on with business as usual until that day arrives.

Today, it is possible to see the beginnings of this with the products that combine cell phones and PDAs. Laptops are getting lighter and have a battery life that exceeds eight hours. Tablet PCs are on the market. Eventually, one device will provide everything people need for communication, either incoming or outgoing, and allow them access to information and knowledge they need wherever it may be. *Eventually*, perhaps, the pocket-size model of this universal communicator will seem too large and cumbersome and the up-to-date knowledge worker will have an implant instead. If you wait for perfection, you'll be out of business long before it arrives.

Input is still a bottleneck. Typing speed severely limits the amount of work people can accomplish each day. You can get some productivity improvements by providing learn-to-type programs with all PCs, thus letting people build their speed without confessing that they need help, but that is not the ultimate solution.

Typing itself is an ancient and slow method of entering information and knowledge into a system. I can talk much faster than I can type and I can think much faster than I can talk. If I could enter knowledge into the system as fast as I could speak, then I could radically improve my productivity as a knowledge worker. And if I could somehow enter knowledge by direct brainwave activity as fast as I could think, then I could really push the limits of speed. But the current systems for speech recognition are not really up to the task of keeping up with spoken communications, and neural interfaces are a remote laboratory dream. At this point, the best we can do is try to get the most out of existing systems for typing and speech recognition and make sure that suppliers know there's a market for better and better input systems for knowledge workers.

Connection speed is another limiting factor. Broadband connections make online interaction almost as smooth as face-to-face, but a company with any sort of global reach still needs a system that can accommodate dial-up connections. As the movement to wireless connections accelerates and expands, the opportunities for ubiquitous connections anytime and anywhere at high speed will open up radically different opportunities to redefine the equation again. The software that you can consider using will have enhanced features that are viable only with high-speed connections. It will allow the merging of data and voice and video into a seamless communication device. This area offers so many opportunities for redefinition that they are too numerous to mention. Focus on wireless and what it can bring to your systems. This will be the foundation for the next big revolution in how we do business.

Global companies run smack into the language barrier. People always function best in their native language, whatever it is, and the more countries you work in the more languages you have to deal with. The ideal would be to set up the network so that people could send and receive communications in their own languages, with translation happening seamlessly on the fly. At Buckman Labs, our associates work in 15-plus languages, but we could "get by" with five. Simultaneous translation into English, Spanish, French, German, and Mandarin would take us a long way into global communications, but even that is out of reach now.

Automated translation on the fly is not a viable possibility at this time, although some good attempts are being made. Unfortunately, more progress is essential to provide a ubiquitous solution to this communication need. It would be nice if Microsoft would embed this feature in Office someday. This would save a lot of time and radically improve global communications in any organization.

Culture

As I said back in Chapter 2, the technology is the easy part. It already allows amazing acceleration of the time equation of work, and developments easily visible on the horizon promise as much again or more. The culture to support these improvements is another matter entirely, however. Taking advantage of the productivity improvements that are possible today requires a dramatic change in outlook at all levels of an organization—and that's far more difficult than installing any amount of hardware and software.

If you go down this road, you will find that about 90% of your effort will be around culture change. It is not technology but culture change that you have to be concerned about—and you do have to be concerned about it. In the end, your organization's speed of innovation is what will determine your customers' view of your merit relative to that of your competition, and that is what will determine your success and even survival in the new marketplace.

Cultural Challenges

As you move forward into the future, you need to think about where you want to go with your organization and how you want to get there. I cannot tell you how to do that. You are unique and your company is unique. You will have to decide how much change your organization can stand at any point in time. You will have to set your priorities for change consistent with your needs at the moment and where you are trying to go.

What I have tried to do with this book is give you some areas to look at that should pay dividends to you and your organization over time. As you look at these areas, here are some things to think about.

- ▶ Anybody in your organization anywhere in the world can have something to contribute to the solution of any problem in the company, no matter where it occurs. How do you organize the company to recognize that fact? How do you organize around the flow of information and knowledge rather than geography?
- ▶ The organization of the future will be made up of shifting communities of individuals that form around issues, deal with them, disband, and reform into other communities around other issues. Most of its decisions will come from focused effort, solving real problems. How do you build communities of people separated by both time and space who trust each other enough to work effectively together? How do you move the entire organization to wherever it is needed at any point in time?
- ▶ Leadership is crucial to getting people to take educated risks. How might you help your people accept the risks of culture change so that the organization can move forward?
- ▶ People who have ideas tend to have a lot of ideas. If their ideas are treated well, then they will offer a lot more. If not, then they will stop coming up with ideas. How do you treat ideas in your company?

▶ People grow in response to the way others see their roles, so look for ways to make each role more expansive. For example, have you ever thought of the receptionist as a concierge for the organization? How do you view your people who are on the front line with the customer? As sales reps? Or as the cutting edge of a knowledge-driven organization? There is a world of difference between the two. Think about changing the perception of what you want your people to be—then give them the opportunity and training to grow into that new perception.

▶ Speed of response to customer needs is becoming of paramount importance in the competitive marketplace. How will you achieve the same speed of response at the furthest reaches of your company?

▶ A sense of urgency is crucial in this fast-changing world. How do you get the customer to drive the sense of urgency in your company? Try hanging out with customers and learning what they want. This is a useful exercise.

▶ If you are interested in being the best in customer service, then you need to look at those companies that are best in the world, not just in your industry. If you want to be better than your competitors, then study those companies that are changing people's views of what's possible, even if they're in a different line of business. This is where you can be a true innovator in your industry, by redefining your own equation.

▶ Look at your markets in ways that you have never imagined before. How do you make your business dramatically different five years out? Do you want to be in control of your future or are you willing to let your competition have that benefit?

▶ Do you have the ability to move faster than your competitors? How might you use a technological breakthrough faster than anybody else? How fast can you close on an opportunity that suddenly presents itself from your customers?

▶ Who are the most innovative people in your organization? How might you bring them together as a team working on a big customer problem or opportunity? How fast can you do it? Can you do it across time and space? Can you support them as they function across time and space? Will their line managers release them to address these problems?

▶ The office as we know it today is becoming redundant to the functioning of the organization. If the cash flow is not generated in the office and the people are not in the office, then why do we have offices? Could we not save that investment?

▶ Everybody has to be engaged with the customer. If people are not doing anything that supports the customers, why are they employed?

▶ The quality of the people that you hire will be critical to your future success. If individual ability to acquire and use knowledge is important, then what is in the collective minds of your associates will determine how well you can function as an organization. How will your human resources department and your learning center respond to this need of the company?

▶ If everybody is critically important to the organization's ability to close the gap with the customer, then it's essential to help associates expand their minds so that they can be the best that they can be. It's now possible to deliver learning anytime and anywhere it's needed. Should you think about hiring more teachers? What about instructional designers who can shift the pedagogical model?

▶ If you wish to achieve change in the knowledge arena, then your organization has to have proactive entrepreneurial support from the top. You will not achieve the change needed by making this journey a project in the IT department. Knowledge systems and knowledge sharing must be treated like any other investment that will redefine the organization. How might you do that in your organization?

▶ Using technology to control costs is a self-limiting effort. What's needed is the entrepreneurial application of technology to gain a competitive advantage in the marketplace. Real progress comes from redefining the time equation of work rather than doing the same thing faster. This means that all processes and activities in the organization are potential areas for a complete rethink. How might you do that in your organization? Where would you like to start?

Fred

Take a look at Fred. He looks like a simple sort of guy, but not that much simpler than the average front-line employee looks to the average command-and-control organization. Nonetheless, building a knowledge-driven organization starts with a single individual like Fred, someone who is out there alone facing the world for his company and who is looking for support. The first step is to consider Fred and come up with ways to shift his role from the bottom of the pyramid to the top of the pyramid.

Once Fred and his cohorts are on top, they will lead the rest of the organization in how best to serve the customer. Everyone more distant from the customer should be working to support Fred and what he is trying to accomplish because that is the way to generate cash flow for the organization. That's *Effective Engagement on the Front Line*—the Buckman Labs recipe for ongoing success.

Fred

But to make this happen, you have to change the culture of the organization so that Fred and his sister and brother associates on the front line and in more specialized positions can each expand their span of influence and reach out with effective engagement to others in the organization. You will find you must spend a great deal of time working with people to shift the culture to a new paradigm.

What's needed is to engage all the minds in the company on this effort. Individually, people are always vulnerable to being beaten. Collectively, the group whose members are most effective at collaborating together can win in any situation.

The mind power of an organization is its most powerful weapon in the competitive arena today. Its collective knowledge, which is changing every minute of every day, is what makes it durably different from its competition. The mental edge is a difference that cannot be copied, because it is as good as your people are today and growing toward being as good as they can be tomorrow. If you can enhance that difference faster than somebody else, you will keep putting distance between your organization and the others.

Where Do You Stand?

Think about your organization's approach to knowledge work. Can your people work smoothly and efficiently when they're outside the office? Can they work in the part of the day or night where they get the best productivity for the time they spend? Have you set things up so everyone can be a knowledge worker?

Think about your investments in physical plant and in transportation. How much could you enhance your return on investment by diverting funds from building and furnishing offices to setting up and maintaining systems for effective communication? How much more could your associates get done if they didn't need to spend two days in airports and away from home so that they can attend a two-hour meeting someplace? What would happen to productivity if you were to take half of the money now spent on moving people around and spend that same amount of money on moving ideas and knowledge around the organization? What if associates who now spend as much as three or four hours a day commuting could use that time to help meet the needs of your customers?

Think about your efforts to build skills and knowledge among your associates. Are you offering opportunities for lifelong learning and setting the conditions so that your associates can grow to be the best that they can be? Are you moving beyond the limits of local language and helping people share knowledge even when they don't share a common tongue?

Think about teamwork. Can your associates build their own virtual teams virtually, from the beginning, without needing to assemble the team face to face before it can get to work? Can they work smoothly and openly with one another, without regard to relative status and location in the world?

And think about your organizational culture—it all begins with culture and returns to it. Are you willing to go through the culture change necessary to radically shift your speed of innovation as an organization?

Fare Well

> And they asked me how I did it; and I gave 'em the
> Scripture text,
> "You keep your light so shining a little in front o' the next!"
> They copied all they could follow, but they couldn't copy my
> mind,
> And I left 'em sweating and stealing a year and a half
> behind.
>
>   —Rudyard Kipling, "The 'Mary Gloster'"

This is a journey, not a project. It is a journey of cultural change and increased opportunities, both individually and organizationally. The speed at which you can innovate is what you need to measure, as this is what will determine your reach.

Building a knowledge-driven organization is not for the faint of heart. It is a messy process that is built on the trust that exists between your associates and your company. Have faith that people will do the right thing. I can assure you that they are all trying to do that to the best of their ability. Building a knowledge-driven organization is about turning your people loose to be the best that they can be.

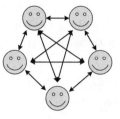

REFERENCES

Adams, Scott. *Dilbert and the Way of the Weasel.* New York: HarperBusiness, 2002.

Allen, Thomas. J. *Managing the Flow of Technology: Technology Transfer and the Dissemination of Technological Information Within the R&D Organization.* Cambridge, MA: MIT Press, 1977.

Baker, Wayne. *Achieving Success Through Social Capital.* San Francisco: Jossey-Bass, 2000.

Buckingham, Marcus. *First, Break All the Rules.* New York: Simon & Schuster, 1999.

Buckingham, Marcus. *Now, Discover Your Strengths.* New York: Free Press, 2001.

Chrislip, David D., and Carl E. Larson. *Collaborative Leadership: How Citizens and Civic Leaders Can Make a Difference.* San Francisco: Jossey-Bass, 1994.

Davis, Stan M., and William H. Davidson. *2020 Vision.* New York: Simon & Schuster, 1991.

Drucker, Peter F. "The Future That Has Already Happened." *Harvard Business Review,* September-October 1997, 75(5), 20, 22, 24, 26.

Drucker, Peter F., Esther Dyson, Charles Handy, Paul Saffo, and Peter M. Senge. "Looking Ahead: Implications of the Present." *Harvard Business Review,* September-October 1997, 75(5), 18-32.

Gleckman, Howard, John Carey, Russell Mitchell, Tim Smart, and Chris Roush. "The Technology Payoff: A Sweeping Reorganization of Work Itself Is Boosting Productivity." *Business Week,* June 14, 1993, 57-68.

Govindarajan, Vijay, and Anil K. Gupta. *The Quest for Global Dominance: Transforming Global Presence into Global Competitive Advantage.* San Francisco: Jossey-Bass, 2001.

Handy, Charles. "The Citizen Corporation." *Harvard Business Review,* September-October 1997, 75(5), 26, 28.

Johnson, Spencer. *Who Moved My Cheese?* New York: Putnam, 1998.

Kerr, Steven. "On the Folly of Rewarding A, While Hoping for B." *Academy of Management Journal*, 18, February 1975, 769-783.

Manville, Brook, and Nathaniel Foote. "Strategy as if Knowledge Mattered." *Fast Company,* April/May 1996, 66.

Moorcroft, Sheila. "Prisoners' Dilemma to the Rescue?" *Gurteen Knowledge-Letter,* 33, March 3, 2003. Available online: http://www.gurteen.com/. Access date: Jan. 13, 2004.

Naisbitt, John. *Megatrends: Ten New Directions Transforming Our Lives.* New York: Warner Books, 1982.

Ostroff, Frank, and Douglas Smith. "The Horizontal Organization (Redesigning the Corporation)." *McKinsey Quarterly,* Vol. I, Winter 1992, 148-168.

Senge, Peter M. "Communities of Leaders and Learners." *Harvard Business Review,* September-October 1997, 75(5), 30, 32.

Senge, Peter M. "Sharing Knowledge." *Society for Organizational Learning,* June 1998. Available online: http://www.sol-ne.org/res/kr/shareknow.html. Access date: Jan. 13, 2004.

Taylor, Frederick Winslow. *The Principles of Scientific Management.* New York: Harper Brothers, 1911.

Toffler, Alvin. *Powershift: Knowledge, Wealth, and Violence at the Edge of the 21st Century.* New York: Bantam Books, 1990.

Weinberger, David. "The Death of Documents and the End of Doneness." *Journal of the Hyperlinked Organization,* March 19, 1998. Available online: http://www.hyperorg.com/backissues/joho-march19-98.html. Access date: Jan. 13, 2004.

Wenger, Etienne C., and William M. Snyder. "Communities of Practice: The Organizational Frontier." *Harvard Business Review,* January-February 2000, 78(1), 139-145.

Wheatley, Margaret J. *Leadership and the New Science: Discovering Order in a Chaotic World.* San Francisco: Berrett-Koehler, 2001.

INDEX

INDEX